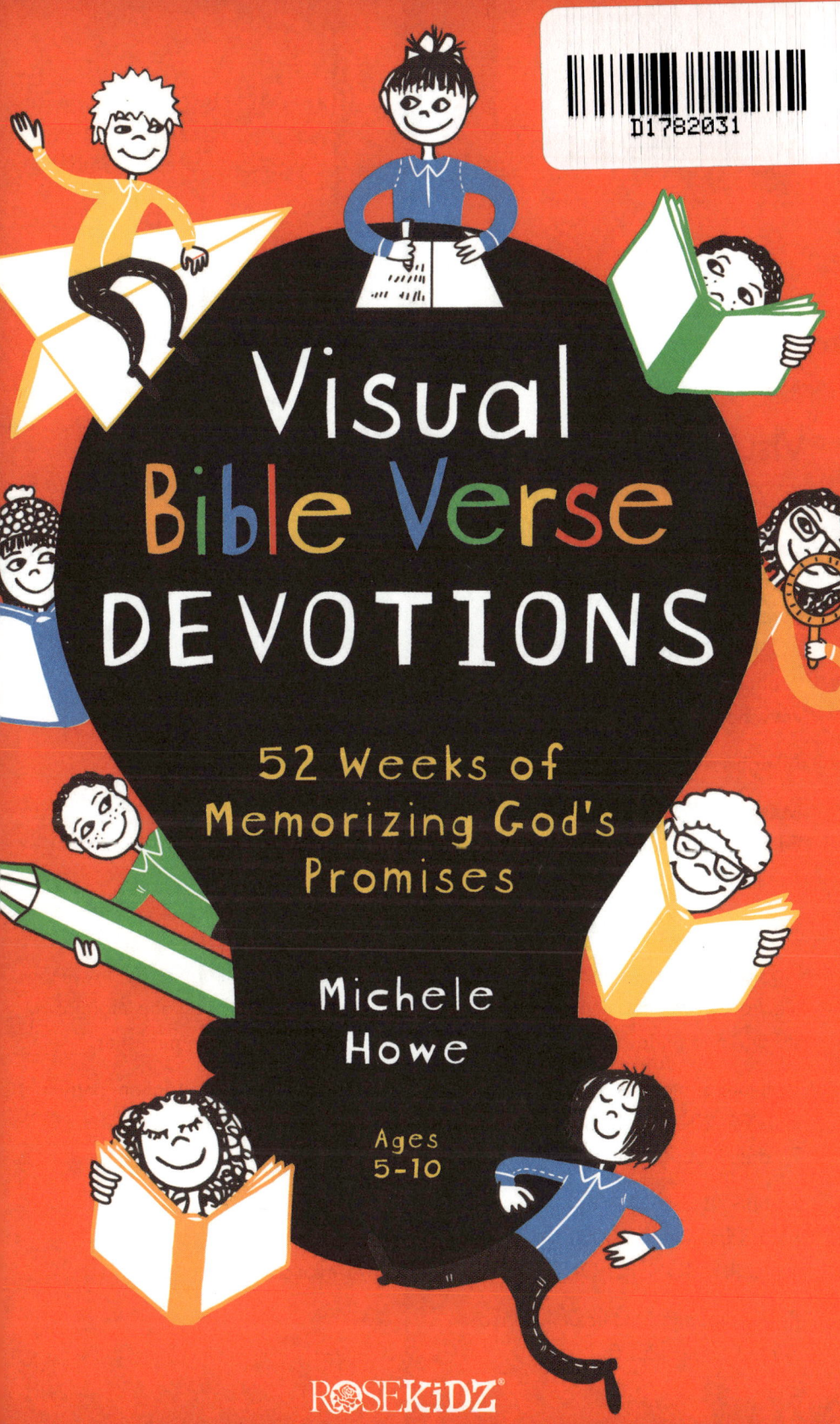

Visual Bible Verse Devotions

Copyright © 2020 Michele Howe

Published by RoseKidz®
an imprint of Hendrickson Publishing Group
Rose Publishing, LLC
P.O. Box 3473
Peabody, Massachusetts 01961-3473 USA
www.hendricksonpublishinggroup.com

All rights reserved.

Managing Editor: Karen McGraw
Editorial and Production Associate: Drew McCall
Assistant Editor: Talia Messina

Cover and Interior Design by Drew McCall

No part of this book may be reproduced or transmitted in any form or by any means, electronic or mechanical, including photocopying, recording, or by any information storage and retrieval system, without permission in writing from the publisher.

Scripture quotations are taken from the Holy Bible, New Living Translation, copyright © 1996, 2004, 2015 by Tyndale House Foundation. Used by permission of Tyndale House Publishers, Inc., Carol Stream, Illinois 60188. All rights reserved.

ISBN: 978-1-62862-841-8
RoseKidz® Reorder #L50047
JUVENILE NONFICTION/Religious/Christian/Devotion and Prayer

Printed in United States of America
Printed August 2020

Contents

Introduction 5
How to Use This Book 6
Week 1: God Is Always with Me (Deuteronomy 31:8) 7
Week 2: Christ Gives Me Victory (Romans 8:37) 14
Week 3: God Will Meet All My Needs (Philippians 4:19) 21
Week 4: God Gives Me Peace (1 Peter 5:7) 28
Week 5: God Makes Everything Possible (Matthew 19:26) 35
Week 6: God Gives Me Strength and Protects Me (2 Thessalonians 3:3) 42
Week 7: Christ Gives Me Wisdom (James 1:5) 49
Week 8: God Forgives Me (Psalm 103:12) 56
Week 9: God Gives Me Strength (Philippians 4:13) 63
Week 10: Everything Is Possible (Luke 18:27) 70
Week 11: Jesus Gives Us Rest (Matthew 11:28) 77
Week 12: God Saves Us (John 3:16) 84
Week 13: God's Grace Is Enough for Me (2 Corinthians 12:9) 91
Week 14: Trust in the Lord (Proverbs 3:5–6) 98
Week 15: Everything Works Together for Good (Romans 8:28) 105
Week 16: God Is Faithful and Just (1 John 1:9) 112
Week 17: God Gives Me Power, Love, and Self-Discipline (2 Timothy 1:7) 119
Week 18: God Is Wisest and Strongest of All (1 Corinthians 1:25) 126
Week 19: Love God, Not Money (Hebrews 13:5) 133
Week 20: I Can Have Eternal Life (John 3:36) 140
Week 21: I'm Not Alone in My Trouble (Psalm 91:15) 147
Week 22: God Gives Me Perfect Peace (Isaiah 26:3) 154
Week 23: The Lord Is My Shepherd (Psalm 23:1) 161
Week 24: God Loves and Delights in Me (Zephaniah 3:17) 168
Week 25: I Don't Have to Worry (Philippians 4:6) 175

Week 26: God Keeps Every Promise (Psalm 146:6) 182

Week 27: God Protects Us (Daniel 6:23) 189

Week 28: God's Hand Holds Me (Isaiah 41:10) 196

Week 29: God Frees Me from My Fears (Psalm 34:4) 203

Week 30: God Always Knows What I Need (Matthew 6:8) 210

Week 31: I Can Speak with Love (Ephesians 4:15) 217

Week 32: The Fruit of the Spirit (Galatians 5:22) 224

Week 33: God Will Comfort Me (2 Corinthians 1:3-4) 231

Week 34: Troubles Become Glory (Genesis 50:20) 238

Week 35: I Can Love What Is Good (Romans 12:9) 245

Week 36: Jesus Knows Me (John 10:14) 252

Week 37: God Understands Everything (Psalm 147:5) 259

Week 38: God Is My Hiding Place (Psalm 32:7) 266

Week 39: Tell the Truth to Each Other (Zechariah 8:16) 273

Week 40: My Body Is a Living Sacrifice to God (Romans 12:1) 280

Week 41: God Owns Everything in Heaven and on Earth (Psalm 24:1) 287

Week 42: We Should Speak as God Would Speak (1 Peter 4:11) 294

Week 43: We Can Be Strong in God's Mighty Power (Ephesians 6:10) 301

Week 44: Love Never Gives Up (1 Corinthians 13:7) 308

Week 45: I Need Faith to Please God (Hebrews 11:6) 315

Week 46: We Must Be Kind and Forgiving to Others (Ephesians 4:32) 322

Week 47: We Must Listen Well Before Speaking (James 1:19) 329

Week 48: Be Humble and Look Out for Others (Philippians 2:3) 336

Week 49: Don't Be Close Friends with an Angry Person (Proverbs 22:24) 343

Week 50: Be Peaceable with Everyone (Romans 12:16) 350

Week 51: Love Is Patient and Kind (1 Corinthians 13:4) 357

Week 52: Help Those Who Are Weak (1 Thessalonians 5:14) 364

Visual Bible Verse Dictionary 371

Activity Answer Keys 377

INTRODUCTION

Put God's Word to work in your everyday life by memorizing Bible verses. When you memorize Bible verses, you'll remember them when you need God's wisdom to guide you.

Whether it's your first time memorizing Scripture, or your hundredth time, this is the book for you!

Filled with fifty-two of God's amazing promises, this book has verses with a difference—many of the words have been replaced with pictures. This makes memorization more like playing a game.

Plus, there are over 100 games, crafts, and other activities that reinforce the visual Bible verses: coloring pages, word searches, verse scrambles, crafts, and more!

You'll also find:

- **Fictional stories about real-life situations!** Enjoy reading stories about kids a lot like you!

- **Over 100 Bible story references to look up and read!** Understand the verses a little bit better by reading these important Bible stories and passages.

- **More than 300 life-application questions!** Discuss these questions with a trusted adult, or write your answers in a journal. It's up to you! Each question will help you understand the verse a little better and see how its truths apply to your life.

- **"Do Something about It" challenges and suggested prayers!** Start using these Bible verses to live your very best life!

Grow closer to God as you learn more about his amazing promises in *Visual Bible Verse Devotions*.

How to Use This Book

As you go through this book, you'll find that seeing a visual Bible verse symbol helps you recall its related verse word. Over time, the symbols will help you memorize each verse. Even when you don't have this book in hand, picturing the visual Bible verse symbols will remind you of God's amazing promises.

Here's how it works:

- Each week begins with a new visual Bible verse. Like the one on page 7.

- Look over each symbol and try to think of what it might mean. Don't worry if they seem difficult at first—once you start seeing the symbols repeat each week, you'll remember what they represent.

- Use the blank lines below the visual Bible verse to write out what you think the verse means. If you feel stuck on a symbol, look it up in the Visual Bible Verse Dictionary on page 371.

- The correct verse is written upside down, just below the blank lines. Use this to check what you've written or use the reference at the end to look up the verse in your own Bible.* It's OK if you make mistakes! You'll have other chances to get it right throughout the week.

Hints for understanding the visual Bible verse symbols:

- Many symbols directly represent what they mean: ☝ = one.

- Most symbols are homophones, or words that have the same sound but different meanings or spellings: 👁 = I.

- Some symbols are like little puzzles: you have to figure out the symbol, and then add or subtract sounds to find out what the word is: 🧈 = but.
  -ter

- Finally, you might recognize some symbols from emoji faces or texting lingo: 👍 = good.

- Have fun!

* All Visual Bible Verses are from the New Living Translation (NLT), so it might be helpful to have an NLT Bible on hand when going through this book. You can also look the verses up online.

Week 1

God Is Always with Me

Look at the visual Bible verse below. Try to figure out what it says. Write the verse words on the blank lines. Use the Visual Bible Verse Dictionary on page 371, if needed.

  neither

nor abandon

_____

_____

_____

_____

_____

The Lord will . . . be with you; he will neither fail you nor abandon you. Deuteronomy 31:8

DAY 1

Never Alone

It was a few days before school was to start and Cassie and Dan were running around the playground outside their school. Their mothers were inside the building filling out paperwork. "Cassie, aren't you excited about starting school next week?"

Cassie said yes and then ran over to the swings. "I can swing higher than you can!" she challenged.

Dan laughed and started pumping his legs as hard as he could. "I don't think so!" Together, Cassie and Dan started going higher and higher until their legs just got too tired of pumping.

As they both jumped off the swings at the same time, Cassie yelled, "Race you to the water fountain!" Off the two ran to get some water and to catch their breath.

After Cassie was done drinking, Dan surprised her by saying, "I'm in the Spanish immersion class, are you?"

Cassie suddenly felt sick inside. Cassie remembered her mom asking her, "You can be in the class that only speaks Spanish or you can choose the English-speaking class. It's your choice, Cassie."

"I want to stay in my regular class," Cassie had told her mom.

It never crossed Cassie's mind that her best friend Dan might choose the Spanish immersion class. Cassie suddenly felt alone and anything but excited about school starting. Dan noticed how quiet Cassie had become, "What's wrong?" Dan asked.

"I didn't know you and I would be in different classes. I'm not sure if I will have any friends in my class if you're not there," Cassie explained.

"Cassie! Remember what we learned in Sunday school? We are never alone. God is always with us! You won't be alone."

No Fear for Joshua

DAY 2

Read about It

Deuteronomy 31:1–8; Joshua 1:1–9

Think about It

1 Today's verse is such a wonderful promise. It comes from our Bible story about Joshua. Joshua heard this promise twice: once from Moses, and once directly from God. This promise is not just for Joshua. It's for everyone who is a member of God's family! God tells us that he is with us . . . and even better . . . he gets there first. God knows what we will be facing even before anything happens (good or hard).

2 How does it make you feel to know that God promises to always, always, always be with us? God never forgets about us.

3 The second part of the verse is just as good as the first. God repeats the same promise using different words! God wants us to really understand that he loves us so much that he sticks close to us every day of our lives.

Do Something about It

When something you planned suddenly changes and it makes you feel like you are all alone, remind yourself of God's promise. We are never alone because God promises to go before us, stay with us, and never, ever forget about us.

Pray about It

Dear God, help me to remember your promise whenever I feel alone. God, you said you would always stay close beside me; I need to always remember this promise. Please help me to remember that you will never forget about me. In Jesus' name, amen.

Coloring Verse

DAY 3

Read the visual verse, and then write each word beneath its symbol. Finally, use fine-tipped colored pens or pencils to color in the pictures.

Deuteronomy 31:8

A New Friend

Cassie was very quiet on the way home from the playground. Her mom asked, "Cassie, did you and Dan argue about something?"

Cassie shook her head slowly back and forth, "No, we didn't argue. Dan told me he chose the Spanish immersion class. I didn't know he was going to do that!" Cassie started to cry. "I don't want to be in a class without any friends!"

Cassie's mom nodded without saying anything. They rode on in a moment of silence. Then Mom said, "Cassie, the Spanish immersion class is filled up. It's too late to change now. But I have an idea."

Cassie looked at her mother in surprise and wondered what idea could possibly make her feel better. Mom continued, "Cassie, I want you to trust me and I want you to trust God. Next week, when you walk into your new classroom, I want you to look around the room and try to find a girl or a boy who is sitting alone. Then, I want you to walk over, smile, and introduce yourself and sit down."

Cassie wrinkled her forehead as she thought about what her mom said. That was just as scary as being alone! Finally, she asked, "Why do you want me to do that, Mom?"

"Because you'll likely be feeling alone, right? Don't you think there are others in your class who will be feeling alone, too? If you go and make a new friend, neither of you will be alone. Does that make sense?"

Cassie nodded. "Yeah . . . It could be really cool to make a new friend." But then she suddenly felt disloyal. She quickly protested, "But Dan is still my best friend!"

Her mom answered, "I know that, Cassie. And you can still see him at lunch and recess. We'll still schedule play dates for you two. Just because you make new friends doesn't mean you lose your old friends."

Cassie bit her lip and thought about that part. Finally, she realized, *There's no way someone could make me less of a friend to Dan!* She decided on the first day of school, she would go into her new classroom and look for a girl or boy that might be lonely. She smiled, thinking about how good she could make someone feel by being a friend.

DAY 5

Paul, Priscilla, and Aquila

Read about It

Acts 18:1–11, 18–26

Think about It

1. Aquila and Priscilla were friends of the Apostle Paul. Sometimes they were together, and sometimes they weren't. Wherever they were, they continued to make friends with others and teach them about God. Who is a friend you sometimes don't get to spend time with?

2. What does it mean to be a friendly person? We smile and we introduce ourselves. We can ask questions that will help us get to know what our new friend likes best. We remember that everyone needs to be loved and respected . . . everyone needs to have good friends.

3. From our story, Cassie can feel better by remembering that God is always with her. Knowing that God always stays close beside us even when we feel alone can help us be strong enough to start looking out for others who need friends, too. Good friends can be found anywhere. But we have to be willing to be a good friend ourselves first.

Do Something about It

When you are going to a new place or are in a new class or group where you do not have any friends, pray and ask God to help you find others who need friends too. Smile and tell others your name and ask questions so that you can learn more about them. Be the friend that you want to have.

Pray about It

Dear God, I am nervous about trying to make new friends. It is easier to just spend time with the friends I already have. But I know that it is a good thing to go looking for others who might be feeling lonely. Help me to have the courage to smile and introduce myself and then ask good questions. Help me to think about others' feelings and make them feel loved. You promise to always stay close beside me . . . this promise helps me be brave even when I don't feel it. In Jesus' name, amen.

Find That Verse!

Look for the symbols from the Bible verse. Circle each one. Then, fill in the blank lines at the bottom of the page with each verse word. Say the Bible verse out loud until you can remember it without looking at the verse.

DAY 6

_____

_____

_____

Deuteronomy 31:8

Week 2
Christ Gives Me Victory

Look at the visual Bible verse below. Try to figure out what it says. Write the verse words on the blank lines. Use the Visual Bible Verse Dictionary on page 371, if needed.

Overwhelming 🏆 is ⏳+s ➡️

✝️ ❓ ❤️+ed US

_____

_____

_____

_____

_____

Overwhelming victory is ours through Christ, who loved us. Romans 8:37

It's Zoo Time

DAY 1

Jon held the permission paper tightly. He needed a parent to sign the form in order to go on a field trip to the zoo with his class. Weeks ago, when his teacher announced the trip, Jon hurried home to tell his mom about it. They were both so excited! They'd snacked on cookies and talked about how much fun they'd have if she came along as one of the parent helpers. Now, it was coming close! All Jon needed was her signature on the paper.

As he got close to his parents' room, Jon stopped in his tracks when he heard his father say, "We are going to beat this. We are!" Suddenly, it all came crashing back. Ever since Jon's teacher passed out the permission papers earlier that day, Jon had forgotten all about his mom's cancer and how sick she was. He was just excited about going to the zoo with her. His heart fell to his feet as he remembered how very sick she was.

Jon wanted his mom to get better so much! He prayed for her every day, "Please God, I know you can make my mom's cancer go away. Please take it out of her body. I love her and I don't like seeing her so sick. In Jesus' name, amen."

As Jon went into his bedroom he felt sad and scared and not at all excited. He held the paper in his hands and tried to decide if he should ask his mom to sign it or not. Jon's dad worked hard during the day and he couldn't take off work to go on the zoo trip. It had always been Mom who had gone on these school trips. Jon wanted his mom to be healthy again. Everything had changed since she had gotten so sick.

Jon dropped down on his knees next to his bed and prayed again. "God, help my mom to get strong again. Help her and help me to be brave, too. In Jesus' name, amen."

Just as Jon got up off the floor, his dad came into his room. "Jon, are you OK?"

"Dad, I was praying for Mom to get better so she could go with me to the zoo with my class. Do you think she can go?" Jon asked.

"I can't give you a for sure answer right now, but I tell you what we can do. We can sit down right now and pray for her together."

Christ Gives Me Victory · 15

DAY 2

David's Victory over Goliath

Read about It

1 Samuel 17:1–50

Think about It

1. In today's story, David is the only one who thought he could win a fight with Goliath. What gave David confidence that he could win?

2. What does the word overwhelming mean? When the Bible tells us that "overwhelming victory" is ours through Jesus, it is promising us that God will give us the strength to face whatever problems we have.

3. How does it make you feel to know that God promises us the strength to overcome everything that seems to scare us? How does it make you feel to know he does this because he loves us so much?

Do Something about It

Write down anything you feel scared or worried about. Ask your parents or another adult to talk with you about these scary situations and then pray together about each one.

Pray about It

Dear God, help me to be brave and to remember to pray when I feel scared. I need to trust you to take care of me. Sometimes I do trust you and other times, I get frightened again. Please show me good things to do when I am scared or worried. In Jesus' name, amen.

Say, Write, Sing, Repeat

Say the verse; write the verse; sing the verse. Repeat these steps until you know the verse!

1. Say the verse aloud. If needed, review the Visual Bible Verse Dictionary at the back of the book to remember what each symbol stands for.
2. Write the verse on the lines below—as many times as you can!
3. Sing it to the tune of "Old MacDonald" or another tune.
4. Repeat Steps 1, 2, and 3 until you can say the verse without help.

Overwhelming 🏆📡 is ⏳+s 🪝 ✝ ❓ ❤+ed US

Romans 8:37

DAY 4
Praying Again

Jon's forehead wrinkled in confusion. His dad just suggested they pray for his mother again, right after Jon had already prayed! "Dad, I prayed for Mom to get better. Why do we have to do it again? Didn't God get the message the first time?"

Dad reached out and put his hand on Jon's head. "Jon, we can never pray enough for the people we love. It's not that God doesn't know or hear our prayers. He does! But praying helps us feel closer to the person we're praying for, and helps us feel closer to God. In the book of Luke, Jesus tells us to keep on praying—keep on "knocking on the door" and the door will be opened. Isn't it wonderful how much Jesus loves us and mom?"

Jon nodded thoughtfully and agreed, "Yes, Dad. Let's pray again for Mom."

Dad began praying, "Father, you already know how sick Jessika is and how weak she feels. We ask you to heal her body and give her strength and energy to do all the things she loves to do. If it is in your will, please make her well enough to go with Jon on the field trip to the zoo. And if she doesn't regain her strength, help us to know how to show her that we love her. In Jesus' name, amen."

Jon and his dad got up and looked at each other, smiling. Dad asked, "Jon, have you shown your mom the permission paper yet?"

Jon shook his head. "No. I was going to ask her but when I heard you talking to Mom, I didn't want to bother her."

"Let's go in together and tell her all about it. And, let's share with Mom how we just prayed for her with Jesus right there with us!"

More Than Winners

Read about It

Romans 8:31–39

DAY 5

Think about It

1 Our Bible verse comes from today's passage of Scripture. This amazing passage is full of encouragement when we are facing something that might frighten us. How does it make you feel to know that God is on your side no matter what?

2 When Jon's mom got sick with cancer, Jon and his family got their courage and strength from God. What are some situations where you would need God's help to overcome fears?

3 Today's Bible verse begins with the words, "Overwhelming victory is ours." Think about the first word: *overwhelming*. Not just victory, but OVERWHELMING victory. There's no question about it. God is promising us that we can overcome in ALL situations. God isn't saying that some of the time we will overcome. Or that most of the time we can overcome. God tells us that in ALL situations, we can have overwhelming victory through him.

Do Something about It

When you feel afraid of something tell God all about how you are feeling. Share your feelings with family members and ask them to pray with you about what frightens you.

Pray about It

Dear God, thank you for giving me the strength to be an overcomer no matter what problems I am facing. Please help me remember to go to family members to share my feelings and ask them to pray with me. In Jesus' name, amen.

DAY 6: Verse Stack

Carefully look over each symbol in the vertical column. Fill in the green bubble. Next, say the entire verse aloud. Write it as many times as you can on the blank lines. Sing the verse like you did on Day 3. Repeat saying it and singing it until you know it!

Romans 8:37

20 · Christ Gives Me Victory

Week 3
GOD WILL MEET ALL MY NEEDS

Look at the visual Bible verse below. Try to figure out what it says. Write the verse words on the blank lines. Use the Visual Bible Verse Dictionary on page 371, if needed.

_____

_____

_____

_____

_____

God . . . will supply all your needs from his glorious riches. Philippians 4:19

DAY 1

Snow Day!

What a great day! Sophie and Sarah were outside playing in the deep snow as the snow kept falling. Big, thick, fluffy snowflakes drifted down on their heads and eyelashes as they played. The girls loved it!

At one point, Sophie called out, "Let's make a snowman family!"

Their mom saw what they were up to and called out, "Girls, here are some old hats and scarves to place on the snow family's heads."

"Thanks, Mom!" the girls replied in unison.

Sophie searched for some broken tree branches for arms while Sarah went inside to get some carrots for noses. For the eyes, they used round stones from the ground near their house's front steps.

When they finished, the girls stepped back and admired their snowman family. "They look real don't they?" Sarah whispered and then beamed with pride.

Sophie suddenly shivered from head to toe. "I'm cold! Let's go inside and ask Mom if we can have some hot chocolate!"

Sarah replied, "You ask Mom while I get the marshmallows out."

Inside the warm house, the girls sipped their hot chocolate. They were contentedly quiet and their eyes became heavy. Mom noticed them both yawning and knew they must be exhausted from all their fun in the snow. "Girls," she said. "I want you to go upstairs, take showers, and change into your pajamas while I make dinner. It's going to be an early night tonight," Mom said.

The girls went upstairs to do as their mom said. Once the girls were all cleaned up, the family settled down to enjoy dinner. Before they realized it, dinner was over and it was time for bed. The girls brushed their teeth, said goodnight to their mom, and read in their bunk beds, snug and warm under their thick comforters and extra blankets.

Suddenly, everything went dark. Both girls gasped and sat straight up.

"Sophie, what happened?" Sarah cried.

"I don't know!" Sophie answered. "I'm scared!"

"So am I!" Sarah whimpered before burying her face in her pillow.

Manna and Quail

DAY 2

Read about It

Exodus 16:1–36

Think about It

1 Today's Bible story is about when God miraculously provided food for the Israelites when they were traveling through the desert after escaping slavery in Egypt. Even though the people were grumbling and complaining, God provided for their needs. Besides food, what are some of the good things God provides for us?

2 This week's verse tells us that God will take care of us even when we feel afraid. Whatever is happening around us, God is already there. God knows what we will need to be OK. What is something you or someone you know needs that you can pray to God about today?

3 We will never have a need God cannot meet. Sophie and Sarah suddenly felt scared when their lights went and it was dark. But God was with them. God wants us to remember his promise to take care of us. Do you believe it would have helped the girls feel brave if they had remembered to pray and ask God for help?

Do Something about It

When you feel afraid because something suddenly happens fast, remember to pray to God and ask him to protect you.

Pray about It

Dear God, sometimes I feel afraid. My heart starts beating fast and I don't want to move. I forget to ask you for help. Please help me to remember that you are always with me even when I am scared. I need to talk to you out loud when I'm most afraid. I know you always hear my prayers. Thank you for your promise to meet every one of my needs. In Jesus' name, amen.

DAY 3: Missing Word

Read the visual verse, and then write each word beneath its symbol. Color the visual verse. One very important word is missing. Write it in the orange bubble. Why do you think this word is so important in the verse? Write your response on the lines provided.

  supply

_____ _____ _____ _____

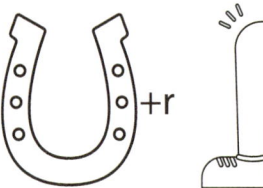+r 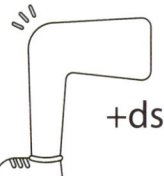+ds *from* HIS

_____ _____ _____ _____

glory + US

_____ _____ _____

Philippians 4:19

_____
_____
_____
_____

24 · God Will Meet All My Needs

When the Lights Go Out

DAY 4

When all the lights went out, both Sophie and Sarah were frozen with fright in their beds. Then, they heard Mom call from downstairs, "Girls, I'll be right up. I'm getting the flashlights."

"I don't like this," Sophie cried.

They heard Mom coming and then saw the light shining bright from her flashlight. "Girls, everything is fine. We lost our electrical power for a few hours because of the snowstorm."

"A few hours!" Sophie despaired.

"I don't want to sleep in our bedroom tonight," Sarah started sobbing. Mom sat down on Sarah's lower bunk and put her arm around her.

"OK, just for tonight you two can sleep on the floor in my bedroom," Mom agreed.

Working together, they brought sleeping bags, blankets, pillows, and a few stuffed animals into Mom's bedroom. Sophie grabbed her mom's hand. "It's too quiet, Mom. I don't like it," she whispered. "I can hear the wind outside. It sounds like it's trying to tear the house down!"

"Girls, what does God say we should do when we feel afraid?"

"Pray," the girls responded.

"Have we prayed yet?" Mom asked.

"Let's pray now," Sophie suggested.

Mom prayed, "Dear God, please help us to go to sleep and not be afraid. Remind us that you are always close by and are looking after us. Even when we feel scared, God you are with us. Give us courage tonight and we thank you for your promise to meet every need we have. Tonight, we need to be brave! Amen."

Mom stood up and brushed her hands together. "Now, girls, I'm going to leave a flashlight on in the hallway so we can see in the dark. But I want you both to close your eyes and go to sleep!"

"We will, Mom!" And they did.

DAY 5

Jesus Is Tempted

Read about It

Matthew 4:1–11

Think about It

1. When Jesus was tempted by Satan, he quoted Bible verses to Satan. We need to follow Jesus' example when we need help, when we're tempted like Jesus was, when we're scared like Sophie and Sarah were—whenever! How can knowing the verses in this book help us when we're in need?

2. One of the best things we can do when we feel scared is pray and ask God for help. Sometimes, we need to know how to figure out a problem. Other times, we need help to be brave. It doesn't matter what kind of help we are asking for, the important thing is that we go to God for everything we need. What could you ask God to help you with today?

3. When Sophie and Sarah felt afraid, they asked their mom for help and then they prayed and asked God for help. We need to remember to ask family members to help us, too. One of the ways God helps us is by giving us families to protect and take care of us.

Do Something about It

Write down a few Bible verses that make you feel brave. Keep them in your room. When you feel scared or need help, get these verses out and say them in prayer to God. You can even say the verses out loud! Also, share your fears with family members and ask them to pray with you about them.

Pray about It

Dear God, help me to remember that you have given me family members and other trusted adults to help protect and care for me. I don't have to do things alone. Help me to tell my family or other trusted adults when I feel scared or when I need help. Thank you for taking care of me and for giving me people who love me. In Jesus' name, amen.

Hot Potato

Gather your family members or friends together. Show everyone this page and review the Bible verse with them. Repeat the verse a couple of times.

Next, sit or stand in a circle and toss a beanbag, small ball, or even a potato back and forth to each other. Each time the Hot Potato is caught, the catcher says the next word in the memory verse. Be sure to have this book open to this page so you can help anyone who has trouble. Continue until as a group, you can play the game and say the verse without help.

Philippians 4:19

Week 4
God Gives Me Peace

Look at the visual Bible verse below. Try to figure out what it says. Write the verse words on the blank lines. Use the Visual Bible Verse Dictionary on page 371, if needed.

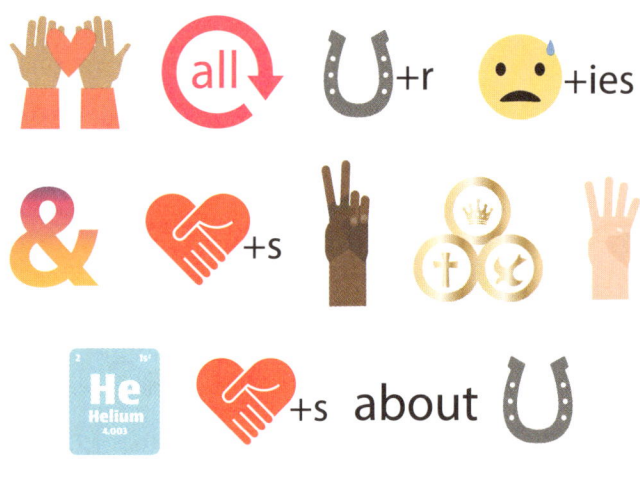

_____

_____

_____

_____

_____

Give all your worries and cares to God, for he cares about you. 1 Peter 5:7

Swimming Season

DAY 1

"Thea! Sean! Please come in here," called their dad from the living room.

The two kids looked up from where they were seated in the dining room, doing their homework. They then looked at each other. Thea shrugged and shook her head no in answer to Sean's unspoken question. Neither Thea nor Sean knew what their dad wanted to talk with them about.

"Coming, Dad," Sean answered. Putting their pencils down and closing their books, Thea and Sean went into the living room and stood waiting for their dad to speak. He was adding something to his calendar.

Putting his phone down, Dad looked up at them and said, "OK, kids, I've just signed both of you up for winter session swimming lessons."

Sean nodded his head. Thea's eyes grew big. Her lip quivered as she protested, "But, Dad . . . I hate the water! I hate getting wet and cold. I hate every part of being near water!" She sniffled pitifully.

"I know you do, Thea." Dad put a comforting hand on her head. "But you want to go to summer camp for a week in July. They require you to know how to swim. And you do not know how to swim," Dad explained.

Thea just stood there staring at her dad. She was torn. Thea wanted to go to summer camp more than anything in the world. This was the first year she was old enough to go. Sean had already gone twice. "I really want to go to camp, but I'm afraid of the water, Dad!" Her eyes welled up. "I don't think I'm brave enough to take swimming lessons," Thea said through her tears.

"I know you're afraid, Thea. That's why I signed you up with a coach who understands how frightening water can be to some people. This coach has helped many children overcome their fears. Plus, Sean will be there with you, even though he already knows how to swim."

God Gives Me Peace · 29

DAY 2

Birds and Flowers

Read about It

Matthew 6:25–34

Think about It

1. What did Jesus say about birds? About flowers? How does it make you feel to know God loves us even more than the other things he cares and provides for?

2. Maybe the best word in this week's Bible verse is the word *all*. Why? Because God tells us to give ALL of our fears, worries, and struggles to him. Why? Because God loves us and wants to take care of them for us.

3. What are some reasons you can trust God to take care of you and handle all your fears, worries, and struggles? Because we know that God is more powerful than all our fears, worries, and struggles, and because we know that he loves and cares for us, there's no reason for us to worry.

Do Something about It

When you start to feel scared or anxious about something, stand up and throw your arms up in the air as if you are giving ALL of your fears to God. Pretend that they are flying away from you and up to Heaven. Then thank God for caring for you and loving you.

Pray about It

Dear God, I don't want to be afraid, but sometimes I am. Please help me to overcome all my fears and not be anxious. Help me to trust that you will take care of me. Remind me that my family and other trusted adults know how to help me overcome my anxieties. I know that I will have to face this fear or it will stop me from doing the things in life that I want to do. In Jesus' name, amen.

Face Swap

Read the visual verse, and then write each word beneath its symbol. In the two faces below, the first is sad, worried, or frightened. In the second face, draw a happy face to show that we can feel happy because we trust that God will take care of us.

_____

     about

_____

1 Peter 5:7

God Gives Me Peace • 31

DAY 4

Shout It Out

After receiving the news that she was going to have to face her fear of water in swimming lessons, Thea returned to the dining room with Sean. They sat at the table and returned to working on their homework until they had finished their assignments. They put their books away.

"Dad, I'm going upstairs to work on my Lego city," Sean called out and then he ran down the hall to his bedroom. Thea went to get some water at the sink and then slowly returned back to the dining room and sat back down at the table. Tears welled up in her eyes. She couldn't stop thinking about the swimming lessons!

After a few moments of silence, her dad walked in. Gently, he said, "Thea, let's talk about this some more. I know that you feel afraid. The thing is, swimming is a skill everyone needs to learn. It will keep you safe all through your life. You may even help keep others safe once you learn to be a good swimmer." Thea looked up sharply, looking at her dad with wide eyes. It had never occurred to her that someday she might help someone else who needed help swimming.

Her dad continued, "And remember, God doesn't want us to live in fear. You know that right, Thea?"

"Dad, I do want to learn to swim, but only because I want to go to summer camp. I understand why you are trying to make me feel better, but I'm still scared," Thea explained.

"Why don't we practice giving all your worries and cares to God like you learned in Sunday school? Remember the empty gift box that your teacher passed around?" her dad said. "You told me that everyone wrote down things that were causing them fear or worry. Then the box was passed around and everyone put their papers in. You all wrapped it up like a gift to give to God!" Thea smiled.

Dad continued, "We have to practice giving all our fears and worries to God and trust that he will take care of us." Dad stood up and brushed his hands together. Then he held one big hand out to Thea. "OK, stand up!" Thea grabbed his hand and stood next to him. "Let's practice right now. We'll take turns calling out anything and everything we are anxious about. In the loudest voice we can!"

Thea smiled. "OK, but first let's get Sean so he can join us!" She giggled. "He's got a tough math test coming up!"

Jesus Heals the Official's Son

DAY 5

Read about It

John 4:43–54

Think about It

1. When we feel anxious, worried, or fearful, God's promises tells us exactly what to do. We are to give ALL our worries and cares to him. In the Bible story, Jesus didn't have to go to the man's house to heal the boy. And the official trusted that. How do you think the official felt when he believed Jesus would heal his son?

2. Thea's dad loved her so much that he knew he had to push Thea a little to overcome her fear of the water. Have your parents or other family members ever pushed you a little to overcome a fear you have? (Encouraged you to sleep in your own bed when you were afraid of the dark; held your hand as you went to a new school; cheered for you the first time you were at bat, etc.)

3. God's love for us is so deep and wide that he doesn't want us to live in fear and worry. God never wants us to be anxious about something we need to do. Instead, he asks us to trust him to care for us.

Do Something about It

When you feel scared or afraid, tell family members or other trusted adults what you are anxious about. Ask them to help you overcome your fears. Do not hide them. With God's help, you will overcome your fears and live bravely.

Pray about It

Dear God, you already know what I am feeling. I get worried that I won't be strong or brave enough to overcome my circumstances. Help me to trust you for the strength to live bravely. I know you love me so much that you don't want me to be afraid of failing or scared of something new or different. Please remind me that you are right by my side no matter where I am. In Jesus' name, amen.

DAY 6

Go Fish!

Read the visual verse, and then write each word on the lines provided.

On separate index cards, draw each symbol or word from the verse. Make four sets. Gather with your family or friends to play a game of Go Fish. (Find instructions for playing Go Fish online.) At the end of each round (when every player has had a turn and play returns to the first player), say the verse aloud as a group.

Alternate activity: Use your cards to play a game by yourself. Try Concentration or Solitaire. For Solitaire, write each set of cards in a different color. Instead of putting cards in number order, put them in verse order.

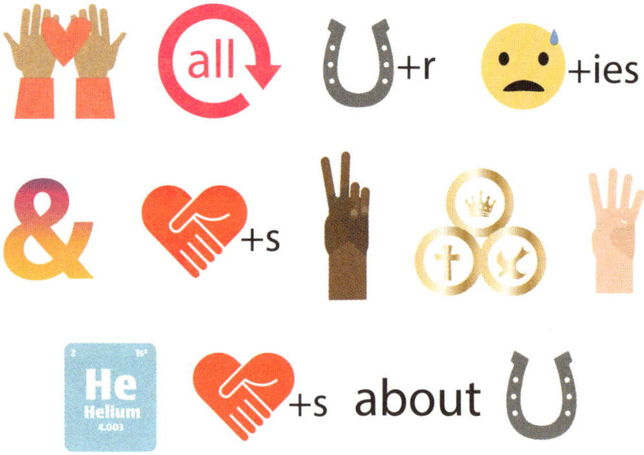

1 Peter 5:7

Week 5
God Makes Everything Possible

Look at the visual Bible verse below. Try to figure out what it says. Write the verse words on the blank lines. Use the Visual Bible Verse Dictionary on page 371, if needed.

_____

_____

_____

_____

_____

_____

With God, everything is possible. Matthew 19:26

DAY 1

No Time for Trevor

"Come on over, Brad!" Trevor called. He was leaning out the open window of his room, waving to his next-door neighbor and best friend, Brad.

"I can't. Not today," replied Brad. He waved before going inside his house and shutting the door. Trevor closed his bedroom window, sighed loudly, and went downstairs. He closed the pantry door harder than he should have, so his mom looked up sharply from where she was stirring stew. One look told her something was wrong with her son.

"Trevor, is there a problem? Are you upset?" Mom asked.

"I invited Brad over again today but he said no." Trevor sat down in one of the stools at the kitchen island.

"Maybe Brad has plans today?" Mom suggested.

"Brad has something going on every day now that Jon moved in down the street," Trevor complained. "He never has time for me now."

"Oh, Trevor. I'm sorry." His mom stopped stirring, turned the burner down, and sat next to Trevor. "I noticed lately you haven't been playing basketball as much at Brad's house, but I didn't think there was a problem between you two," Mom's eyes were kind. "Did you argue or disagree about anything?"

"No . . . we didn't . . . It's just that . . ." After pausing for a moment, Trevor continued in a rush. "Everything changed after Jon moved here! He invites Brad to his house EVERY DAY! They never include me!" Trevor shook his head sadly.

"Trevor, I am sad for you about your friendship with Brad. Sometimes relationships do change. Sometimes we lose friends we thought were our closest friends." Mom put a hand on Trevor's head. "It hurts, I know. But don't give up on Brad yet. He may surprise you."

Mom sat up straight. "I think we should tell God all about this situation right now. Don't you?"

Trevor scrunched his eyebrows together and looked at her, surprised. "I guess," he said.

A Sick Woman

DAY 2

Read about It

Mark 5:24–34

Think about It

1. In our Bible story, we read about a woman who had been sick for a very long time. She'd been to many doctors, but none were able to help her. She was likely told again and again that it was impossible for her to be well. But everything is possible with God and Jesus healed her! How do you think the woman felt when Jesus healed her? What do you think was the first thing she did?

2. Trevor was feeling hurt and sad about his friend Brad ignoring him but until Trevor's mom suggested praying, he never thought about it. God cares so much about us that he waits for us to tell him all our feelings and thoughts. Have you told God today how you are feeling?

3. This week's verse is powerful and encouraging because it reminds us that even when we feel like we can't change anything at all, God can. We need to put our trust in God to work out problems that are way too big for us. This gives us lots and lots of hope. There will be times when we feel so sad and so discouraged that we want to give up. But what does God want us to do instead?

Do Something about It

When you feel sad or discouraged and want to give up, remember to go to God and tell him how you feel. Share with God everything you are hurting about. Ask him to help you have hope. Then trust in him to work things out.

Pray about It

Dear God, sometimes I feel sad and disappointed—and my heart hurts. Please help me to be strong and not get angry and bitter. I want to trust you to work out my problems. Give me wisdom to trust you will do what seems impossible to me. In Jesus' name, amen.

DAY 3: Filling In the Possible

God often works behind the scenes on our behalf. We may face something that seems impossible, but everything is possible with God. He is capable of doing more than we can even imagine. Read the visual verse, and then write each word beneath its symbol. Next, color the word POSSIBLE below by making lots of dots. Use a different color of crayon or marker for each letter. Before you begin coloring a new letter, repeat the verse aloud.

  everything

Matthew 19:26

POSSIBLE

38 · God Makes Everything Possible

Don't Give Up on Friends

DAY 4

Trevor sat beside his mother in the kitchen. His mom began to pray,

"Dear God, please help Trevor to work through all his hurt feelings about his friendship with Brad. Give Trevor your wisdom. Teach him to be a caring friend even when someone doesn't seem to care about him. And God, would you help Brad to see how hurt Trevor is? Whatever happens, God, we love you and trust you. We know that everything is possible for you. You can do what seems impossible in situations that we have no control over. In Jesus' name, amen."

Trevor's mom leaned over and gave him a big hug. Trevor smiled and admitted it felt good to pray, "But it still hurts, Mom," Trevor said.

"Hurt feelings don't just immediately disappear, but telling God how we feel is the first step in healing our hearts," Mom encouraged. "Don't give up yet on Brad! He may be struggling with something you don't know about. Pray for him, Trevor."

Trevor put his head down for a moment, thinking about what his mom just said. Finally, he looked up. "I will, Mom. I will pray for Brad."

Later that night, as he lay in his bed and stared at the glow-in-the-dark stars on his ceiling, Trevor decided to talk to God.

"Dear God, you know I miss Brad. We used to have so much fun playing together. But now it seems like he wants to have fun with Jon. I wish he would at least invite me to go with him to Jon's house. I feel so bad, it's making me not like Brad or Jon! But I don't want to feel that way. Brad's a great guy. That's why he's been my friend all these years. And Jon seems nice, too. I kinda liked him before he and Brad started spending all their time together without me. Lord, help me be a good friend to both Brad and Jon. Help me find ways to show your love to both of them. In Jesus' name, amen."

Trevor turned on his side, closed his eyes, and immediately fell into a deep, peaceful sleep.

God Makes Everything Possible

DAY 5

Sarah Laughs

Read about It

Genesis 15:1–6; 18:1–14; 21:1–7

Think about It

1. Sometimes it's hard when something seems out of our control and impossible to fix! Abraham and Sarah wanted a son, but were so old, they were sure it was impossible. Sarah even laughed when God promised her a son! She'd forgotten that everything is possible with God. How do you think Sarah felt when her son Isaac was born? How did Abraham feel?

2. This week's Bible verse is full of encouragement and hope. Knowing these verse words and remembering their truth can help us feel positive even in impossible situations. When Trevor and his mom sat down to pray about his "impossible" friendship problem with Brad, God was listening. Trevor still felt sad feelings but he knew he had done the right thing in praying for Brad. Have you ever been angry with someone and then obeyed God by praying for that person? How did it make you feel?

3. Trevor's mom was right when she explained to Trevor that sad feelings don't always go away immediately, but when we talk to God about our impossible situations, we can be full of hope. God can do anything. Anything! What seemingly impossible situation do you want to pray about today?

Do Something about It

When you feel like you can't do anything to fix a problem, and you're feeling hopeless, remind yourself of this week's Bible verse. God says that everything is possible with him. Tell God about your problems. Then trust him to care for you in the very best ways.

Pray about It

Dear God, when I feel sad and discouraged, help me to keep trusting you to work things out. Remind me to keep praying every day—even when nothing seems to have changed. I need your courage and strength to not be hopeless. In Jesus' name, amen.

Rhythm Verse

Reread the visual verse below. Then, say it several times aloud. Refer to page 35 if you need help. Finally, come up with motions for each of the three phrases shown below: clap on each syllable of the word, stomp your feet, hop on one foot, pump your fists, etc. Write what you want to do on the lines under each phrase. Then practice saying the phrase and doing the motion several times. After you've practiced, perform your rhythm verse for your family or friends.

  everything

With God,

_____
_____
_____

everything is possible.

_____
_____
_____

Matthew 19:26

_____
_____
_____

Week 6

God Gives Me Strength and Protects Me

Look at the visual Bible verse below. Try to figure out what it says. Write the verse words on the blank lines. Use the Visual Bible Verse Dictionary on page 371, if needed.

The   +ful

+en  &

from: The evil

_____

_____

_____

_____

_____

Bus Bullies

Elina sat cross legged on the floor, watching a movie about a girl her age. The girl was getting bullied every day as she rode the bus to school. Elina's eyes got big and round, and she clasped her hands as she listened to the terrible names two boys were calling this girl. The girl in the movie didn't do anything to make the boys angry. They were just mean.

In the movie, the little girl went home and told her parents what was happening. Her parents went to the school and told the school principal. Those bully boys were taken off the bus so that they wouldn't tease anyone else.

Elina felt better about the ending of the movie than she did about watching the girl being teased and hurt. Still, Elina couldn't forget the look in the little girl's face when it was happening.

"Elina! Time for lunch," her father called.

"I'm coming!" Elina answered. Elina and her parents sat down to a yummy lunch of veggies, fruits, cheese, and crackers. But Elina didn't feel very hungry. She pushed her food around a bit before looking up from her plate and saying, "Dad, do you think there are any bullies on my bus this year?"

Dad looked at Elina, "No, I don't think so. Why? Has someone been unkind to you, Elina?"

"No . . . ." replied Elina. "But it could happen anytime, right? Even Monday?" Monday was the first day of school for the new year.

"Why are you worrying about being bullied, Elina? We've always told you to talk to an adult right away if you see someone being hurt, with words or with fists. Have you seen that happen?" Dad asked.

"No, but I was watching a movie about a little girl who was bullied by two boys. And now I feel scared it might happen to me," Elina explained.

DAY 2

Singing from Jail

Read about It

Acts 16:16–40

Think about It

1 In the Bible story, Paul and Silas were beaten, arrested, and put in jail. They could have been really worried about what was going to happen to them next. Instead, they were singing songs of praise to God! They trusted that God would protect them, even though terrible things had happened to them. Why do you think Paul and Silas were able to sing in jail?

2 This week's verse is a wonderful promise that tells us three important facts:
- First, that God is faithful.
- Second, that God will strengthen us.
- Third, that God will protect us from the evil one (Satan).

How does it feel to know that God is always faithful?

3 Now think about the third part of the verse: how God promises to protect us. Sometimes God will use people who love us—like parents and other family members—to protect us from danger. Other times God will use adults like teachers, coaches, and bus drivers. Our part is to make sure we tell an adult when we are being hurt. Is there anything you need to tell an adult today?

Do Something about It

If you start to feel scared about something that might happen to you, remember this Bible promise about God being faithful to strengthen and protect you. Tell an adult how you are feeling so that you can talk to each other about it.

Pray about It

Dear God, help me to stop worrying about bad things that might happen, and instead think about everything that is good. Please give me courage in my heart to not be afraid of something that hasn't even happened. And if something bad has happened to me, please give me the courage to talk to a trusted adult about it. In Jesus' name, amen.

Verse Word Search

Read the visual verse, and then write each word beneath its symbol. Then, find each verse word in the word search.

Note: Some words appear more than once in the verse, but they'll only be in the puzzle once. Also, don't forget to find *Thessalonians*!

    from: The evil

---

2 Thessalonians 3:3

```
F X E U K I U G L H X L R C H
I N O V J D J Z T W E D W H N
F Y W F I E P X K V H A I K T
Z S I U A L O Z G Z I M L H H
F F H D Y I M N G P E D L I E
R R R S B E T R E S D M S G N
U O O Z G S U H G N M X T T L
L M M E A D D R F B Q V R M N
U G D Z N S X L D U S W E L L
S U C V D O R W Y W L S N A Z
U A O N I S I B C K N O G A G
A R C H D E A U Q W A U T A S
E D C I F B H U M K C T H F W
C K R U C U Z V Y K O Z E B H
X T H E S S A L O N I A N S K
```

Answer Key on page 377.

DAY 4: Rating Reasons

After Elina told her parents about the movie she'd watched, and how it had worried her, she saw her dad and mom looking at each other before looking back to her. "Elina, what were you watching on television? Was it a movie that we gave you permission to watch?" her mom asked.

Elina hung her head down and mumbled, "No."

"Why did you watch something without asking us first?" Dad said.

"I don't know. It looked good. I didn't think I would feel scared after seeing it!" Elina cried.

"Didn't you notice the rating? They always announce it at the beginning of the movie. What was the movie rated?" Mom asked.

Elina's head dropped down even lower. "TV 14," she whispered.

"Honey, this is exactly why we have rules in our house. To protect you, not to stop you from having fun," Dad said.

"I know. I made a bad choice," Elina said through her tears, "And now I can't get the bad parts out of my mind."

Elina's parents got up from the table and knelt down beside her. "Let's pray," Dad said.

> "Dear God, please help Elina to understand that we love her so much that we need her to follow the rules to protect her. Help her to learn from this lesson of watching something that frightened her. And please help Elina to never forget that you, God are faithful and will always strengthen and protect her from evil. In Jesus' name, amen."

Elina wiped her tears and felt so happy that her parents were there to love and protect her. "I won't forget, Dad," Elina smiled.

"I'm glad," Mom said.

"I'm glad, too," said Dad. "But you still disobeyed the rules and there are consequences for that."

"Can you think of what might be an appropriate consequence, Elina?" Mom asked.

"Since I broke the rules by watching something I shouldn't have . . . maybe I should be grounded from television for a week," Elina suggested.

Paul Asks for Prayer

DAY 5

Read about It

2 Thessalonians 3:1–5

Think about It

1 Today's Bible passage contains this week's Bible verse and tells of many things Paul asked the Thessalonians to pray about. One of these things is protection from the evil one. That's another way to ask for protection from the temptation of sin—the feeling of wanting to do wrong things. God promises that he will strengthen us and help protect us from temptation, but God expects us to make good choices, too. Have you ever disobeyed family or school rules and had things get even worse?

2 This week's verse promises us God's strength and protection. Elina's parents wanted her to understand that they will protect her, too. The rules they set in place are one way they protect her. Elina's parents know that if we start thinking about scary stuff or watch scary movies, it becomes harder to think about good things. How do you think Elina felt after she realized she made a mistake by watching that scary movie?

3 Obeying God and our parents and other trusted adults is one way we can be protected from real danger as well as from scary thoughts. God wants us to live bravely and be courageous, but our part is to make good choices even when no one else is watching.

Do Something about It

When you are tempted to make a bad choice and disobey God or your parents, stop and pray. Ask God to give you the strength to make a good choice. Then, talk to your parents or other family members about what you were thinking. Finally, ask them to pray for you.

Pray about It

Dear God, please remind me to always obey you and the adults you have given to care for me. I know that you only want what is best for me. Help me to remember that the rules in my family are there to protect me, not to stop me from having fun. In Jesus' name, amen.

Mirror Writing

This week's visual Bible verse is backwards! Write each word beneath its symbol. Then, color the symbols. Finally, hold a mirror up to the picture to read the verse.

2 Thessalonians 3:3

48 · God Gives Me Strength and Protects Me

Week 7
God Gives Me Wisdom

Look at the visual Bible verse below. Try to figure out what it says. Write the verse words on the blank lines. Use the Visual Bible Verse Dictionary on page 371, if needed.

 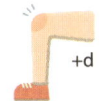+d +dom

 generous  &

  it

_____

_____

_____

_____

_____

If you need wisdom, ask our generous God, and he will give it to you. James 1:5

God Gives Me Wisdom

DAY 1

On the Ball

Dan walked to school every morning with his best friend Cory. They had so much fun running and walking and tossing their football into the air. Dan would start by calling out, "Cory, catch this if you can!" He would then hurl the ball as far down the road as he could.

Cory would run forward with arms open wide and grab for the football. "Got it!" Then it was Cory's turn to yell, "Catch!" and chuck the ball and watch, laughing, as Dan tried to catch the football before it hit the ground.

Every morning, Dan and Cory walked the same route to school. Every morning the boys tossed the same football to each other. Then one morning Dan and Cory saw a boy named Jason from school wiping away tears from his eyes. They stopped.

"Are you OK, Jason?" Dan asked. Jason nodded but didn't answer.

"You're all dirty and your nose is bloody," commented Cory. Jason still didn't say a word. Dan and Cory looked at each other and shrugged their shoulders.

"Come on, Jason, walk with us to school or we are all going to be late," Dan encouraged. Jason wiped his nose with his sleeve and followed behind Dan and Cory. Jason didn't say a word about what happened or anything else.

The boys rounded the corner in front of the school just in time to hear the first warning bell ring out. "Hurry, we have to put our coats and books in our lockers!" Cory shouted. The three boys barely made it to class in time, but Dan and Cory still hadn't solved the mystery of what had happened to Jason.

Solomon Seeks Wisdom

DAY 2

Read about It

1 Kings 3:1–14; 4:29–34

Think about It

1. What did Solomon ask God for? Why did he want that? Solomon sought wisdom from God in order to lead God's people. And God helped Solomon know the best thing to do in any situation. That same wisdom is available to us. Just like Solomon, all we need do is ask!

2. This week's Bible promise is special because God encourages us to come to him when we need wisdom. What is wisdom? Wisdom helps us understand what to do or say when you are faced with a problem. In the story, Dan and Cory need wisdom to know how to help Jason.

3. When was a time you felt confused or puzzled about a problem? Maybe it was something a friend said to you and you didn't understand. Or maybe it was a problem at home between you and another family member. God's promise to give us wisdom is good for every situation we face. Have you asked God for wisdom? If you haven't and you are facing a confusing problem that you cannot figure out, pray right now and ask God to show you what to do.

Do Something about It

When you feel confused or puzzled about a problem, pray and ask God for wisdom to figure it out. It might be a problem with schoolwork, or with family or friends . . . It doesn't matter what the problem is. The important thing is to go to God for help.

Pray about It

Dear God, sometimes I have a confusing problem and I can't figure out what to do. Will you please help me? Please give me the wisdom I need to understand. Help me to think about this problem and consider how Jesus would handle it. Give me your good thoughts and ideas for solving this problem in a way that pleases you. In Jesus' name, amen.

God Gives Me Wisdom

Hidden Visual Verse

Review this week's visual Bible verse. The symbols and words are hidden in this picture. Can you find them all? Each symbol or word is hidden once.

Answer Key on page 377.

52 · God Gives Me Wisdom

Mystery Solved

DAY 4

Just as the final bell rang, Dan, Cory, and Jason were taking their seats. Mrs. Mitchell turned from the board where she had been writing, smiled brightly and said, "Good morning, class!" The smile quickly faded from her face when she saw Jason and his bloody nose. "Class, the opening journal assignment is on the board. Get out your notebooks and start writing. I'll be back in a moment."

Dan and Cory and all their classmates watched their teacher walk straight to Jason, hold her hands out to him, and whisper, "Let's go to the nurse." She walked Jason out into the hallway and the door closed behind her.

As soon as the door shut, Dan and Cory heard Ted laugh. Ted leaned over to the boys sitting near him and whispered. "I got him good. And Jason won't tell anyone what I did to him or I'll hit him again!" Dan and Cory looked at each other. Now they understood. Jason was afraid of getting hit again by Ted. That's why he wouldn't tell them what had happened.

Dan whispered to Cory, "Remember what we learned in Sunday school about asking God for wisdom? That when we don't know what to do we can ask God? Well, I just prayed. I think we need to tell Mrs. Mitchell what happened because Jason won't."

Cory nodded in agreement. "We'll stay in during recess and tell her after everyone leaves," Cory whispered.

Dan's eyes suddenly got big and his voice quivered as he whispered. "What if Ted finds out we told on him? He might come after US!"

"We have to do what is right, Dan. If somebody hurt you, I would tell someone," Cory whispered.

Dan slowly nodded. "Yeah, you're right. I just got scared for a minute."

"Let's ask Jason to walk with us to school from now on," Cory suggested. Dan nodded and both boys got to work on their writing assignment.

DAY 5: A Solid Foundation

Read about It

Matthew 7:24–29

Think about It

1. Jesus taught that anyone who follows his teachings will be building their life on a solid foundation. This means that we can become wise and make good, solid decisions if we listen to and learn from God's wisdom in the Bible. What are some ways you are learning from the Bible?

2. This week's Bible promise is important to memorize and remember because there isn't a day in our whole lives when we won't need God's wisdom. We will need his thoughts to guide us at home, at school, on the playground, from the minute we wake up until we close our eyes to sleep at night. We need God's wisdom as kids, and we need it when we're adults.

3. Dan and Cory did make the wise choice of going to their teacher after Ted had hurt Jason. Even though it might have been a little scary, the boys knew it was right. God gives us wisdom because he knows there will be many times in our lives when we will be confused. He doesn't want us to struggle with confusion. He wants to help us with wisdom! Is there anything you would like to ask God for wisdom to deal with today? You can!

Do Something about It

When you feel scared or confused about doing the right thing, ask God for wisdom. And if you need to, ask for courage, too. Sometimes it can feel scary to do the right thing. In spite of everything, know that God wants you to choose wisely for every decision you make.

Pray about It

Dear God, thank you for giving me wisdom to know how to handle problems and other confusing situations. Help me to be wise even when it feels scary. Help me remember to take care of other people like I hope they will take care of me. I know that you want me to always do the right thing even when other people may not like it. Give me your wisdom, courage, and strength to obey you. In Jesus' name, amen.

Symbol Memory

Remember what the symbols are for the verse and draw each one above the appropriate word. (Turn to p. 49 if you need help!)

DAY 6

if   you   need   wisdom

ask   our   generous   God

and   he   will   give

it   to   you   James 1:5

Week 8

GOD FORGIVES ME

Look at the visual Bible verse below. Try to figure out what it says. Write the verse words on the blank lines. Use the Visual Bible Verse Dictionary on page 371, if needed.

 has removed

as  from:  as

 from:

_____
_____
_____
_____
_____

[God] has removed our sins as far from us as the east is from the west. Psalm 103:12

The Colored Book

"Lili!" Amelia cried out her younger sister's name when she opened the door to her room. She'd just gotten home from a tiring day at school, and was looking forward to just laying on her bed and reading one of her library books. And this is what greeted her!

All of her books were on the floor. Worse yet, Lili had used color markers to scribble all over the book Amelia was halfway through. Now Amelia would have to pay for it. Amelia's eyes filled with angry tears.

She marched into her sister's room where Lili was playing with her dolls. "Lili, I'm telling Grandma what you did!" She waved the colored book under her sister's nose.

Lili was surprised by how angry Amelia was. She knew she wasn't supposed to go into Amelia's room without permission. But she'd been bored and Grandma was downstairs cleaning. She wanted to be like her big sister, so playing with Amelia's books was what Amelia did the most. And coloring the book . . . Well, Lili was too young to read. Coloring is what she did with all her books.

Lili's lip started to quiver and fat tears rolled down her cheeks. "I . . . I'm sorry," Lili apologized.

"Lili, I hate you! I hate you! I hate you!" cried Amelia at the top of her voice.

Amelia pushed past her sister, stormed out of Lili's room, and slammed the door hard. That's when she realized Lili had scribbled in several of the books. Amelia's anger grew as she discovered each additional book that Lili had scribbled in. She gave up trying to clean. She was just too mad!

Amelia plopped down on her bed, looked around at the mess in her room, and replayed in her mind all the awful things Lili had ever done. *My stuff just isn't safe when I'm at school,* she thought. *Not with Lili in the house! I will never forgive her!*

"Amelia," called Grandma from the hallway, "Please come out here now, I want to talk with you."

Amelia did not want to talk to her grandmother. Amelia wanted to be alone and be angry.

"Amelia, did you hear me?"

"Yes, I'm coming," Amelia reluctantly answered.

God Forgives Me • 57

DAY 2: The Unforgiving Servant

Read about It

Matthew 18:21–35

Think about It

1. Jesus told this story so that we would know that God wants us to forgive other people. Just like we have been forgiven by God, we need to forgive others. How do you feel when someone tells you that you've done something wrong? How do you feel when you are forgiven for that thing?

2. This week's Bible promise tells us that God tosses our sins away as far as the east is from the west (that means it is so far no one can make them meet). God forgives all of our sins, big ones and little ones. If God forgives us, shouldn't we forgive others?

3. It's fine that Amelia was upset about her favorite books being drawn on. Lili was wrong to have touched and then ruined Amelia's books. Still, when someone asks us for forgiveness, we are disobeying God when we refuse to forgive. Have you ever refused to forgive someone for hurting you?

Do Something about It

When you feel so angry with someone for hurting you or doing something mean to you, pray. Ask God to help you forgive that person. Remember this week's Bible verse. It will remind you that God always forgives you and that you should obey God and forgive others.

Pray about It

Dear God, I know I need to forgive others, but sometimes it is so hard. I need your help to be forgiving. Please give me the strength I need to forgive others, even when it is hard. In Jesus' name, amen.

As Far As East Is from West

Our verse promises that "[God] has removed our sins as far from us as the east is from the west." Our world is round, so east and west never meet. That means when God forgives us, our sins are gone forever!

Look for the visual verse symbols and words on the world map. Circle each one. Write the verse at the bottom of the page in verse order. Each symbol or word is hidden once.

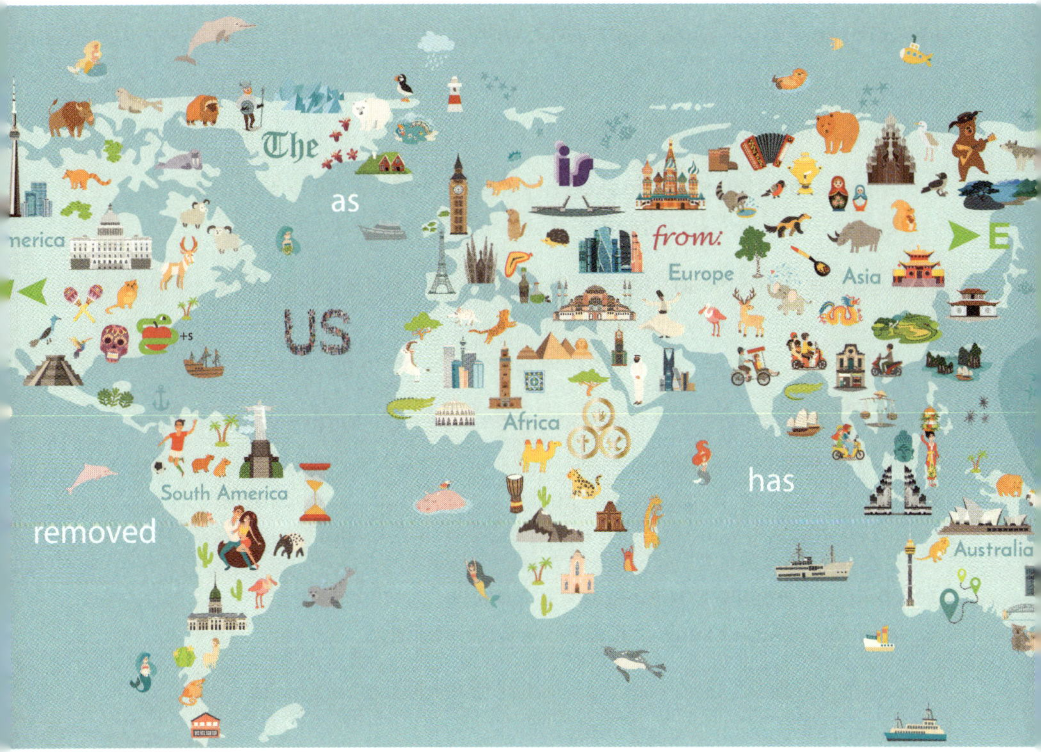

_____

_____

_____

_____

Psalm 103:12

DAY 4

Forgiveness or Anger?

Amelia opened her bedroom door. She walked slowly into the hallway where her grandmother and sister stood waiting.

Grandma began, "Amelia, I understand you're upset with Lili. What happened?"

Amelia responded loudly and quickly, "Lili went into my room WITHOUT permission. She threw all my books around and then she scribbled on some of them with her markers! She ruined a LIBRARY book! That's against the law or something, isn't it?" Amelia finished, crossing her arms across her chest.

"I said I'm sorry!" Lili spoke up, "I am sorry!"

Grandma looked at Amelia. "Lili shouldn't have touched your books. She will use her birthday money to replace the book she ruined." Amelia smiled smugly.

Grandma wasn't done. She looked at Amelia. "But we still need to talk about why you screamed that you hated her."

The smug look left Amelia's face as her cheeks turned red and her eyes welled up with tears. Amelia finally looked up at Grandma. "I know I shouldn't have said that. But I was so angry! Lili knows better than to go in my room!" Amelia replied.

"Yes, she does, Amelia. But when someone asks us to forgive them, we have a choice. We can hold a grudge and maybe try to make them feel bad or seek revenge. Or we can forgive them. Remember the Bible verse that tells us God forgives our sins and he removes them as far as the east is from the west?" Grandma asked.

"Yes, but . . . " Amelia started to protest, but her voice trailed off when she couldn't think of any more words to say.

"There are no 'buts.' God commanded us to forgive others as he forgives us," Grandma stated firmly.

"That means we're sinning if we refuse to forgive and stay mad, huh?" Amelia asked.

"That's exactly right," Grandma nodded. "So is there anything you want to say to Lili?"

"Lili, I forgive you," Amelia said.

Grandma smiled. "Now, why don't the two of you go and clean up that mess together?

Philemon and Onesimus

DAY 5

Read about It

Philemon

Think about It

1. Paul reminded Philemon that Jesus loves everyone so much that he was willing to die so that we can be forgiven. When we remember how much Jesus has done, it makes us want to forgive others. What are some ways you can be encouraged to forgive others?

2. This week's verse makes it clear that God is serious about forgiveness. He wants us to be serious about forgiveness, too. Try to imagine how far the east is from the west. You can't do it! And that is God's point. He wants us to know that he throws our sins so far away from us that we can never find them again.

3. Have you struggled to forgive someone this week for hurting you? Have you talked to God about forgiving this person? Whenever you find it hard to forgive, ask someone from your family or a trusted friend to sit down and pray with you. Together you can ask God to give you the love and strength needed to forgive.

Do Something about It

If you think about a time when someone hurt you even after you have forgiven them, you might start to feel angry all over again. Pray and ask God to give you the strength to keep forgiving. Ask God to help you put that anger as far away from you as the east is from the west. Think about other things—good things—and don't keep thinking about what made you feel angry and hurt.

Pray about It

Dear God, help me to always remember your great forgiveness. Help me to forgive others the way you forgave me. Please help me to think about good things, and not keep replaying bad things in my mind. I know I make mistakes and sometimes I hurt others. I want them to forgive me just like you do. So I need to be willing to forgive, too. Thank you for your love and forgiveness. In Jesus' name, amen.

Backwards Words

Write each backwards word correctly on the blank line next to it. Number the words in the correct order. Then, match each word to its symbol on the right by drawing.

morf	_____
devomer	_____
sah	_____
sa	_____
raf	_____
tsew	_____
eht	_____
tsae	_____
ruo	_____
doG	_____
si	_____
morf	_____
su	_____
sa	_____
eht	_____
snis	_____

Psalm 103:12

62 · God Forgives Me

Answer Key on page 378.

Week 9
Christ Gives Me Strength

Look at the visual Bible verse below. Try to figure out what it says. Write the verse words on the blank lines. Use the Visual Bible Verse Dictionary on page 371, if needed.

_____

_____

_____

_____

_____

I can do everything through Christ, who gives me strength. Philippians 4:13

DAY 1: Soccer Strong

Brianna and her friends listened carefully to their teacher. Mr. Williams was making the daily announcements, "Fall soccer tryouts are coming up this Friday at 3:30. Be sure to get a parent or guardian signature on the permission form available at the office."

Brianna had never played soccer before, but she really wanted to try. All of her friends had played before and were always talking about how much fun it was. Brianna hated missing out. She also knew with all their experience, she wouldn't be as good as any of them. Still, she wanted to be on the team.

At recess, Brianna ran up to her friend, Ellie. "Hey, Ellie!" Brianna asked, "Do you think I could be on your soccer team even though I haven't ever played before?"

"Sure! We weren't very good last year, but it was still so fun. You have to try out. You have to!" Ellie encouraged. Brianna nodded her head in agreement, but inside she didn't feel as confident.

Brianna went home that afternoon with the information on soccer tryouts and the permission form. She gave them to her parents to read. "OK, Brianna. Give us a chance to read the materials and talk this over." Brianna nodded and headed to her room to do her homework.

At dinner, Brianna's dad said, "I think this is a great idea, Brianna. But just remember, you haven't played soccer before so it might be harder than you think to learn the skills you need."

Brianna replied, "I thought of that, but Ellie told me their team wasn't very good last year. Ellie told me not to worry."

Dad nodded. "OK. Well, know that if you join the team, we want you to finish the whole season. Even if it's hard, don't quit."

Brianna answered, "I'll remember. And I still want to try!"

Samson and Delilah

Read about It

Judges 13:2–5,24; 16:4–31

Think about It

1 In the Bible story, Samson prayed for physical strength, and God gave it to him. God gives us physical strength when we need it. But this week's verse is talking about more than physical strength when we're sick or weak. God will give us mental strength when we need confidence. God will give us emotional strength when we're worried or afraid. God gives us whatever strength we need! What kind of strength do you want to ask God for today?

2 This week's promise from God has a great word, *everything*. *Everything* tells us that God gives us exactly what we need to be strong in all the ways we need. When was a time when you felt weak but God gave you the strength you needed?

3 In our story, Brianna's father told her to finish the whole season of soccer even if she wanted to quit. Do you think that was fair? Why or why not?

Do Something about It

When you begin a new sport, or a new class, or even a new hobby. Pray for strength. If you start to feel discouraged because it is harder to learn or do than you thought it would be, turn to God. Ask God for the strength to keep going, growing, and learning.

Pray about It

Dear God, please help me to keep trying my best every day even when I want to give up. Give me the strength to do what I need to so that I can learn the skills to succeed. In Jesus' name, amen.

DAY 3: Say, Write, Sing, Repeat

Say the verse; write the verse; sing the verse.
Repeat until you know the verse!

1. Say the verse aloud. If needed, review the Visual Bible Verse Dictionary at the back of the book to remember what each symbol stands for.
2. Write the verse on the lines below—as many times as you can!
3. Sing it to the tune of "London Bridge" or another tune.
   I can do everything, everything, everything!
   I can do everything through Christ, who gives me strength!
4. Repeat Steps 1, 2, and 3 until you can say the verse without help.

Philippians 4:13

66 · Christ Gives Me Strength

A Kick Too Hard

DAY 4

It was the first day of soccer practice and Brianna sat on the bench next to Ellie. The coach was explaining what was expected of each team member and how the practices would run. He even demonstrated the most important skills they would be learning.

"Ellie, those don't look as hard as I thought," Brianna whispered.

Ellie nudged Brianna and giggled, "They're easy! At least until we start playing a real game against another team!"

"Oh," Brianna replied. She started watching more carefully.

Then practice started. All the girls lined up along the side of the field. The coach and his assistant coach each took one half of the girls. The drill was to kick the soccer ball to a partner a few feet away. When it was Brianna's turn, she kicked the ball so hard it flew past her teammate. Brianna felt embarrassed. Her coach had told her to kick it to her teammate not right past her.

"Let's try these passes again," Coach said. The girls lined up in their positions and one by one each girl kicked the ball to her partner. "I can do this!" Brianna told herself. When it was Brianna's turn, she kicked the ball too hard again.

"Oh no!" Brianna said out loud. She felt like crying.

Coach walked over to Brianna and said, "Hey, Brianna, that was better this time. Let's keep practicing until you get it right!" And she did. Brianna kicked that ball so many times into the field she forgot about everything else.

Ellie ran over to watch Brianna when her practice was over. "Brianna, you did it! See I told you could."

Brianna smiled at Ellie and said, "I did . . . but it was a lot harder than it looked. I'm so tired I need a rest!"

"You earned it. Come and have some water and a snack," Ellie replied as she grabbed Brianna's hand and pulled her toward the table with the drinks and snacks.

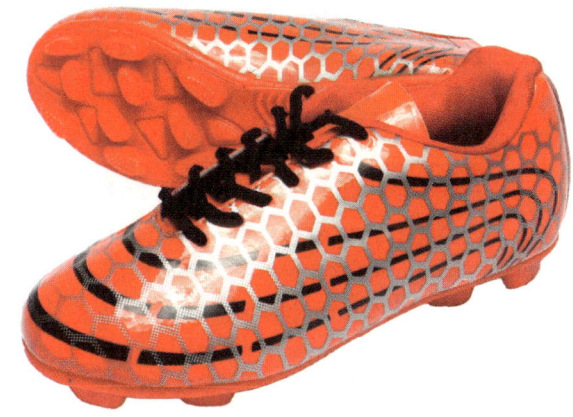

DAY 5: Run the Race

Read about It

Hebrews 12:1–4

Think about It

1. Our Bible passage compares living the life God wants for us to running a race. Who does the passage tell us is our champion? Looking to Jesus' example of how to live is one way we can have strength.

2. When we ask God for the strength to keep trying, we have to remember that we have to work hard, too. That means we have to do our very best and not give up when we feel discouraged or when it gets too hard. Have you ever been so tired you have wanted to quit? Did you? Or did you keep going?

3. Brianna had to work harder than she expected when she was learning how to kick that ball into the right place. She was tired but she didn't give up. Her friend Ellie wasn't struggling, but she helped Brianna. Sometimes we will feel strong and our friend might feel weak. What can we do to encourage them to keep trying?

Do Something about It

When you start to feel tired, do not quit. Ask God for the strength you need. If you have a friend who feels discouraged, encourage them to keep trying, too. Pray for them to be strong.

Pray about It

Dear God, when I am exhausted and want to quit doing your will, help me remember that you promised to give me all the strength I need. Help me learn the lessons I need to live life in the right way. Thank you! In Jesus' name, amen.

Soccer Symbols

DAY 6

On their shirt, each soccer kid has a symbol or word from the verse. Write the correct word on the blank line under each kid. Then, circle the kid with the first word of the verse. Draw a line from that word to the kid with the next word. Continue until you have completed the verse with the reference.

Philippians 4:13

Challenge: Get a family member or friend to play a bouncing game with you. Use a Ping-Pong ball to play inside or a larger ball to play outside. Players bounce the ball to another player, saying one word of the verse on each bounce. If you are playing alone, bounce the ball against a wall.

Week 10
Everything Is Possible

Look at the visual Bible verse below. Try to figure out what it says. Write the verse words on the blank lines. Use the Visual Bible Verse Dictionary on page 371, if needed.

_____
_____
_____
_____
_____
_____

What is impossible for people is possible with God. Luke 18:27

An Early Christmas

DAY 1

It was the first day of November. Jeremy and Joel were helping their parents decorate their Christmas tree. "Why are we decorating our tree so early this year, Dad?" questioned Jeremy.

"Well, I didn't want to miss one of the best parts of Christmas! I love bringing the tree down from the attic, putting it together, and spending the evening decorating with you and Joel," Dad explained, "This year I might not be home for Christmas. Even so, I want everything to be all ready for you boys and your mom."

Jeremy and Joel both froze and looked at their father, mouths open and eyes wide. After a moment, Jeremy found his voice again. "What do you mean you might not be here for Christmas?" demanded Jeremy.

"We have already talked about this, Jeremy. The army moved up my departure date by four weeks so that there is a better chance of us being here by Christmas Eve," Dad explained again.

"Oh," both boys said quietly. Jeremy and Joel remembered when their dad and mom sat them down a week earlier and told them about Dad being on duty near Christmas time. They felt sad and didn't want to think about Dad missing Christmas. Maybe that's why they just forgot he wouldn't be there.

"OK, boys, each of you take a box of ornaments and carefully hang them on the tree." Mom said. Dad will take one, too. When you're done, I'll have hot cocoa and cookies ready." With that, Mom disappeared into the kitchen.

"Dad, you take this box." Jeremy handed him a box. Then he handed one to Joel. "Joel, you take this one and I'll take that last one." Jeremy continued his instructions. "Joel, you work on the bottom part and I will reach the above you. Dad, you're in charge of the top!" Dad looked at the boys and smiled.

Working together, the tree was all decorated before they knew it. It looked beautiful. Mom came out with the hot cocoa and cookies. But even with the fun and excitement of a wonderful early Christmas tree, Jeremy and Joel couldn't shake all their sad thoughts that Dad might miss all the REAL Christmas fun.

Everything Is Possible · 71

DAY 2: The Rich Man

Read about It

Luke 18:18–30

Think about It

1. This week's verse comes from the Bible story we just read. In this story, we read about an encounter Jesus had with a rich, young ruler. Peter and the other disciples thought if a rich man couldn't get to heaven, it would be impossible for a poor person like them. But Jesus explained that what seems impossible to men is possible with God. Have you ever prayed and asked God to help you do something that seemed impossible? Write about what happened.

2. This week's verse reminds us who God is and who we are. God is all-powerful. Nothing is impossible for him. We are humans and are not all-powerful. In fact, we are often weak and afraid. God is never weak, never afraid, because his power rules over everything in Heaven and on Earth.

3. How does it make you feel to know that God can do anything he chooses? How does it make you feel to know that you can tell your worries to God and ask him for the impossible?

Do Something about It

Instead of worrying and feeling afraid, talk to God every day about what is happening in your life. Tell him if you feel happy or sad, excited or discouraged, brave or fearful. Pray and talk to God in the morning and when you go to bed at night. God loves you so much and he wants to talk with you!

Pray about It

Dear God, I am going to tell you all about what is happening in my life every day. When I wake up in the morning and am getting dressed, I will talk with you. When I lay down in my bed at night, I will tell you everything that happened during the day. I am so thankful that you love me so much that you want to spend time listening to me and talking with me. I am so grateful that you are powerful and nothing is impossible for you. I feel safe knowing that you can do anything. In Jesus' name, amen.

Christmas Tree Verse

All the words to this week's verse are decorating the tree. Try to remember what each symbol means. Then, write the verse in the correct order on the lines below.

Luke 18:27

DAY 4

Impossible Things

"Mmm, this is so good, Mom!" commented Jeremy, "Can I have another marshmallow?"

"Sure! Take two more. You boys did such a great job decorating." Mom said with a smile.

"Dad, when will you know if you will be home for Christmas?" Joel asked uncertainly.

"Boys, I probably won't know until the week before Christmas. It all depends on when we finish our current assignment."

Mom said, "Boys, what verse did we learn last week? The one about God doing the impossible? Do you remember?"

Jeremy jumped up and ran to the bulletin board on the wall. "Here," he cried, "It says, 'What is impossible for people is possible with God' Luke 18:27."

Dad and Mom looked at each other and smiled. Dad asked, "Do you boys believe that God can do the impossible?"

"Yes!" both boys said enthusiastically.

Then Mom asked, "Should we talk to God right now and ask him to let Dad be home for Christmas?"

"Yes!" both boys yelled.

"God is the one who decides to say yes or no when we ask him to do the impossible. If he says no and Dad doesn't get home in time for Christmas, we still have to accept that answer and trust God. Can you trust God even if he says no?" Mom questioned.

Jeremy and Joel didn't answer right away. They wouldn't like it, but could they trust God anyway? "I will," spoke up Joel. "God's will is always best. If he decided Dad can't be home for Christmas, then it's up to us to be brave and celebrate Jesus' birth anyway."

"I will, too!" agreed Jeremy.

"OK then, why don't we all go sit in the living room, turn off the lights, and sit near the Christmas tree while we pray?" Mom suggested.

Dad and his two boys jumped up and cried, "Yes!"

Jesus Is Alive

DAY 5

Read about It

Mark 15:21 — 16:8

Think about It

1. Our Bible story is the most amazing story in the history of everything. Jesus died, but he is alive again! Jesus died to take the punishment for our sins. Because of Jesus, we can be forgiven of our sins and become members of God's family. If this is something you are interested in doing, please tell an adult family member or other trusted adult.

2. Have you ever thought about what the word *impossible* means? Another way to understand this word is to think of other words that mean the same thing. What are other words that mean impossible? (No way; out of the question; unimaginable and inconceivable, etc.)

3. Have you thought about what the word *possible* means? What are some other ways to describe something that is possible? (Potential; maybe; it can work; I can see it happening, etc.)

4. Compare these two sets of words. How do the impossible words make you feel? How do the possible words make you feel? Remember with God all things are possible even those things that people cannot do.

Do Something about It

When you believe that something important to you cannot happen (it seems impossible), talk to God about it. Pray for him to do the impossible. Remember that God may not say yes; and if he doesn't, thank God for hearing your prayer and choose to trust him.

Pray about It

Dear God, I am glad that I can ask you to do the impossible. I know that you can do all things. Help me to trust you even if you say no to my prayers. Thank you for listening to me pray and for always doing what it best for me. In Jesus' name, amen.

DAY 6: Criss-Cross Verse

Read the visual verse, and then write each word beneath its symbol. Next, solve the puzzle by filling in the words of the verse. Tip: Count the letters in each word before you put them in the boxes.

_____ _____

_____ _____ _____ _____

_____ _____ _____

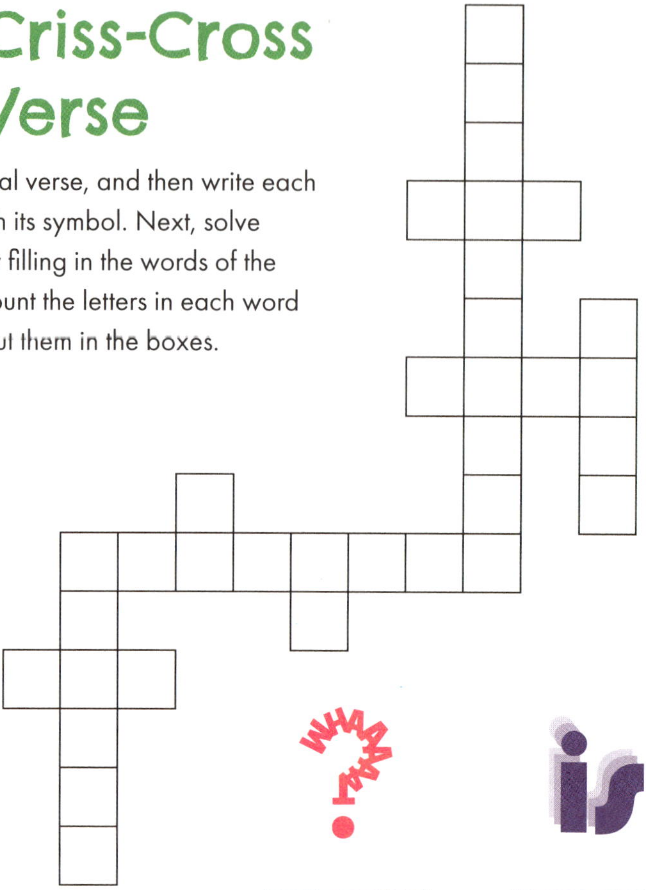

Luke 18:27

Week 11

JESUS GIVES US REST

Look at the visual Bible verse below. Try to figure out what it says. Write the verse words on the blank lines. Use the Visual Bible Verse Dictionary on page 371, if needed.

_____

_____

_____

_____

_____

_____

Come to me, all of you who are weary and carry heavy burdens, and I will give you rest. Matthew 11:28

DAY 1

Lazy Saturdays

Every Saturday morning Noel was allowed to sleep in late because it wasn't a school day. She loved sleeping in! When she did wake up, there would be yummy smells coming from the kitchen. This particular Saturday, Noel tried to guess what breakfast was from the smells. "Mmm . . . pancakes . . . and bacon!" Noel whispered to herself and smiled.

Noel climbed out of bed and reached under her bed to find her bunny slippers. "There you are!" She put them on and slung her bathrobe over her shoulders. "I'm coming, Mom," Noel yelled before dashing into the bathroom.

Minutes later, Noel sped down the stairs and into the kitchen. "Yes! I was right. Pancakes and bacon!" Noel cheered.

Mom smiled, "Sit down, Noel. Eat before it all gets cold."

After gobbling up two large pancakes and three pieces of crispy bacon, Noel put her fork down and sighed, "I'm full!"

"Noel, make sure you finish all your chores before doing anything else today," Mom said.

"Oh no . . ." Noel moaned. "I told Sarah she could come over this morning to play."

"She can come over after your chores are finished," Mom explained.

Noel got up and walked over to the bulletin board where Mom hung the weekly calendar and checked out her chores. "No!" Noel screamed.

Mom jumped. "What is wrong, Noel?"

"I have five chores to do today and it's going to take me all day!" Noel complained.

"Noel, first of all, it won't take you all day. Second, those are the chores you failed to do during the week, so today you have to finish them all," Mom said patiently.

"But . . ." Noel started before Mom cut her off.

"No buts. You know the rules. If you had finished one chore each day like I suggested, today would have been a free day to do whatever you liked."

God Rested

DAY 2

Read about It

Genesis 1—2:3

Think about It

1. When God finished with his creation of the world and everything in it, he rested. He then set aside the seventh day of the week as a day of rest. God gave us an example of resting because he wants us to know that rest is important. How much time do you set aside each day to rest? Each week? Do you rest on Sundays or are those busy days?

2. Our visual Bible verse is a wonderful promise from God that if we come to him, he will give us rest. God knows that when we work hard at school or sports or around our house doing chores, that our bodies and minds need time to rest. God tells us in his Word, the Bible, to make sure we get the rest we need every week.

3. Have you ever felt so tired after school or after practice that you just wanted to plop on your bed and go to sleep? Everybody feels that way. Sometimes, in our hearts we may feel sad and tired, too. God promises that if we come to him and tell him about how we feel, he will give rest to our hearts as well as our bodies.

Do Something about It

When you feel tired and weary in your body and your mind, lay down and be quiet for a while. As you are resting, tell God how you are feeling and ask him to give you new strength.

Pray about It

Dear God, sometimes I work hard on my homework or other activities. I feel so tired and I just want to lay down and go to sleep. Other times, I have lots of energy, but my heart hurts because of something bad that happened. Please help me to remember that you want me to rest. Help me find rest when I am tired and especially on Sundays. I am thankful that I can talk to you and tell you how I am feeling. Thank you for giving me strength. In Jesus' name, amen.

DAY 3

Noel's Messy Room

Circle the symbol for each word that is hidden in the picture. Then, fill in the blank lines at the bottom of the page with each verse word in order. Each symbol only appears once.

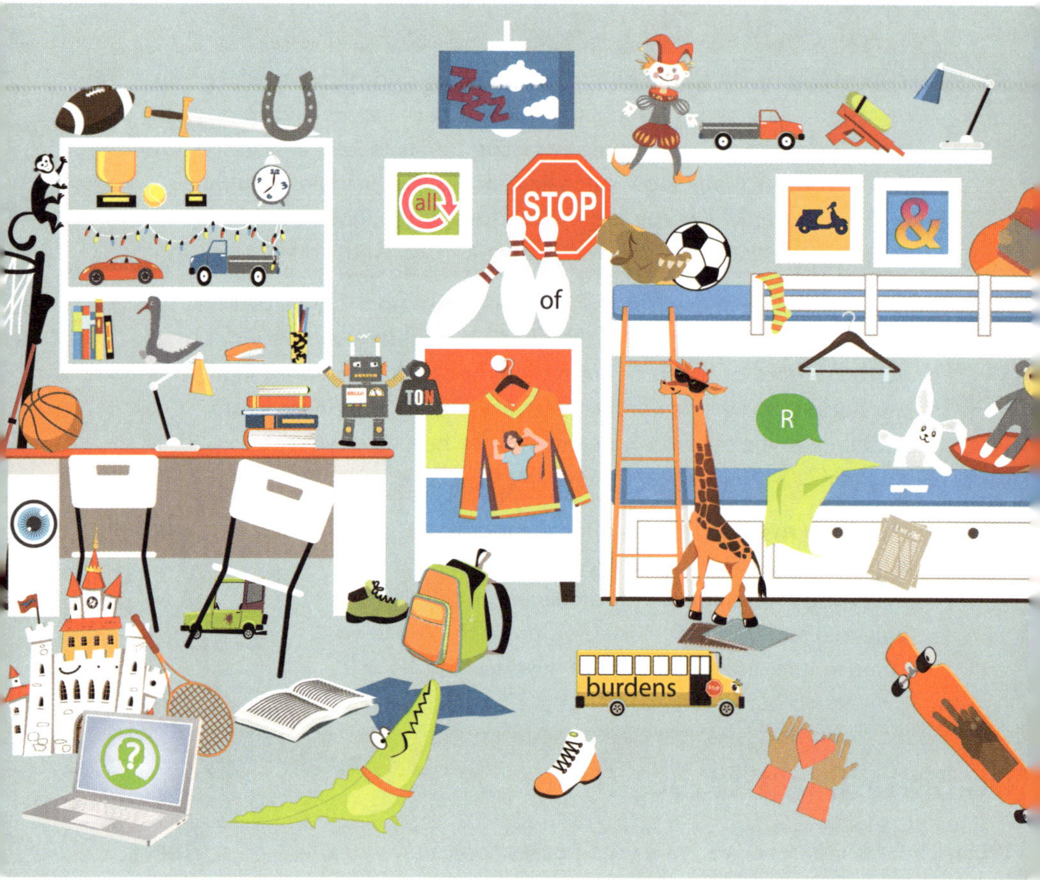

Matthew 11:28

Answer Key on page 378.

Chore Time!

DAY 4

Noel wasn't happy about spending all morning doing her chores. But her mom was right. It didn't take her all day.

Noel cleaned up the clothes from the floor of her closet and folded them. Then, she put all her toys and books away. "I don't like cleaning out your smelly cage, Priscilla, but it is dirty," Noel admitted to her hamster. "I'm sure you'll be happier in a less smelly place."

"There, three done! Two more chores to go!" Noel cheered as she raced past her mom on her way out the back door. After making sure the backyard was all cleaned up so that her father could mow their grass, Noel only had to vacuum the living room and the dining room. "Almost done!" Noel chorused happily.

"Good job, Noel!" Mom said after walking around with her and checking Noel's work.

Noel plopped down on the couch. "I might be done with my chores, but now I'm too tired to play," she complained. Mom sat down next to her and took her hand.

"Noel, remember we talked about how doing our best is important? How working hard at whatever we do pleases God?" Mom asked.

"Yes," answered Noel.

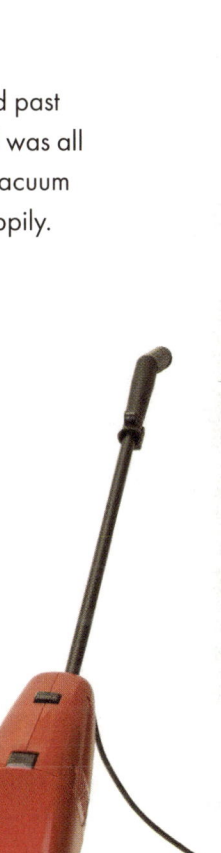

Mom continued, "We also talked about how important it is to rest. God tells us to come to him when we are tired or when we feel worried or sad, too. He wants us to get the rest we need. Sometimes that rest might be taking a nap. Other times, it can be by avoiding having to work too hard. And if you had finished one chore each day after school, you wouldn't be so tired today. It was your choice to wait until Saturday to do all your work. I'm not surprised you feel tired," Mom explained.

"I know I should have done my chores each day . . . I just didn't feel like it," Noel shared, "But next week, I will! I would like to have two days of rest each week . . . Saturday and Sunday!" Noel laughed.

Jesus Gives Us Rest · 81

DAY 5: Elisha's New Room

Read about It

2 Kings 4:8–37

Think about It

1 In the Bible story, the woman and her husband showed kindness to Elisha by giving him a room to rest in and food to eat. They understood how important it was to have a restful place for Elisha. Sometimes we might see someone who is feeling tired or sad. We show those people God's love when we are kind to them, or find a way to give them rest. If someone in your family is feeling tired or sad this week, what can you do that will give them rest or ease their mind?

2 Isn't it great that God loves us so much that he tells us to rest every week on Sunday? That doesn't mean we don't get to rest at other times, too. But God wants us to remember him and talk to him and thank him for loving us. What are some ways you find rest on Sundays? On other days?

3 The word *weary* and the phrase *carry heavy burdens* from our verse refer to when we feel tired or weak or sad about something. The verse goes on to say that God tells us to come to him. When we talk to God about how we feel, he promises to give us rest on the inside and the outside. What can you tell God about how you are feeling today?

Do Something about It

When you are feeling weary (tired) and carrying heavy burdens (sad), talk to God about your feelings. Then, look around at your family and friends to see if you can do something to give them some rest.

Pray about It

Dear God, I am glad that I can come to you and tell you all about how tired or sad I feel. I know that you love me and want what is best for me. Help me to remember to obey you on Sundays and take time to rest. I work hard at school and I need to rest before starting back at school on Mondays. And please help me to notice if someone else is feeling tired too. I want to show your love by doing something to give them rest. In Jesus' name, amen.

Find That Verse!

Look for the symbols from the Bible verse. Circle each one. Then, fill in the blank lines at the bottom of the page with each verse word. Say the Bible verse out loud until you can remember it without looking at the verse.

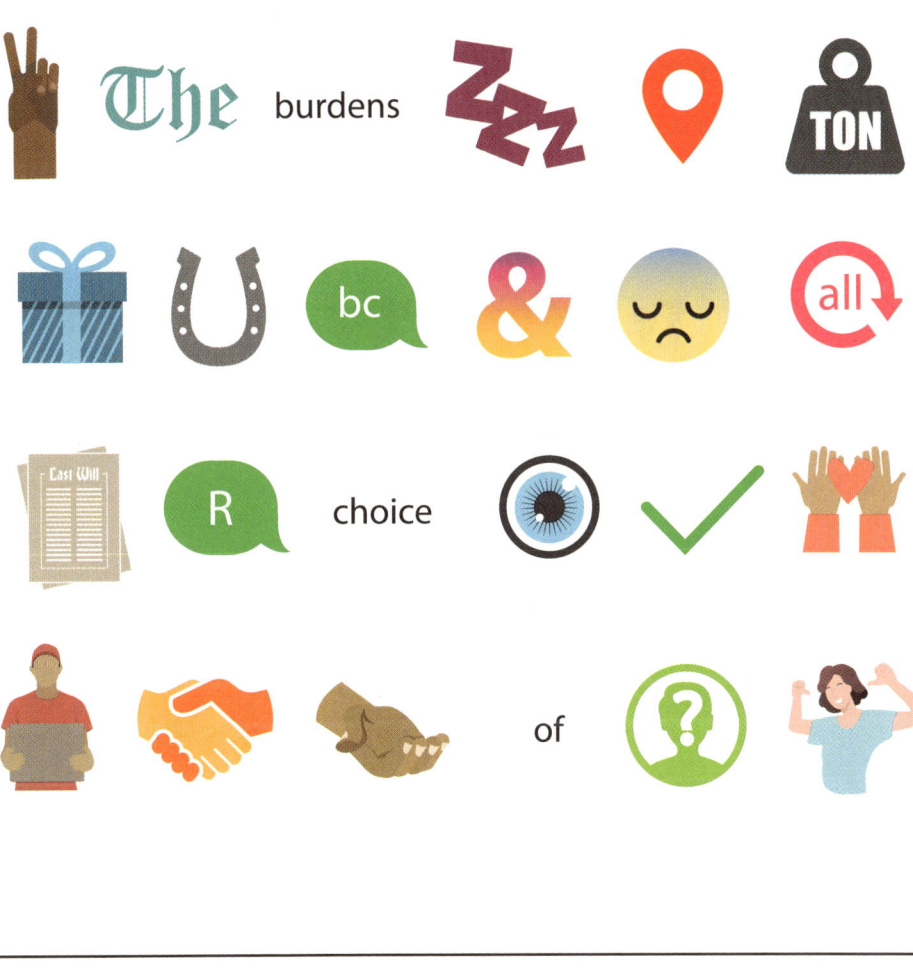

_____

_____

_____

_____

Matthew 11:28

Week 12

God Saves Us

Look at the visual Bible verse below. Try to figure out what it says. Write the verse words on the blank lines. Use the Visual Bible Verse Dictionary on page 371, if needed.

_____

_____

_____

_____

_____

For this is how God loved the world: He gave his one and only Son, so that everyone who believes in him will not perish but have eternal life. John 3:16

Bicycle Blues

DAY 1

Will sat on the edge of his desk chair trying to finish his homework. But he just could not concentrate. Instead, angry thoughts swirled in his head. *I am so angry at Danny! I can't believe he took my bike without asking me! Now it's all muddy and the tire has a hole in it. I will never forgive him. Never!*

He knew he needed to forgive his brother because God's Word tells us to forgive. *But how can I forgive him? He did the wrong thing by taking my bike!* Will wondered. *Why is it so hard to forgive?*

Will's father knocked on his door and then opened it, leaning in. "Will, are you almost finished with your homework?" he asked. "We are getting ready to go out for ICE CREAM." Will's dad smiled big as he said the words, *ice cream*.

Will turned to his father with a scowl on his face, "I'm not finished with my homework. And I don't even want to go."

"Will, what is wrong? You look upset," Dad asked. He was still leaning in the doorway.

"I am so mad at Danny! He took my bike out today . . . without asking my PERMISSION. And he got it all muddy. But the worst thing is the back tire is flat now, too!" Will cried.

Will's dad nodded. "Yes, your mom told me all about it. Danny is going to pay for a new tire and he will wash your bike on Saturday."

"I know. Mom said so. But I don't care! I'm still mad! I don't want to see him or talk to him or ever be around Danny ever again EVER!" complained Will. Despite his best efforts to hold them back, angry tears ran down his face.

"We need to talk about this, Will," Dad said as he sat down on Will's bed.

God Saves Us • 85

DAY 2: Nicodemus Asks

Read about It

John 3:1–21

Think about It

1 Today's Bible story contains our verse for this week. This verse tells us that because God sent Jesus to die on the cross as the punishment for all of our sins, we can be forgiven. When we accept God's forgiveness through Jesus, we become members of God's family and will one day live with him in Heaven forever. What do you think Heaven will be like?

2 Jesus never sinned because he is God. Because Jesus never sinned and he took all of our sins away from us by forgiving us, God wants us to forgive others in the same way. Have you ever struggled with forgiving someone who hurt you like Will is struggling to forgive his brother?

3 God understands that we sometimes feel angry when another person sins and it hurts us. But God still tells us we must forgive if we want to be forgiven. What is something you remember doing that was wrong? Did you ask for forgiveness from God and anyone you hurt? If you didn't, you can still ask for forgiveness today.

Do Something about It

When you feel angry because someone has sinned against you, ask God to give you the strength to forgive, even if you don't want to. Remember that Jesus never ever sinned but he still died on the cross so that you can be forgiven of every sin you have ever committed. Forgiving others is not only obeying God, but shows that you love God.

Pray about It

Dear God, I know it is wrong for me to refuse to forgive others. Jesus died on the cross to forgive me of all of my sins. If I love Jesus, I'll do what he asks and forgive others. Will you please give me the strength to forgive like Jesus forgives me? In Jesus' name, amen.

Cross-Out Verse

Can you tell what's wrong with this verse? Cross out the symbols that don't belong to reveal this week's visual Bible verse. Then, read the verse aloud.

 this

+ed

   +ly

that

    perish  -ter

     John 3:16

God Saves Us

DAY 4: Time to Forgive

"Sit next to me, son." Will moved to sit next to his father on the bed.

"Will, I'm going to read you something from the Bible. I want you to think hard about what God wants you to do." He opened Will's Bible to John 3:16.

Together, Will and his father read the verse out loud. "For God so loved the world that he gave his one and only Son that whoever believes in him shall not perish but have eternal life."

His father closed the Bible and looked at his son, "God sent his son Jesus to die on the cross so that you and I and everyone in the world could be forgiven for all of our sins. But we have to ask Jesus for that forgiveness. I know you are angry with Danny for how he sinned against you by taking your bike and ruining it."

"That's right. He did. And I'm still mad, but maybe not as mad as I was before," Will admitted.

"You know, Will, I remember when you have sinned, too," Dad said. Will hung his head, knowing it was true. "Did your mother and I ever refuse to forgive you when you asked us to?"

"No." Will answered quietly.

"Do you think we would have been right to be angry at you for what you did?" Dad asked.

"Yes, but this is different . . ." Will protested.

Dad chuckled. "It might feel different to you, Will. But it isn't. Sin is sin. God forgives us. God tells us to forgive others. It is that simple," Dad said. "Every person who has ever lived has sinned. Every person needs the forgiveness of Jesus. When we tell God we will not forgive someone, we are sinning! God's love is so big for us that he sent Jesus to die on a cross! Because Jesus died and came to life again, we can be forgiven, become members of God's family, and live forever with Jesus in Heaven. How can we say no to God by choosing not to forgive?"

"OK, I will forgive Danny. But . . . Dad? First, I need to ask Jesus to forgive me for my sins. Can I do that right now?" Will asked.

"Yes! Let's pray together," Dad said as he took Will's hands in his. They closed their eyes and bowed their heads to pray.

Saul Is Saved

DAY 5

Read about It

Acts 9:1–31

Think about It

1 Before he met Jesus on the road to Damascus, Saul was angry. He believed everyone who followed Jesus was going against God. And he was determined to stop them. But after meeting Jesus, Saul was forgiven and he wanted to do good things. The Bible tells us Saul, also known as the Apostle Paul, went on to do many wonderful things for God. When we know Jesus, God gives us the desire to do good things, too. What are some of the good things God's given you the desire to do? Has he ever helped you forgive someone even when you didn't want to?

2 When we think about all of the sins we have committed, we understand that every person has to ask Jesus for forgiveness. Have you ever asked Jesus for forgiveness for your sins?

3 God's great love for us is shown by what he asked his Son Jesus to do for each of us. God sent Jesus to earth to be born a baby, grow up, and then die on the cross so that we can be forgiven. Remember that Jesus never sinned but he still died for our sins. How does that make you feel when you think about what Jesus did for each of us?

Do Something about It

Ask an older family member or trusted adult to talk with you about what Jesus did on the cross. Think about your own sin and how Jesus promises to forgive you. Then, forgive others who have sinned against you, the way Jesus forgave you.

Pray about It

Dear God, I know that I have sinned and hurt others with my poor choices. I am thankful that I can be forgiven because of what Jesus did for me on that cross. Jesus never sinned but he died for my sins. I want to ask Jesus to forgive me for every sin I have committed. Then, I need to think about anyone I have not forgiven. Please help me to be a person who always forgives others when they sin against me. In Jesus' name, amen.

DAY 6: Verse in Motion

Read the visual verse and write each word beneath its symbol. For each phrase, write down some motions you can do as you say the verse. Then, practice saying the verse and doing the motions several times. Practice the motions and try to teach it to someone or video yourselves saying the verse and doing the motions.

John 3:16

Week 13

God's Grace Is Enough for Me

Look at the visual Bible verse below. Try to figure out what it says. Write the verse words on the blank lines. Use the Visual Bible Verse Dictionary on page 371, if needed.

_____

_____

_____

_____

_____

_____

My grace is all you need. My power works best in weakness. 2 Corinthians 12:9

DAY 1: Waiting Room

Micah couldn't stop fidgeting in the doctor's waiting room. He kicked his legs back and forth and squirmed so much his mom gently put her hand on his arm. That was his mom's way of saying, "Please stop," without using words. Micah and his mom used all sorts of silent hand signals to communicate with each other—especially when they were out in public places like the doctor's office.

"How much longer?" Micah whispered to his mom.

She looked at her watch, "Shouldn't be too long now," his mom answered.

Micah wanted to get up and run out of the door. Last night, after dinner, his mom explained that they needed to come to this appointment. The school nurse had called and suggested to his mom that they see the doctor. The nurse was concerned that Micah's hearing loss was getting worse. Micah understood what that meant.

I do not want to wear those ugly hearing aids! Micah thought to himself. *I WON'T wear them,* Micah determined.

Just as Micah was trying to figure out a way to avoid wearing a hearing aid, the nurse called out, "Micah Zimmerman?"

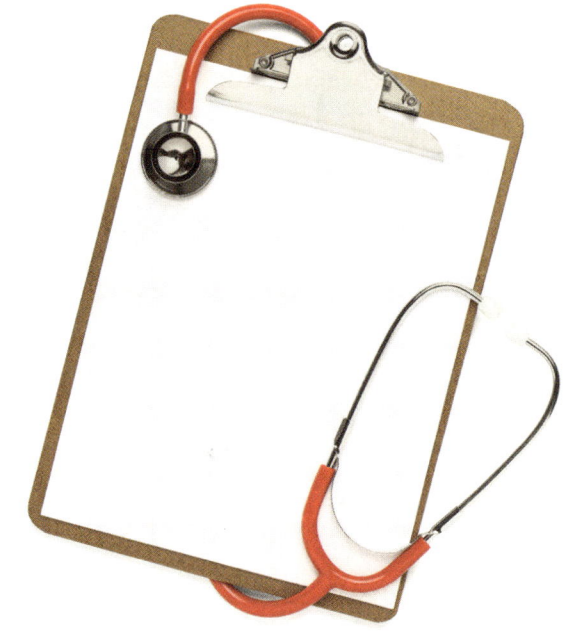

"Come on, Micah, that's you," Mom said as she got up. Micah just sat there frozen to his seat in the waiting room. Mom turned around, "Micah," she motioned with her hand that he was to come with her. Micah got up and followed his mom and the nurse into one of the patient rooms walking as slowly as he could.

Gideon, Mighty Hero

DAY 2

Read about It

Judges 6:11–24

Think about It

1. The Bible story tells us Gideon was hiding from the Midianites, when an angel of the Lord came and called him "mighty hero." Gideon must have felt anything other than *mighty* or a *hero*! How do you think you would have felt if an angel came and called you a "mighty hero"?

2. God understands that we are often weak and do not have the strength we want and need. But this week's verse is a two-part promise. God promises us that his grace is enough plus God's power (working inside of us) is made perfect through our weakness! This means that even when we feel very weak we can count on God's power inside of us to give us the strength we need. How does it make you feel to know that God promises to give you enough grace and strength to handle whatever is troubling you?

3. When we face something that feels too hard or too big for us to handle, we need to ask God to give us his grace and strength. We can be thankful that our weakness is made powerful through God. What can you do today to show your thankfulness to God?

Do Something about It

When you feel weak and do not have the strength you need to face something hard, ask God. Thank God for his power that is stronger than all your weaknesses.

Pray about It

Dear God, I know that you promise to give me the grace and strength I need when I feel weak and afraid. Remind me to come to you whenever my strength is not enough for what I need to do. You are my all-powerful God and you promise to overcome all my weaknesses. Help me to understand what this means by trusting in you to supply everything I need in every situation. In Jesus' name, amen.

DAY 3 Roll On

Roll a pair of number cubes. Look up the word associated with each number and write it on the appropriate blank line. Keep playing until you have rolled every number that corresponds to the words in the verse.

1 m+ 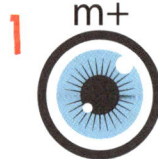   2    3

_____   _____   _____

4    5    6 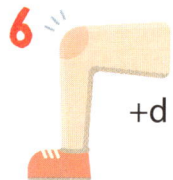 +d

_____   _____   _____

7 m+ 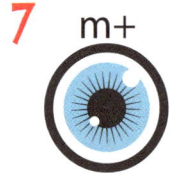   8    9  +s

_____   _____   _____

10    11    12  +ness

_____   _____   _____

Challenge: Using separate sheets of paper, play this as a game with family members or friends. See who can complete the verse first!

Now Hear This

DAY 4

Micah sat in the examining chair and waited for the doctor to come and check his hearing. "What kind of test is the doctor going to do today?" asked Micah.

"His nurse explained there will be a few different ways he will test you. He needs to see how much your hearing loss has increased. It won't hurt, Micah," Mom assured him.

"I'm not afraid of the tests. I'm afraid of wearing a hearing aid to school!" Micah announced loudly.

"Micah, we have already talked about this so many times. You have to get a hearing aid for your right ear so that you can hear your teacher talk. You can't hear her when she turns toward the board and writes. You told me this yourself. This will help make school so much easier for you because you won't have to guess anymore what she is saying," Mom explained.

"You're wrong, Mom. The hearing aid might help me hear better, but I will also hear all the other kids make fun of me, too," Micah said.

"Oh, Micah, your true friends would never laugh at you . . . never. You know that. And if someone does laugh I want you to explain to that person why you need a hearing aid," Mom coached. "Will you try that?"

"I guess," replied Micah. "Micah, remember that Bible verse you learned last week at Sunday school? The one that promised God's grace is enough? Can you say it for me right now?" Mom asked.

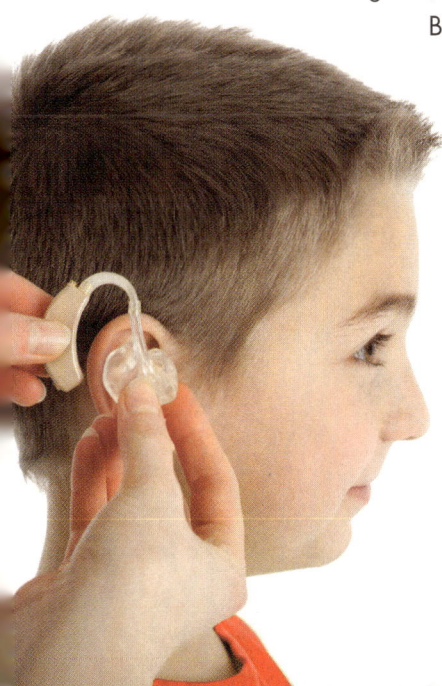

"'My grace is all you need. My power works best in weakness.' 2 Corinthians 12:9. That one?" Micah asked.

"Yes! Now let's talk about how you can apply that promise right now!" Mom said with a smile.

DAY 5: Queen Esther Is Strong

Read about It

Esther 2:1–17,16–20; 3:1–11; 4—5:1–8; 7:1–10

Think about It

1. In the Bible story of Esther, she knew that her life would be at risk if she went to the king as her cousin Mordecai requested. So she prayed, and asked Mordecai and the other Jewish people to pray for her. When we need God's help and strength, we can pray and ask others to pray for us, too.

2. This week's verse is full of power and promise because we can apply it to every area of our lives. When we feel weak or worried about something at school, at home, on the playground, even on vacation, we can say this promise out loud to remind ourselves that God's grace and strength is always enough for us. How does it feel to know that God has exactly what you need for any situation?

3. Micah needed to wear a hearing aid because his right ear couldn't hear the words his teacher and other people were saying. Micah understood that the hearing aid would help him, but he was afraid the other children would laugh at him. When is a time you were afraid other people might laugh at you?

Do Something about It

When you wonder about how others will treat you and feel worried, say this verse out loud. Think about how God is always with you, and how he will give you the grace and strength you need.

Pray about It

Dear God, I am sometimes worried that kids will laugh at me. Help me to remember that you are always with me and that I don't have to be afraid. You promise to make my weaknesses into strength. Thank you for taking such good care of me. In Jesus' name, amen.

Telephone Verse

Read the visual verse, and then write each word beneath its symbol.

With family members or friends, play a game of Telephone, using this verse as your secret message. Stand or sit in a circle. Whisper the verse in the ear of the person on your right. That person then whispers it in the ear of the person on their right. Continue until the verse has gone all the way around the circle. The last person then says the verse aloud. Repeat the process, until the last person says the verse correctly.

Alternate Idea: Instead of playing Telephone, repeat the verse into a recorder (cell phone, dictation machine, etc.) Play it back. Then record yourself again, but this time use a really high or really low voice. Continue recording and listening to the verse. You can say it fast or slow, in a silly voice, in a frog's voice, and so on. Use your imagination!

_____ _____ _____ _____

 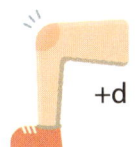  

_____ _____ _____ _____

_____ _____ _____ _____

2 Corinthians 12:9

Trust in the Lord

Look at the visual Bible verse below. Try to figure out what it says. Write the verse words on the blank lines. Use the Visual Bible Verse Dictionary on page 371, if needed.

_____

_____

_____

_____

_____

Trust in the LORD with all your heart; do not depend on your own understanding. Seek his will in all you do, and he will show you which path to take. Proverbs 3:5–6

A Weekend with Dad

DAY 1

"Well, that's all for math!" Gemma said as she slammed her math book closed. Mom looked up from the other end of the dining table where she was working on her laptop. "And that's the last of my homework!" Gemma was all set to settle down and dive back into her library book. She grabbed the book and headed to her favorite reading spot in the window seat.

"Gemma, did you pack all your clothes for this weekend yet? Your dad will be here in one hour," Mom said.

"No," Gemma answered.

"Better get on it," Mom said and put her attention back to her computer.

Gemma reluctantly switched directions and headed to her bedroom to pack. *I don't want to go to Dad's this weekend,* Gemma thought to herself. *I don't know why I have to live in two different houses. I hate it.* When her father moved out of their home right before school started, Gemma had been so angry with him. And sad. She remembered crying every day because she missed him so much. Eventually, Gemma got used to living alone with her mom and visiting her dad two weekends a month. But every now and then it just seemed like a pain. Like now.

Gemma was still sitting on her bed with her book in her hand. She was thinking about how much harder it was to spend time at her father's place. Gemma's dad had moved into an apartment and he never had anything good to eat in the kitchen. All of Gemma's favorite games and toys stayed at her mom's house. "I don't want to go! I'm not going. I'm not!" Gemma complained out loud.

A moment later, Gemma's mom came into her bedroom. "Just checking on your progress. I brought up some clean pajamas from the dryer," Mom said. She looked at Gemma just sitting on the bed with no suitcase in sight. "Oh . . . I see you haven't started packing at all . . . Tell me what's going on." Mom said.

"I am angry at Dad for leaving us and I don't want to spend the weekend with him. I hate where he lives," complained Gemma.

"Honey, I know it's hard, but we don't have a choice about your visits with Dad. It is what he and I agreed to." Mom said gently.

DAY 2

God Guides Job

Read about It

Job 1—2:10; 42

Think about It

1. Today's Bible story tells about a man named Job and how he had some VERY difficult times. Through it all, Job praised God and never lost faith in God. God doesn't promise that we're going to have a life free from difficulties. But God tells us to trust in him with all of our heart. We don't have to try to figure out why things happen. Instead, we can simply trust and obey God and he will show us which path to take.

2. There will be many difficult times in our lives. At those times, we will need to trust God. Often, like Gemma, we don't understand why difficult things happen in our families but as we trust and obey God he guides us along the right paths. What is something difficult that is happening in your life, or in the life of someone you love? What can you do to feel stronger about trusting in God to guide you through that difficult time?

3. Sometimes when difficult things happen and we feel confused and hurt, we want to know why. But often there are no reasons or at least no answers. When are some times kids your age might have to trust God? Why can we trust God, even in hard times?

Do Something about It

When you feel confused and hurt, write down your questions for God. Then talk with an adult family member about your questions. Finally, pray and ask God for the strength needed to trust and obey him—even when your questions may not be answered.

Pray about It

Dear God, I don't understand why things are difficult. Please help me to trust you and obey you even when I don't get all my questions answered. You promise to help me do the right thing even when I feel confused and hurt. Thank you for loving me and helping me make right choices. In Jesus' name, amen.

Which Path?

DAY 3

Find your way through the maze from start to the finish. Along the correct path, you'll find symbols and words for today's verse. Write each word in the order you find them on the lines below.

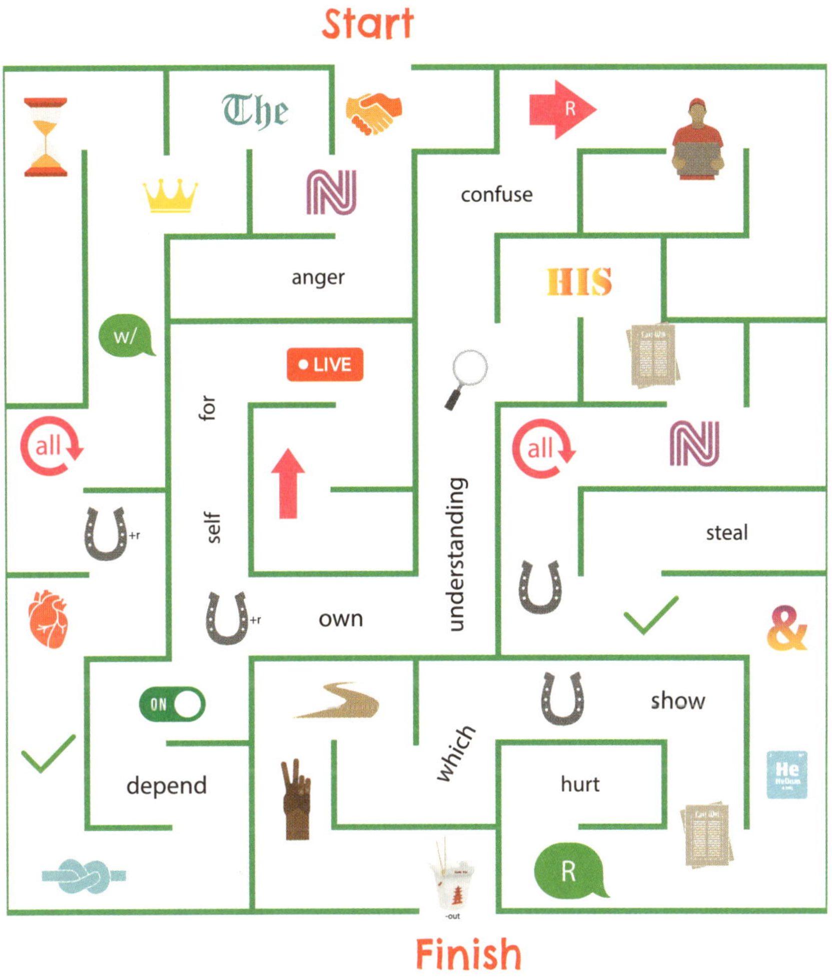

Start

Finish

_____

_____

_____

_____

Proverbs 3:5-6

DAY 4

Why Ask Why?

Gemma was mad. She didn't really want to discuss with her mom why she didn't want to go to her father's place for the weekend, but here was Mom. Sitting on her bed, trying to talk about it. "Gemma, when your dad moved out at the end of the summer, it was a hard time for all of us. We all felt hurt and sad. Your dad felt that way, too. I know that you felt angry at him for leaving but I thought you had gotten over your anger. Didn't you?" Mom asked.

"I don't feel angry ALL the time now. But I don't like spending the weekends at his apartment because it reminds me that he doesn't live with us." Gemma's eyes stung with tears as she explained. "And that hurts. I just want to understand why he left. Why, Mom? Why?" Gemma wiped away a tear that had snuck its way down her cheek.

"I can't answer that question, Gemma. You see . . . I don't know! I don't think your dad knows either. But I pray for him every day and that helps me not feel angry at him," Mom said.

Gemma sniffled and wiped her eyes before speaking. "I pray, too. I ask God to help me understand," Gemma confided.

"That's the best we can do . . . That and trust God and obey him by doing the right things. I believe today that the right choice is going to visit with your dad. You agree?" Mom asked.

Gemma nodded. "Yeah, I mean . . . If I'm feeling sad without Dad here, he must feel really lousy!" Mom and Gemma laughed and then hugged each other.

Mom brushed the hair out of Gemma's face. "This is the verse I will pray for you to think about this weekend. If you start to feel confused or hurt, 'Trust in the LORD with all your heart; do not depend on your own understanding. Seek his will in all you do, and he will show you which path to take' (Proverbs 3:5–6). We won't always understand why things happen, Gemma, but we can always trust God to help us walk through hard times."

Ruth and Naomi

DAY 5

Read about It

Ruth 1:6–22; 2:1–23; 4:9–17

Think about It

1. At the beginning of Ruth's story, there has been nothing but bad things happening to her and her mother-in-law. But by the end of the story, we learn that Ruth has been a blessing to Naomi, and Naomi has been a blessing to Ruth. Even when we're going through difficult times, one of the ways God provides for us is by giving us people to help and guide us. Who are some of the people who guide and care for you? What are some of the things they do?

2. Trust and obey are two commands that always go together. God wants us to trust him, and then obey him. But it can be really difficult to either trust or obey when you're confused about things that are going on! What are some things you can do to help you trust and obey God, even when you are confused?

3. Sometimes we don't understand what happens to us, but there are times adults don't understand either. Ask an adult family member to share with you a time when they didn't understand, but they chose to trust God. Then, ask them how everything turned out!

Do Something about It

When you have questions that you cannot find answers to, ask adult family members or other trusted adults for help. Talk to them about times they choose to trust and obey God, even though they had questions or were confused, too.

Pray about It

Dear God, please help me to not get upset because I don't have answers to my questions. Help me to trust you, God, obey you, and make good choices every day. I want you to guide my path through life, and that begins with me choosing to trust and obey you. Thank you for loving me so much and for helping me every day. In Jesus' name, amen.

DAY 6: Which Way?

The phrases to this visual Bible verse have gotten out of order. Help them get back on the right path by drawing a star where the verse begins. Then, draw lines to connect the end of that phrase to what should come next. Continue until all the phrases are connected in order. Finally, write the verse on the lines below.

own understanding

 which

   w/

   &   show

   depend

Proverbs 3:5–6

Week 15

EVERYTHING WORKS TOGETHER FOR GOOD

Look at the visual Bible verse below. Try to figure out what it says. Write the verse words on the blank lines. Use the Visual Bible Verse Dictionary on page 371, if needed.

_____

_____

_____

_____

_____

We know that God causes everything to work together for the good of those who love God and are called according to his purpose for them. Romans 8:28

DAY 1

Room for Grandma

"Logan! Tyler! Come inside please," Dad called from the window.

"One more time, Tyler!" Logan encouraged his younger brother. Tyler was just preparing to ride the zip line in their backyard. Tyler took hold and zoomed across the yard, with Logan following right behind.

"Whoa . . . that was fast!" Tyler exclaimed. His landing was a bit sloppy, and he fell down as he let go. Logan helped him stand up, and Tyler brushed the dirt from his pants. Both boys reluctantly walked into the house together. Inside, they dropped their jackets on the floor and bent down to remove their shoes.

"We're in here," Dad called from the living room.

"Coming!" Logan replied.

"Sit down here, boys, by the fireplace to get warm," Mom encouraged.

"Boys, you know how sick Grandma has been in the last few months?" Dad asked as both Logan and Tyler nodded up and down. "Well, your mom and I have decided that Grandma is going to move in here with us until she recovers from her operation. That means you two will be sharing a bedroom again," Dad explained.

Logan looked at Tyler. Tyler looked at Logan. "So whose bedroom is Grandma going to be staying in? Mine or Tyler's?" Logan asked with a frown.

"Your mom and I already decided that we think Grandma would be more comfortable in your room, Logan. It's closer to the bathroom and already has a double-sized bed in it," Dad said.

"But Dad . . . what will happen to all of my stuff? Where will I put my blocks and my books and my games?" Logan cried.

"Logan, we will move all of your belongings into Tyler's room. Remember we are all going to have to sacrifice something when Grandma comes. But it is the best thing for her to be close to us. Understand?" Dad said. Logan didn't answer because he was too busy grumbling inside his head.

106 · Everything Works Together for Good

Remembering God's Goodness

Read about It

Nehemiah 8

Think about It

1. Nehemiah and Ezra knew how important it was for people to remember how God had cared for them in the past. So they read God's Word. All the people were happy to remember God's great care, and wanted to obey him. There may be times that God cared for your family that you don't remember. Look through some family photos with an older family member and see if you can remember them.

2. Do you believe that all things work together for good even when it doesn't seem that way? Logan was having a difficult time understanding how his grandmother's living with them could be a good thing. Could you explain how helping his grandmother is good even when it may be hard for those caring for her?

3. This verse also tells us something important about God. He is the one who is working to make even the difficult things in life good for his children. If we love God and obey him, then even the hard times are made good for us. Can you think of something that was hard for you, but after you did it, God did something good?

Do Something about It

When you feel upset or angry because you have to give up something of your own for someone else, say this verse out loud. Then, pray and ask God to help you find the good in the situation.

Pray about It

Dear God, please help me to look for the good in every situation. Help me to trust you are doing good things even in situations where I'm not happy. Please help me to obey you with my actions and in my heart by not complaining or grumbling. In Jesus' name, amen.

Conversation Starters

DAY 3

Read the requests in each conversation balloon. In the empty balloon, write a response that would show you trust God to work things for good. Then, write this week's verse from memory on the lines below.

Put your video game down and do your homework!

Your room is such a mess! Please clean it up. While you're at it, pick out some clothes and toys to give to charity.

_____

_____

_____

_____

Romans 8:28

Move On Over

DAY 4

The family worked together to move Logan's things into Tyler's smaller bedroom. Mom and Dad noticed how quiet Logan was while they worked. Logan's brow was furrowed, and his head was down.

Suddenly, Logan found his voice when he wasn't able to fit his clothes into Tyler's closet. "These aren't going to fit! I knew it! This room is too small for both of us," Logan grumbled.

"Logan, take a deep breath and calm down." Dad advised.

Mom continued, "Remember, honey, it's important to have Grandma living here with us until she is strong enough to go back home. This is the best way we can show Grandma we love her. I know you love her."

"I do love Grandma . . . I'm just not happy about giving up my room and having to sleep with Tyler again." Logan said.

"We get that," Dad said. "But as a family, we need to pull together and help each other when someone needs help. And right now, Grandma needs us. This isn't easy for her either. She needs you, Logan, to help her. Can you do that?"

Logan's heart dropped. He'd only been thinking about how he was feeling. "I'm sorry, Mom and Dad. I haven't been thinking about Grandma at all—just myself." He took a deep breath. "I will stop complaining and think about all the good ways I can help Grandma get better," Logan said.

Logan grinned. "Yeah, but this is a huge sacrifice. Tyler snores!" Logan laughed.

"And you don't?" Tyler said. Dad ruffled Logan's hair as everyone laughed.

"Now, that's the attitude God wants us all to have: willingly giving up something for the sake of others. I'm proud of you for understanding how important this is to Grandma," Dad said encouragingly.

"OK! Let's finish up moving all this stuff into Tyler's room and then we will take a pizza break," Mom said.

"Yes!" Logan and Tyler shouted.

Everything Works Together for Good

DAY 5

Joseph's Life in Egypt

Read about It

Genesis 45:1–11

Think about It

1. Every time something seemed to be going well for Joseph, something bad happened and it looked like his life was ruined. (If you want to read the whole story of Joseph's life in Egypt, read Genesis 39—45.) The Bible tells us that God was with Joseph, and Joseph never stopped trusting and obeying God. Joseph is a great example to follow. What is something you can do today to show you trust God like Joseph did?

2. Sometimes we may not like what is going on around us, but God is always busy making us stronger, wiser, kinder, and better servants when we ask him to help us have attitudes that please him. Why does God use his power to transform difficult things into good things for us?

3. Logan wasn't happy about moving his belongings into his brother's room and he grumbled a lot. What helped Logan stop complaining? What are things you can think about that might help you stop grumbling and complaining? When we ask God for help to see difficult things from his perspective, he makes it easier to accept what is happening. God is always working to change us and he is working to bring what is best into our lives.

Do Something about It

When you start to feel selfish, pray and ask God to help you to find a way to serve another person. Talk to adult family members about ways to see the good things God is always doing. Think about how God is making you a stronger, wiser, kinder, and better servant.

Pray about It

Dear God, please help me to be happy to serve others—especially when I don't get what I want. Help me to look for others who need my help, and then give me the strength to serve them. I don't want to complain or grumble, but please forgive me when I do. In Jesus' name, amen.

Verse Stack

Say the word for each symbol aloud. Fill in the missing words on the blank lines. Next, make up motions to do with the verse. Repeat until you know it by heart. Finally, draw pictures or write about things this verse reminds you of.

DAY 6

WE
💡
_____

🔱
_____

✌️
⚙️
🤝
✋
The
👍
_____

🧠
❤️
🔱
&
💬R
📞+ed
_____

✌️
HIS
_____

✋
THEM

Everything Works Together for Good · 111

Week 16

God Is Faithful and Just

Look at the visual Bible verse below. Try to figure out what it says. Write the verse words on the blank lines. Use the Visual Bible Verse Dictionary on page 371, if needed.

_____

_____

_____

_____

_____

Coin Theft

DAY 1

Kyle carefully pressed his brand-new quarter into its slot. Kyle's dad had given him a collector's coin book to save all fifty of the United States quarters inside. "Dad, I only have to find two more quarters and the book is finished!" called out Kyle to his father.

"After dinner, I'll go out and check in my coin box. I might have the coins you need. We can look together," Dad said.

Kyle was so excited to spend time that evening with his dad. He went to his room, dropped the coin book on the bed and then went outside to play.

When Kyle returned to his room later in the day, his coin book was on the floor, and all of the coins were missing! "What happened to my coins?" he yelled.

Kyle's dad appeared in the doorway. "What's wrong, Kyle?" he asked.

Just then, his little sister Kayla appeared next to Dad. "I put your money in my piggy bank! I wanted to keep them safe."

"Give them to me!" Kyle yelled. "What were you doing in my room anyway?"

Kayla burst into tears. "I was looking for you! When I saw how many quarters you have, I was afraid a burglar would steal them, so I put them in my piggy bank!"

"The only burglar around here is YOU!" Kyle yelled.

"OK, Kyle, that's enough. Kayla didn't mean to upset you. We'll get the coins back and return them to your book after dinner. OK? No harm done."

"I am sorry, Kyle," Kayla sniffled.

Kyle shuffled his feet for a moment. He really did love his sister and hated to see her so sad. "I forgive you, Kayla," he said. He walked over to give his sister a hug.

That evening, as Kyle and his dad were putting the quarters back in the book, his dad said, "Kyle, I'm proud of the way you forgave Kayla today. That shows real maturity. Maybe on Saturday we can run over to the coin store together. I'm looking for some good deals for my coin collection, too," Dad offered.

"Really? I have never been to the coin store. Yippee!!!" Kyle said excitedly. "I can't wait!" Kyle cheered.

God Is Faithful and Just

DAY 2: Zacchaeus Is Forgiven

Read about It

Luke 19:1–10

Think about It

1. The story about Zacchaeus shows how Jesus forgave even people others didn't like and who were considered bad people. Everyone can receive forgiveness from God! It's one of his greatest promises. That's what this week's verse is about. Not only does God forgive us, he makes our hearts clean from wickedness. What are some other words that mean *wickedness*?

2. When we ask God for forgiveness he will give it to us. When God cleans our hearts from sin, we feel better on the inside because we have obeyed God. When have you asked God to forgive you for doing something wrong? How did you feel afterwards?

3. One of the best parts of this Bible verse is its promise that God is faithful and just. Those two words, *faithful* and *just*, mean that God always does what is good and right. What are some other words you can think of to describe God?

Do Something about It

When you know that you have made a poor choice and have sinned, ask God to forgive you for your sin. Then thank him for how good he is to always forgive you and clean your heart of wickedness, no matter how many times you sin.

Pray about It

Dear God, please forgive me for sinning. When I sin, it's usually because I'm only thinking about what I want. Please help me to make good choices that show I am listening to what the Bible tells us is right. Thank you for forgiving me and making my heart clean again. In Jesus' name, amen.

Verse Word Search

Read the visual verse, and then write each word beneath its symbol. Then, find each verse word in the word search.

Note: Some words appear more than once in the verse, but they'll only be in the puzzle once. Also, don't forget to find *John*!

```
M I S E T S S G H O M U V A R
W S W V J X L I S R T J I S R
V R G L K E K K T Z A H F H Q
F A I T H F U L U U E W C P Z
K B K F G C L W S R E D L C A
Q L W J W A V I I M V H E O M
Q N A J Y D K C S T D B A N N
D K P I M L Z K G L X E N F C
F F O R G I V E B W X I S E F
H R H F X A N D W E J F E S K
S T O J C E X N W K O E U S A
I H I M T J W E E G H J U S T
N P U K O O Y S M X N Q B D Z
S H H A U Q P S J B Q Y V Q T
V M W E R S I T M C X M W T V
```

  confess

  just

    from   wickedness

1 John 1:9

The Coin Store

When Kyle and his father arrived at the coin store, Kyle couldn't believe his eyes. There were coins everywhere!

"I'll be over on this side looking for the coins I need, Kyle. The quarters are over there," Dad pointed across the room. Kyle grinned and made a beeline to where Dad pointed.

Kyle started searching for the two quarters he still needed to complete his collection. "Ohio and California, Ohio and California, Ohio and California . . ." he repeatedly muttered the state names under his breath. He looked and looked and looked. His frustration grew along with his certainty that the store didn't have what he needed.

After several minutes, Kyle's father completed his shopping and joined Kyle in the quarter corner. "Kyle, have you found your quarters?" Dad asked.

"No!" answered Kyle in frustration. He was on the verge of angry tears.

"Well, calm down, son. Let's look together," Dad offered. After searching for a long time, Dad finally said, "We need to get going, Kyle. Your mom is waiting for us."

"But . . . I didn't get what I came for," Kyle complained.

"We can come back next week. Maybe they'll have what you need," Dad replied.

"I am so mad! I never found those dumb quarters," Kyle grumbled on the ride home.

"OK, Kyle, I understand that you are disappointed, but your words are not respectful. And your tone is not thankful. How about you think about what your response should be. What do you think would please God?" Dad said firmly.

Kyle sat silently for several minutes. "OK, I guess God wouldn't be happy that I got so upset," Kyle answered. As soon as the words were out of his mouth, he realized how true they were. "I'm sorry, Dad. It was great that you took me to the store with you. And I definitely want to go with you again. Will you forgive me for getting so mad?" Kyle asked.

"Of course, son. I love you," Dad said as he squeezed Kyle's shoulder.

"And I need to tell God I'm sorry, too." Kyle added.

"I'm really proud that you realize that, Kyle. Why don't you take a moment to talk with God now?" Kyle closed his eyes and did just that.

Jesus Forgives Peter

DAY 5

Read about It

Matthew 26:31–35, 69–75; John 21:1–24

Think about It

1. Our Bible story tells us that Peter denied knowing Jesus three times after Jesus was arrested. Then, after Jesus came to life again, he visited Peter and some other disciples on a beach. Three times, Jesus asked Peter if he loved him and instructed him to feed his fish. This was Jesus' way of telling Peter he was forgiven. Jesus hadn't given up on Peter! And God doesn't give up on us when we do wrong things, too.

2. Kyle's grumbling and complaining because he couldn't find the coins he wanted came out in his angry words. Can you think of how Kyle could have responded to his disappointment instead of getting upset? Sometimes we just think bad things and don't say them out loud. Even when we just think bad thoughts, we need to ask for God's forgiveness—remember, God knows our every thought. Have you had any bad thoughts recently that you need to talk with God about?

3. God is faithful and just to forgive us from our sins when we ask. Have you ever not asked God to forgive you for a bad attitude you had? How did you feel on the inside knowing that you were thinking bad thoughts but you wouldn't ask God for forgiveness?

Do Something about It

When you are feeling upset and angry on the inside, ask God to help you make good choices with the words you say. Ask him to help you think about your attitude and words before speaking out loud.

Pray about It

Dear God, please help me make good choices about the words I say out loud. When I am feeling peaceful and happy it is easy to speak good words. But when I get upset, it can be easy to say words that do not honor you. Help me to have the self-control to not speak words that hurt you and others. In Jesus' name, amen.

DAY 6
Coin Toss

Gather your family members or friends together. Show everyone this page and review the Bible verse. Repeat the verse a couple of times.

Next, sit or stand in a circle and toss a quarter back and forth to each other. Each time the quarter is caught, the catcher says the next word in the memory verse. Be sure to have this book open to this page so you can help anyone who has trouble. Continue until as a group, you can play the game and say the verse without help.

1 John 1:9

118 · God Is Faithful and Just

Week 17

God Gives Me Power, Love, and Self-Discipline

Look at the visual Bible verse below. Try to figure out what it says. Write the verse words on the blank lines. Use the Visual Bible Verse Dictionary on page 371, if needed.

 has   +n

 spirit of   timidity  -ter

of  self-discipline

_____

_____

_____

_____

_____

God has not given us a spirit of fear and timidity, but of power, love, and self-discipline. 2 Timothy 1:7

DAY 1

Stuck Drawer

Luke and Mandy were doing their before-school, bedroom cleanup when Luke heard banging coming from his foster sister's room. Luke stuck his head in her room and saw that Mandy was trying her best to force a drawer shut on her clothes dresser. "Let me help you, Mandy," offered Luke.

"No!" Mandy replied anxiously. "I can do it myself," she said firmly.

"OK . . ." Luke replied, shrugging before he left the room. Once Luke was gone, Mandy quietly opened the drawer again and looked inside to make sure all of her things were there. Then she used her whole body to push it shut. Once Mandy was sure she had closed the drawer completely, she exhaled a sigh of relief and went downstairs to breakfast.

Sitting at the table eating their oatmeal and sizzling hot bacon for breakfast, Luke and Mandy gobbled up their food. Any minute now, Dad would be calling them to get their coats on and their backpacks ready for school.

Sure enough, just as Mandy finished chewing the last of her bacon, they heard Dad yell from the garage, "Come on, kids! Time to leave."

Mandy and Luke put on their jackets, grabbed their backpacks, and were out the door. "Have a great day," Mom called out as she finished folding the laundry.

Mom went to Luke's room to put everything away. Then, she went to Mandy's room. She tried to open Mandy's dresser drawer, but it wouldn't budge.

That's odd, Mom thought and she tugged on the drawer again. It took all of Mom's strength to force it open. What she found inside made Mom so sad. *Tonight, I'll have another talk with Mandy . . . I feel so bad for her and what she has been through,* Mom thought to herself.

Moses and the Burning Bush

DAY 2

Read about It

Exodus 3:1—4:17

Think about It

1 This Bible story tells about Moses being called to lead the Israelites out of slavery in Egypt. Moses was terrified at the thought! He had one excuse after another why he didn't think he was the right guy for the job. But God persisted, because God always knows best. God promised to be with Moses and to help him. That same help from God is available to us every day.

2 This week's verse has a three-part promise to us. God promises to give us power, love, and self-discipline because he knows that we will need all three of these every day of our lives. Read the verse and say aloud the three things God promises to each of us. Which of these three things do you think you need the most?

3 God also reminds us that because we have the Holy Spirit living within us we do not have to be timid—or afraid, or scared, or frightened, or worried. The Holy Spirit is always with us and gives us the power, love, and self-discipline we need to think good thoughts and make good choices.

Do Something about It

When you feel like you're not strong enough to make a good choice, say this promise out loud. It will remind you that because the Holy Spirit is with you, you have the power, the love, and the self-discipline you need for every decision you have to make.

Pray about It

Dear God, sometimes I struggle to make good choices. I need you to help me. Thank you for giving us the Holy Spirit to be with us and help us when we need it. Thank you for promising to give me the power, love, and self-discipline to make right choices. Please help me to think good thoughts so that I will make good choices. In Jesus' name, amen.

Brain Maze

Find your way through the maze from start to finish. Along the correct path, you'll find symbols and words for today's verse. Write each verse word down in order on the blank lines below.

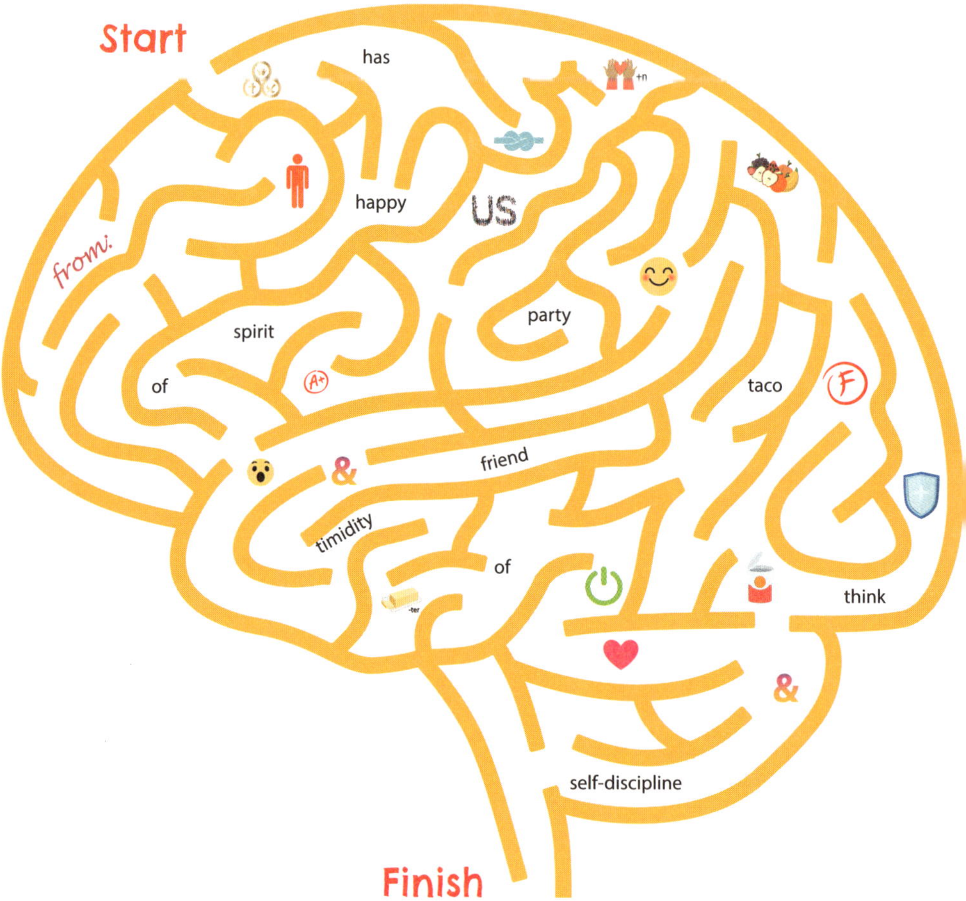

Start

Finish

_____
_____
_____
_____

2 Timothy 1:7

No More Fear

DAY 4

As soon as Luke and Mandy walked in the door after school, Mom had a snack waiting for them on the kitchen counter. "Oh, good, veggies and hummus!" Luke said happily. "Come on, Mandy, let's eat."

Mandy smiled and carried two small plates over to the counter, handing one to Luke. A few minutes later their stomachs were full and Luke and Mandy were ready to relax and enjoy some free time before dinner.

"Mandy, can you come in here please?" Mom called. Mandy went to find Mom and found her sitting on Mandy's bed. She motioned to Mandy to sit next to her. When Mandy did, Mom took her hand gently in her own. "Mandy, I found something today that I want to ask you about. Honey, why are you hiding food in your drawer?" Mom asked gently.

Mandy's face turned red and she started to cry, but no words came out. "Please tell me what's wrong, Mandy," Mom said encouragingly. "I want to help if I can."

Mandy looked sad and ashamed and even scared as she cried. "When I was living in a different foster home we never had enough to eat. So I started trying to hide as much food as I could. That way, I would always have something to eat. I'm sorry. I shouldn't have taken the food and hidden it," Mandy cried.

Mom stroked Mandy's hair and spoke softly. "Mandy, in this house you will always have enough food. You don't ever have to hide it." Mom said. "God loves you too much to want you to live afraid. He wants you to know that you are loved. I want you to know that we love you. We promise to take care of you and God promises to care for you, too. How about we sit together right now and ask God to take away your fears and worries?" Mom asked.

Mandy nodded yes. So they bowed their heads together as Mom prayed, "Dear God, please help Mandy to understand how much you love her and how much we love her. Please help her not to be afraid. Help her to trust in your perfect protection and care for her. Help her to know that you sent us to care for her because you love her. In Jesus' name, amen."

God Gives Me Power, Love, and Self-Discipline

DAY 5: Elisha and the Widow

Read about It

2 Kings 4:1–7

Think about It

1. In this Bible story, Elisha needed food. So God told him to ask a poor widow for food. And then God provided food for Elisha, the widow, and the widow's sons! God loves to provide us with more than enough.

2. Everyone goes through scary times now and them. And some people have been through LOTS of scary times. We may not always understand why others think or act the way they do. Mandy was hiding food because she was afraid of going hungry. There had been times in her life when she didn't have enough food to eat. In her mind, it was smart to hide food. God wants us to face our fears, talk about them with people who love us, and then trust him to care for us. How do you think Mandy feels now that her foster mom understands what happened to her?

3. God gives us the Holy Spirit living inside of us so that we can have the power, the love, and the self-discipline we need. Mandy had never thought about this before, but now when she starts to feel afraid she can say this Bible promise out loud to herself!

Do Something about It

When you remember something from the past that hurt you or made you feel afraid, remember that God has given you the Holy Spirit to be with you and to help you. Pray and ask God to help you be brave and to think good thoughts instead of dwelling on hard, scary, or sad times from the past.

Pray about It

Dear God, sometimes I think about difficult times that happened in the past. Some days it's all I think about! Thinking about these things makes me feel sad or scared again. Help me to trust you to take care of me. Help me to talk to with people I love about my fears. Thank you for giving me the Holy Spirit to be with me, help me think good thoughts, and help me make good choices. In Jesus' name, amen.

Complete the Comic

Read the visual verse, and then write each word beneath its symbol. Complete the comic strip using your own words and drawings. Work the verse into your comic strip.

 has    spirit of

_____

& timidity  of  & self-discipline

_____

2 Timothy 1:7

"Hey, what's wrong?"

Week 18
God Is Wisest and Strongest of All

Look at the visual Bible verse below. Try to figure out what it says. Write the verse words on the blank lines. Use the Visual Bible Verse Dictionary on page 371, if needed.

_____

_____

_____

_____

_____

This foolish plan of God is wiser than the wisest of human plans, and God's weakness is stronger than the greatest of human strength. 1 Corinthians 1:25

Thump, Thump, Thump

DAY 1

Cough, cough, cough! Charis coughed. *Thump. Thump. Thump.* Julissa sat next to her younger sister, Charis, thumping on her back. The thumping was to help loosen all the thick mucus that would get caught in Charis's lungs. Julissa had done this so many times before, that she didn't even need to think about how to move her hands up and down Charis's back. *Thump. Thump. Thump.*

Charis was only eight years old and her cystic fibrosis had changed everyone's life in a big way. Charis liked to play games on her phone to distract from the coughing. "Charis, did you see that? Move the screen over so I can see it better," Julissa said as she continuing thumping.

"Can you see it now?" Charis asked.

"Yes, now try to get to the next level before I finish thumping," Julissa challenged.

After Julissa had finished her part, she called to her mom to do the rest, "Mom, I'm done with Charis. It's your turn!" called Julissa.

Mom came into the living room and asked Charis to lie down on the floor. "OK, honey, let's get you all loosened up." Just then, Charis started to cough. "Do you feel alright? Are you getting sick, Charis?" Mom asked as she bent low over Charis's chest to hear her breathe better.

"I feel OK, Mom," Charis replied.

Julissa left the room and started worrying about the possibility of Charis getting sick . . . again. *We have the weekend all planned out. We're going to the county fair. And this is the first time I can go alone with my friends to walk around and ride the rides. . . . Charis cannot be getting sick again,* Julissa stated firmly to herself. The more she thought about it, the angrier she got that she might miss out on having fun at the fair with her friends. *There's nothing FAIR about me missing the fair!*

Julissa went to the kitchen to get a glass of water. Julissa overheard her mom asking Charis more questions about how she was feeling. Suddenly, Charis started coughing a second time. *Oh, no!* thought Julissa.

God Is Wisest and Strongest of All

DAY 2: The Wisest Man in the World

Read about It

1 Kings 3:5–14; 10:1–13

Think about It

1. In our Bible story, King Solomon asked God for wisdom to be a wise ruler. God gave Solomon the wisdom he wanted. Solomon may have been the wisest man in the world, but he never could have grown that wise on his own. It was a gift from God, the wisest ever in Heaven or Earth!

2. This week's verse is fun to learn because it is comparing opposites. God is telling us that even if God were foolish (and he is not) our best wisdom wouldn't compare with God. Our best strength, wisdom, love—everything!—is nothing compared to God's strength, wisdom, and love. How does it make you feel to know this about God?

3. Knowing that God is both wise and strong and that he loves us is important. It is especially important when we feel overwhelmed or afraid. Our trust in God and our confidence in his plan for us can be secure because we know who God is. God is wise. God is strong. And God loves us. Which of these three things means the most to you—that God is wise? That he is strong? Or that he loves us? Why?

Do Something about It

When you are frustrated about something that you don't like or don't understand, say this verse out loud. It will remind you that God is both wiser and stronger than you are. Trust God to know what is best for you and to take care of you because he loves you.

Pray about It

Dear God, I don't always understand why some things happen. I feel bad when I get upset that our family can't always do the things we plan. Please help me to be kind and helpful when difficult things happen—even if I don't understand them. And please help me to trust you, God, even if I don't like what is happening. In Jesus' name, amen.

Verse in Motion

DAY 3

Read the visual verse and write each word beneath its symbol. Write some motions you can do for each phrase. Then, practice saying the verse and doing the motions several times in front of a mirror, for your family or friends, or for your stuffed animals. Teach it to someone to do with you and video yourselves saying the verse and doing the motions. Keep it up until you know the verse by heart.

1 Corinthians 1:25

God Is Wisest and Strongest of All

DAY 4: A Cinnamony Morning

Julissa woke up several times that night from Charis's cough. She wasn't angry anymore. She was scared.

Just when Julissa felt like she was drifting off to sleep again, her father shook her awake. "We need to take Charis to the hospital. Grammy is on her way over to stay with you," Dad said.

"OK, Dad, I'll be praying for her," Julissa said.

Some hours later, Julissa woke up and smelled something yummy. *Grammy makes the best cinnamon rolls!* Julissa thought to herself as she rolled out of bed.

"Hi there, kiddo! Did you sleep alright?" Grammy asked. A delicious looking pan of cinnamon rolls sat by the oven.

"Yes, I didn't even hear you come in," Julissa explained.

"How about we pray for Charis? Your dad called and said she's fine, but the doctor wants to keep her one more night."

Julissa paused. "Grammy?" she finally said. "Yesterday, I was kind of mad about Charis being sick. I was worried about our trip to the fair . . . I wasn't thinking about Charis at all! Doesn't that make me the worst sister ever?"

Grammy put an arm around Julissa's shoulder. "No. It just makes you human. We all can get caught up thinking of ourselves instead of others. But being sick isn't Charis's choice. We don't always know why God plans things the way he does, but the Bible tells us that even a plan of God's that seems foolish to us is wiser than any plan we could have."

Julissa looked up. "So being mad is like being mad at God?"

"In a way, yes," Grammy admitted.

"I've got even more to pray about now" Julissa said. "Dear God, I'm sorry I was thinking about myself. I'm sorry that being mad like that was like being mad at you. Help me understand that your ways are always the best ways. Please be with Charis now as she's in the hospital. In Jesus' name, amen!"

"Amen," Grammy agreed. "Now, let's dig in to those cinnamon rolls!" Julissa grinned and reached for the pan.

Jesus Heals a Blind Man

DAY 5

Read about It

John 9

Think about It

1. When some of Jesus' friends asked him who was responsible for the man being blind, Jesus told them it was so that God's power could be seen. When Jesus used God's power to heal the blind man, people better understood how powerful God is. What is something that helps you know how strong and wise God is?

2. The first part of this week's verse tells us that the foolishness of God is wiser than human wisdom. When we don't like or understand difficult things in life—like Julissa not understanding or liking how her sister was so sick—we need to trust God and trust his wisdom. When is a time it might be hard for a kid your age to trust God's wisdom?

3. The second part of this week's verse tells us that the weakness of God is stronger than human strength. What are some examples of God's strength and power? If you're having a hard time, think of all the strong and powerful things you see in nature (animals, nature, etc.), and then remember that God made all those things and he controls them!

Do Something about It

When you see others who are sick and weak in their bodies, tell God how grateful and thankful you are for your healthy body. If you have sickness or weakness in your body, ask God to help you get better. And then thank God for the things you are strong in. Find ways to help others who aren't strong at the things you are strong at.

Pray about It

Dear God, I am thankful for the strengths and wisdom that you have given me. Please help me to use them in ways to help others. Give me good ideas for making their lives easier when I serve them. Help me to put myself in their place and love them like I would like to be loved. Help me to do all these things so that you can have all the glory. In Jesus' name, amen.

Two Times

Below you will see the visual Bible verse twice. In the top verse, fill in the missing words. In the bottom verse, draw all the missing symbols, and color them in.

____ 🗓️+ish ____ 👑 is 🦉+er

____ The 🦉+st ____ 🧍 📋+s &

👑's 🔗+ness is 💪+er ____

The gr8+est ____ 🧍 🏋️

This			of			
than			of			
				than		
		of				

1 Corinthians 1:25

Week 19
Love God, Not Money

Look at the visual Bible verse below. Try to figure out what it says. Write the verse words on the blank lines. Use the Visual Bible Verse Dictionary on page 371, if needed.

satisfied    ½

_____

_____

_____

_____

_____

Don't love money; be satisfied with what you have. Hebrews 13:5

DAY 1: Counting On It

Meg shook every last coin out of her piggy bank and pulled out every last dollar bill inside. She then put all the coins in a neat pile. Next to those piles, she put all the bills in piles with all the faces pointing up!

Meg liked to count her money every few days. Last week, she'd had a birthday so Meg's savings had increased even more. Aunts, uncles, grandmas, and grandpas who couldn't come to her party had all sent cards with cash inside.

I have one hundred and eighty-two dollars and seventy-three cents, Meg whispered to herself. Meg smiled. Her goal was to save two hundred dollars. Her dad said when she'd saved two hundred dollars, he would help her open a savings account. *I'm only seventeen dollars and twenty-seven cents away!* Slowly, Meg replaced all the money back into her piggy bank and placed the rubber stopper in the bottom.

Just as she was putting the piggy bank back in its corner on her desk. She heard her mother calling. "Meg, come downstairs please."

"Coming!" Meg stopped just inside the laundry-room door as her mom began to fold the clothes fresh from the dryer.

"Good. You're here. Meg, I wanted to remind you of Grace's birthday party next Saturday. We need to go shopping for her gift. I'd like your help putting this laundry away so we can go before starting dinner," Mom explained.

"Ah . . . I decided not to go to her party . . . " Meg said with embarrassment.

Mom stopped folding clothes to look at Meg. "But you already told her you were coming. Why don't you want to go?" Mom asked.

"Well, I . . . I don't want to spend my money on a gift . . . I'm trying to save enough to open my own savings account . . . " Meg shared.

"Honey, we have already discussed this . . . you do chores every week and we give you money. Some of that money is to be spent on gifts you need to buy others . . . did you forget that?" Mom asked with a frown.

"No . . . but I think it's more important for me to save it all . . . " Meg said defensively.

"Let's sit down and talk this through . . . "

The Rich Fool

DAY 2

Read about It

Luke 12:13–21

Think about It

1 Jesus' story tells us about a man who foolishly did everything he could to save money, but then wouldn't be around to enjoy it. God wants us to know that there are things that are more important than money, and we shouldn't get confused about that. What are some things that are more important than money to you?

2 This verse gives us two instructions. First, it tells us to keep our lives free from the love of money. Why do you think God wants us to make sure we don't love money? Who are we supposed to love more than anything or anyone else?

3 The second part of this verse tells us to be satisfied with what we have. Have you ever wanted more of something? More toys? More food? More friends? More money? When we are not content with what God gives us how do we feel on the inside?

Do Something about It

When you start to feel dissatisfied because you don't have everything you want, start thanking God for everything you do have! Remember that God really is the owner of everything on Earth—and that includes everything you have. God gives you things to use wisely and share with others. Instead of thinking of ways to keep these gifts for yourself, think about ways you can share them with others.

Pray about It

Dear God, I don't think I love money, but maybe I do. Please help me to be satisfied with whatever I have. Please help me to love you and others more than I love money. Help me to be happy to share the things I have with others. In Jesus' name, amen.

# This Little Piggy

Read the visual verse, and then write the words on the lines below.

   satisfied

_____

_____

_____

_____

Hebrews 13:5

Instead of looking at your piggy bank as something that money comes out of, think of it as something that can spark ideas! What are some ways you could use money to serve God and help others? Draw or write your ideas in the space below.

Lemonade Lessons

Meg sat at the kitchen counter while Mom poured two glasses of strawberry lemonade. "I know that you are so good at saving your money, Meg, but there are times when the best choice is to use some of that savings for others. We give you chore money each week not to just save it but to learn how to spend it wisely," Mom explained.

Meg burst in saying, "But I don't want to spend it!"

"Right now, it seems like you love your money more than you love your friend Grace. Am I right?" Mom asked gently.

"No . . . I don't think so . . . but what about my goal of opening my own savings account? I'm only seventeen dollars and twenty-seven cents away!" Meg asked.

"Of course those things are important. But some things are more important. Will it really make a difference if you have to wait to open that savings account?" Mom asked.

"Oh, Mom!" Meg groaned. She wanted to be a good friend to Grace and buy her a gift, but she also wanted to open a savings account—and sooner rather than later.

"Think about how Grace will feel if you suddenly decide not to attend her party? Is that the loving choice?" Mom inquired.

Meg had a feeling Mom was right, but she just really wanted that bank account!

"Think about this. How would you have felt if Grace hadn't come to your party last week because she didn't want to spend her money on a gift for you? " Mom asked.

Suddenly, it became very clear to Meg. "Terrible. I would think she didn't like me . . . Or at least didn't like me as much as she liked her money," Meg answered, feeling ashamed of her hesitation.

"Well, then . . . I think you have your answer," Mom said.

"Yeah. You're right, Mom. I will buy Grace a gift for her birthday and I'll be content to wait longer to open my savings account."

"Great! Now let's finish up that laundry!" Meg laughed as she followed her mother back to the laundry room.

DAY 5: A Jar of Perfume

Read about It

John 12:1–11

Think about It

1 Our Bible story shows us two different people who had very different reactions to an expensive gift. The woman was happy to use her expensive perfume to wash Jesus' feet. Judas was upset that she had "wasted" the money. The passage also tells us that Judas loved money and even stole from Jesus and the other disciples. Which of these two reactions do you think pleases God—being generous or being greedy?

2 Learning to use our money wisely is a good thing. Money is a powerful tool and we can learn how to use it to both save and to spend wisely. The choice to use money in a way that pleases God might mean we need to share it. When is a time you or someone in your family was able to share with others? How did it make you feel afterwards?

3 When we are satisfied with what we have, God is pleased. God is the true owner of everything on earth and the Bible helps us understand what matters most to God. How can you use money this week in a way that will please God?

Do Something about It

When you hear about someone who has a need and you have the money to help them, think about asking your parents if you can spend your money to help. Pray about how to save and spend your money in ways that will please God. Be thankful every day for what you have.

Pray about It

Dear God, I am thankful that you have given me money and other things that I need. Please help me to be satisfied with what I have. Help me to make wise choices about saving and spending my money. Remind me that everything on Earth really belongs to you and that you have given it to me to use wisely. In Jesus' name, amen.

Verse Order

Read the visual verse, and then write the verse on the lines below.

    satisfied

_____

_____

_____

Hebrews 13:5

On separate bills of play money or index cards, draw each symbol or word from the verse to make verse cards. Make as many sets of cards as you will have players. Shuffle each set of verse cards, and give one set to each player. On your signal, players race to put the verse cards in order. At the end of each round, everyone says the verse aloud as a group.

Or, to play by yourself, make two copies of verse cards, lay them out face down in a grid, and turn two at a time over, trying to make a pair. If the cards match, take them out of the grid and place on the side. Continue until all the cards are matched.

Week 20
I Can Have Eternal Life

Look at the visual Bible verse below. Try to figure out what it says. Write the verse words on the blank lines. Use the Visual Bible Verse Dictionary on page 371, if needed.

_____

_____

_____

_____

_____

Anyone who believes in God's Son has eternal life. John 3:36

Pizza Party

Trees zipped past the window as Zoe sat next to her brother Zack in the backseat on the car ride home from school. Zack was super excited. That day, his class enjoyed a pizza party they'd won for reading the most books in the school's Battle of the Books reading competition.

"Mom, we each got to eat as many pieces of pizza as we wanted! Then, we had a pizza piñata and took turns hitting it until it fell apart. I have so much candy and toys in my bag!" Zack declared loudly.

"That sounds like so much fun, Zack! You and your classmates worked hard to read enough books to win that party. I'm so happy for you," Mom smiled as she glanced in her rearview mirror to the backseat. "What's wrong, Zoe?" Mom asked.

"Nothing!" Zoe crossed her arms and stared at the trees zipping by.

"Uh, I can tell by your tone that 'nothing' isn't correct. Something's bothering you. Tell me what it is," Mom persisted.

Zoe took a deep breath and then let everything spill out. "I just don't think it's fair that Zack got to have a pizza party when I read just as many books as he did. It's not fair," Zoe complained.

Zack opened his mouth to speak, but Mom shut him down. "Zack, let me handle this." Mom glanced again at Zoe in the backseat, meeting her daughter's angry eyes. She looked back at the road before speaking. "Zoe, Zack's class read the most books total. I know that you read as many as Zack, but his class read more than yours."

Mom pulled onto their driveway, and then into the garage. Zack opened his door, grabbed his backpack, jumped out of the car, and ran into the house. Zoe was just opening her door when Mom spoke again. "Zoe, stay here for a minute please. I want to talk with you," Mom said.

"Why do we have to talk? What did I do?" Zoe whined.

"It's not something you did, Zoe, it's the way you are thinking that's a problem," Mom said.

I Can Have Eternal Life · 141

DAY 2: This Man Has Done Nothing Wrong

Read about It

Luke 23:32–43

Think about It

1. This Bible passage tells of how Jesus was put on a cross to die. There were two others put on crosses at the same time. One of the men mocked Jesus, but the other believed in him. The believing man talked about how unfair it was that Jesus had to die. Why do you think Jesus was willing to suffer and die for us?

2. This week's verse explains the importance of what we believe. If we believe in Jesus and ask him to forgive us for our sins, we can have eternal life—live with him in paradise (Heaven). Do you know what the word *eternal* means? It means forever and ever.

3. What we believe about God and Jesus—and even sin—shapes how we think and talk about everything in life. When we see someone doing something bad and they are forgiven, it doesn't always seem fair does it? But Jesus tells us when we believe and ask him for forgiveness we are forgiven. Jesus wants us to believe and to follow him even when life doesn't seem fair.

Do Something about It

If you have questions about believing in Jesus and asking for forgiveness for all your sins, talk with an adult family member or whoever gave you this book.

Pray about It

Dear God, thank you that you forgive me for my sins. Please help me to remember all that Jesus did for me. Help me to believe with my heart and my mind. Please help me to read the Bible and remember your promises every day. In Jesus' name, amen.

Over and Over

Eternal life is life that goes on forever. The visual verse seems to be going on forever on this page! Draw lines to separate each instance of the verse, and then write out the verse on the lines at the bottom of the page.

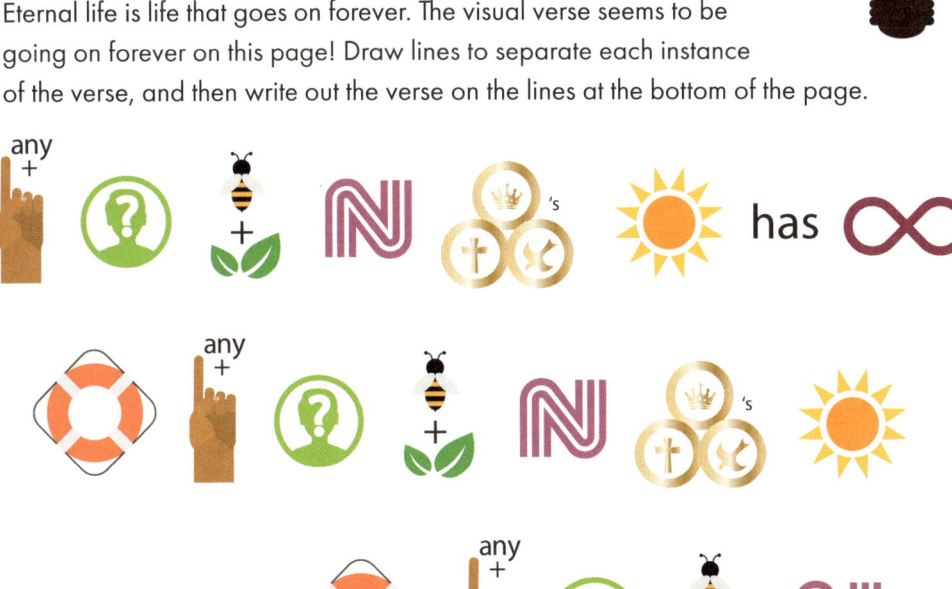
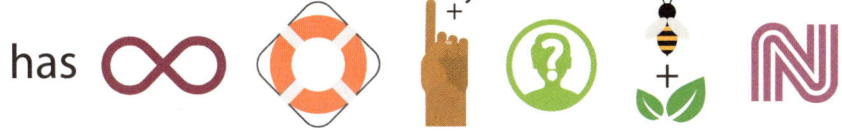

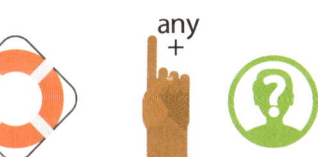

_____
_____
_____
_____
_____

John 3:36

DAY 4: Power to Choose

Zoe and her mom were still sitting in the car after Zack went inside. Mom looked at Zoe. "Honey," she said gently. "This won't be the last time something like this happens. Life just isn't always fair. Think about this: Jesus died on the cross for us. Did Jesus ever do anything wrong?"

"No," Zoe answered. "He never sinned."

"That's right. Never. Was it fair that he had to die?" Mom asked.

"No," Zoe said slowly. "I guess not, but I never thought about it that way."

"Jesus knew it wasn't fair, but he willingly died because he loves us." Mom said. "I know how hard you worked. It isn't fun when you work as hard as someone else and they get rewards that you don't."

"It might feel unfair, but is it?" Mom asked. Zoe looked up at her, surprised. "You knew how the contest worked before you read the first book. What would have happened if your class had read more books?" Mom asked.

Zoe understood. "I would have had the prize and Zack would have missed out even though he read as many books as me. Maybe he'd feel like I do—that it was unfair!"

"And you'd probably feel bad if he were upset about it. You have no control over others. But you do have control over how you react. You have that power."

This caught Zoe's attention. She'd never thought about things like this before. *What kind of power is Mom talking about?* she wondered.

Mom continued, "You can choose to be angry or you can choose to be happy for your brother," Mom explained. "And not just for Zack's sake. For your own. Which feels better: being angry or being happy?"

"Happy," Zoe said.

"That's a choice you have," Mom said and then smiled at Zoe. "So what's it going to be, Zoe? Do you choose to be angry or happy?"

"Well, I think I can manage to not be angry, but I don't think I'm ready to be happy just yet." Zoe said. They both laughed, got out of the car, put their arms around each other, and headed into the house.

Jesus Predicts His Death

DAY 5

Read about It

Luke 18:31–34

Think about It

1. In the Bible story, we read that Jesus predicted his death and resurrection. This means that Jesus knew what was going to happen to him, and he chose to go through with it. Even though it wasn't fair that he was punished for everyone else's sins, Jesus lovingly chose to obey God. How does it make you feel to know that Jesus was willing to suffer and die for you?

2. Jesus willingly died so that we can be forgiven of our sins and become members of God's family. This is the most important event in the history of the world. If you have any questions about becoming a member of God's family, be sure to ask someone in your family who follows Jesus. Or ask the person who got this book for you.

3. Sometimes life doesn't seem fair—and it isn't. But what are some things we can do when we start to feel upset about life not being fair?

Do Something about It

When you start to get upset because life doesn't seem fair, remember that it wasn't fair for Jesus to die on a cross for everyone else's sins. But Jesus loves us so much, that even though he was sinless, he died for everyone—including you!

Pray about It

Dear God, sometimes I feel angry and upset because life isn't fair. Please help me to remember what Jesus did for me on the cross. Help me to think about the truth that Jesus never sinned, but he chose to die for me. I need to always remember that Jesus took my sin and erased them after I asked him to forgive me. Even when life isn't fair, I can still choose how to react. In Jesus' name, amen.

I Can Have Eternal Life • 145

DAY 6

Symbol Memory

Remember what the symbols are for the verse and draw each one above the appropriate word.

"Anyone	who	believes
in	God's	Son
has	eternal	life."

John 3:36

Week 21

I'm Not Alone in My Trouble

Look at the visual Bible verse below. Try to figure out what it says. Write the verse words on the blank lines. Use the Visual Bible Verse Dictionary on page 371, if needed.

When they call on me, I will answer; I will be with them in trouble. I will rescue and honor them. Psalm 91:15

DAY 1
Cookie-Dough Dough

Joey, Lindsay, and Janna were asked to count up all the orders for their soccer team's fundraiser. Their team was selling buckets of cookie dough to families and friends and neighbors. Everyone on their soccer team was so excited about this fundraiser! They figured everyone loves cookies and they should be able to sell enough dough to meet their goal. If they could raise enough money, each team member could go to a three-day training camp during the summer.

Joey and Lindsay divided all the orders into two piles: those who had already paid and those who had not. Janna filled out two lists: those who had already paid and those who had not. The friends worked together well.

All the team members had worked hard to sell as much cookie dough as possible. It looked like they had sold over 150 buckets of dough. That was more than enough to reach their goal!

"Wow," Joey exclaimed, "I never thought our team would sell this many."

"I have already counted eighty buckets sold in my pile," said Lindsay.

"And I have the names and addresses of fifty customers in my book," shared Janna.

The three friends continued to add up the paid and not-paid orders. Suddenly, Joey said, "Wait . . . Mr. Meyers paid too much for his cookie dough. He paid twice!"

"Are you sure?" asked Lindsay.

"Yes, he gave me forty dollars instead of twenty," Joey explained.

"Hmm, that means we have an extra twenty dollars?" Janna asked.

"We will have to give it back to him," Lindsay said. Joey and Janna didn't answer her. They just looked at each other.

Then Joey said, "I think we should just keep the money and add it to the money we raised . . . I mean, we will reach our goal that much faster right? It isn't stealing if we don't keep the money for ourselves right?"

"I think that's a good idea, Joey," agreed Janna.

Lindsay was upset. "We can't do that! It's stealing from Mr. Meyers. He made a mistake giving us forty dollars instead of twenty," Lindsay told her friends.

The Soldier's Psalm

DAY 2

Read about It

Psalm 91

Think about It

1 This Bible passage contains this week's verse. It is sometimes called the Soldier's Psalm because it is said that during World War I, many members of the U.S. Army recited Psalm 91 every day. The key idea in the psalm is that we can take refuge in God. There is nothing he can't save us from! How does it make you feel to know that God can keep you safe from anything?

2 This week's verse has two promises God gives to us. When we pray and ask God for help, God first promises to answer us. The second promise is that God will be with us when we are in trouble. Even when you have done something that would not please him, God wants you to call out to him. When was a time you felt so bad about something that you didn't want to pray about it?

3 When we are in trouble we need God's help. When have you felt alone or scared but you were afraid of telling God? You don't ever need to be afraid to talk with God about something . . . God already knows everything about us.

Do Something about It

When you make a poor choice and feel guilty because you know that you sinned, call out to God and ask him to forgive you. Then ask him for his help so that you can make things right.

Pray about It

Dear God, sometimes I make a poor choice and feel guilty and ashamed. Sometimes I don't know how to make things right. Help me to remember to come to you to ask for forgiveness. Please give me your wisdom so that I do not make the same mistakes again. Help me to be wise and know how to make things right. Give me the courage to do it. In Jesus' name, amen.

Verse Pictures

DAY 3

Review the visual verse on page 147. In each box, write or draw what you think of when you think about those words from the verse.

When they call on me,	I will answer;
I will be with them in trouble.	I will rescue and honor them.

Psalm 91:15

The Right Thing

DAY 4

The three friends were at a stalemate. Lindsay thought they needed to return the extra money Mr. Meyers had paid them. Joey and Janna thought they should just add it to the fundraising money.

"But keeping the money would be wrong," Lindsay said firmly.

"Well, it's two against one, so we're doing it our way!" Janna decided.

"You better not tell on us, Lindsay!" Joey warned.

"If you tell, you will get us into trouble," Janna said angrily.

The three teammates got back to their jobs organizing the orders and payments. Joey and Janna continued to give Lindsay mean looks. They pretended Lindsay wasn't even in the room.

Lindsay felt like she could cry. *How could they want to do this bad thing to Mr. Myers, and then be so mean to me, too? I thought they were my friends,* Lindsay thought to herself as she fought back tears.

The rest of the time they worked, Joey and Janna would talk and laugh—and ignore Lindsay if she asked a question or said anything.

When the counting was done, Joey looked at Lindsay and warned her one more time, "You better not say anything, Lindsay."

Walking out to her mom's car, Lindsay felt tears in her eyes as she prayed, "Dear God, I think I know the right thing to do, but I don't want my friends to get angry at me. Please give me the courage to be honest and tell the truth. I need your help right now . . . In Jesus' name, amen."

After she prayed, Lindsey felt better. And she felt confident about what the right choice was for her to do. Lindsay would wait until she got home, and then she would tell her parents what had happened. Lindsay was sure they would talk to the coach about it and he would give Mr. Meyers his money back. Lindsay would try to keep Joey and Janna out of the whole thing, if she could.

After that, well, it would be up to Joey and Janna whether or not they wanted to be mad at Lindsey. She felt sure they'd be OK once they realized she wasn't trying to get them into trouble.

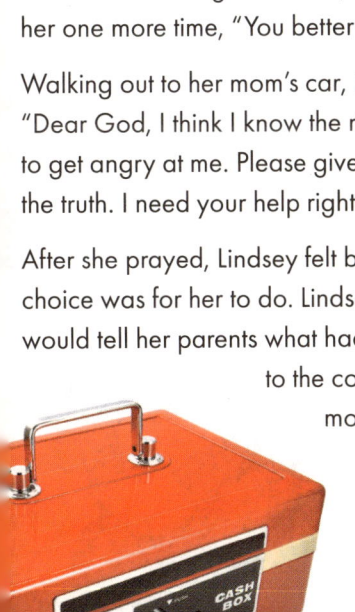

I'm Not Alone in My Trouble

DAY 5: Joy Comes in the Morning

Read about It

Psalm 30

Think about It

1. This psalm was written by King David. You may not have to worry about enemies wanting to kill you like David did, but what are some of the things that can be frightening to a kid your age? God wants us to call out to him in good times and in bad.

2. Lindsay tried to get her friends to make the honest choice and give back the extra money, but they said no. Lindsay realized her friends were upset with her . . . for doing the right thing! Sometimes other people will get angry with us when we obey God. When has that happened to you? If it hasn't happened to you, what do you think you would do?

3. When we call out to God, he promises to answer us. Sometimes God's answer will be helping us to remember a Bible verse that tells us the right choice to make. Other times God's answer may come through people who give us wise advice. God promises to be with us in trouble. He is always close by to love and care for us.

Do Something about It

When you feel upset because others are treating you badly, stop and pray. Ask God for the strength you need to obey him and do the right thing. Say this verse out loud to remind yourself that God promises to be with you in times of trouble.

Pray about It

Dear God, sometimes I feel all alone. Help me remember that you are always with me. Thank you for staying close to me and listening to me when I pray. In Jesus' name, amen.

Call Out the Verse

"Call out to God" by calling out the verse. First call out loudly. Then call out softly, in a high voice, in a low voice, in super-slow motion, as fast as you can, in a silly voice! Remember: God hears us call out anytime, anywhere, all the time!

Bonus Idea: Make it a game with your family. Gather everyone together and take turns calling out a different way each time.

THEY 📞 ON 💪

👁 📄 Q&A 👁 📄 🐝 w/

THEM N ⚠ 👁 📄

rescue & honor THEM

_____
_____
_____
_____
_____

Psalm 91:15

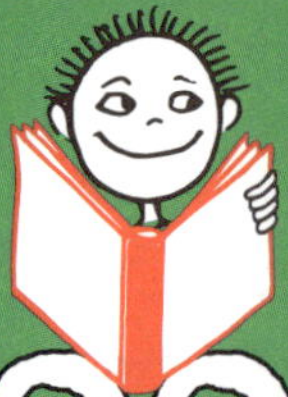

Week 22

God Gives Me Perfect Peace

Look at the visual Bible verse below. Try to figure out what it says. Write the verse words on the blank lines. Use the Visual Bible Verse Dictionary on page 371, if needed.

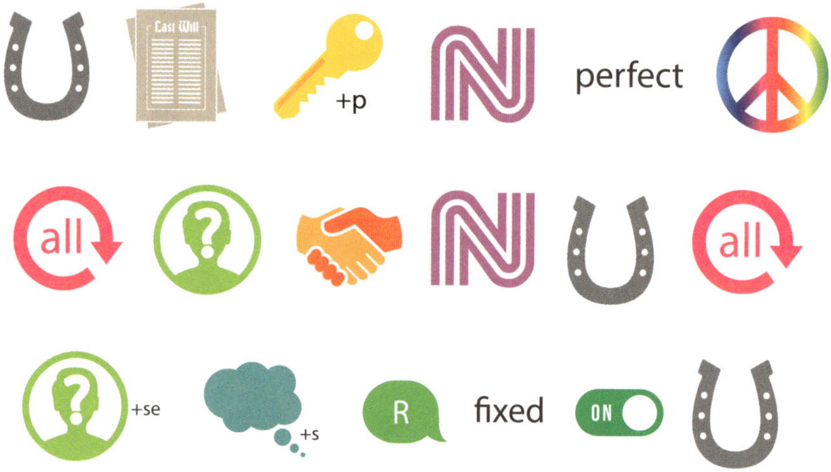

____

____

____

____

____

____

You will keep in perfect peace all who trust in you, all whose thoughts are fixed on you! Isaiah 26:3

Fish Tales

DAY 1

It was the last day of summer vacation and Eden was pulling in another fish. "I got it! I got it!" Eden announced happily. "That makes five for me and only four for you, Grampy. I caught more fish than even you did today!"

Eden's grandfather smiled as he helped Eden take the fish out of the net and remove the fishhook from its mouth. "There you go, Eden. Now let's measure this big guy," Grampy instructed as he pulled out the tape measure.

The fish flopped and flipped around. Eden reached in to help Grampy hold him down. "Eew! . . . He's so squirmy . . ." Eden said as she wrinkled her nose and grimaced. Eden loved fishing, but she did not like touching the fish.

"Fourteen inches! That beats your record for the week. We are going to have a wonderful fish fry tonight," Grampy beamed.

"Can I try for one more before we go back in? Please?" Eden begged.

Grampy looked at his watch and nodded yes. "I think we have time for one more try."

As Eden and Grandpa stood with their fishing poles dangling in the lake water, Eden sighed. Grampy glanced over at the sound. "What's on your mind, Eden?" Grampy asked.

"Oh . . . I'm just thinking about school starting next week. I'm nervous. None of my friends are in my class this year. I won't know anybody," Eden explained with another big sigh.

"Oh, Eden, you will make friends. There is no reason to worry. None at all."

"But Grampy, I'm not like you . . . I never know what to say to people I don't know . . ." Eden said sadly.

God Gives Me Perfect Peace • 155

DAY 2: Shadrach, Meshach, and Abednego

Read about It

Daniel 3

Think about It

1. In our Bible story, Shadrach, Meshach, and Abednego were threatened with being burned if they didn't worship an idol of King Nebuchadnezzar. That didn't scare them! And it didn't make them bow to something other than the one true God. They were able to be brave and have peace that God would take care of them. When are times that a kid your age might need God to help them in a scary situation?

2. This week's Bible verse is terrific because it helps us when we feel nervous or afraid. It reminds us to keep our thoughts on God. When we think about Jesus and trust him, our hearts will not be afraid.

3. This Bible verse includes things that we are supposed to do and things that God promises to do—God's part and our part. God's part is giving us perfect peace inside our hearts. What is our part? What are we supposed to do?

Do Something about It

When you start to worry or feel nervous, stop, sit down, and pray. Ask God to help you keep your thoughts on him and trust him to take care of you. Remember how faithful God has been to you in the past and thank him.

Pray about It

Dear God, sometimes I worry. Maybe it's about something that is going to change or something new in my life. When these times come, please help me to not be afraid. Help me to keep my thoughts on you and to trust you to take care of me. Please help me to forget about being scared and look for ways to help others. In Jesus' name, amen.

Fishy Maze

DAY 3

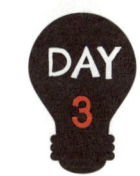

Find your way through the maze from start to finish. Along the correct path, you'll find symbols and words from today's verse. Write each word on the lines below in the order you find them.

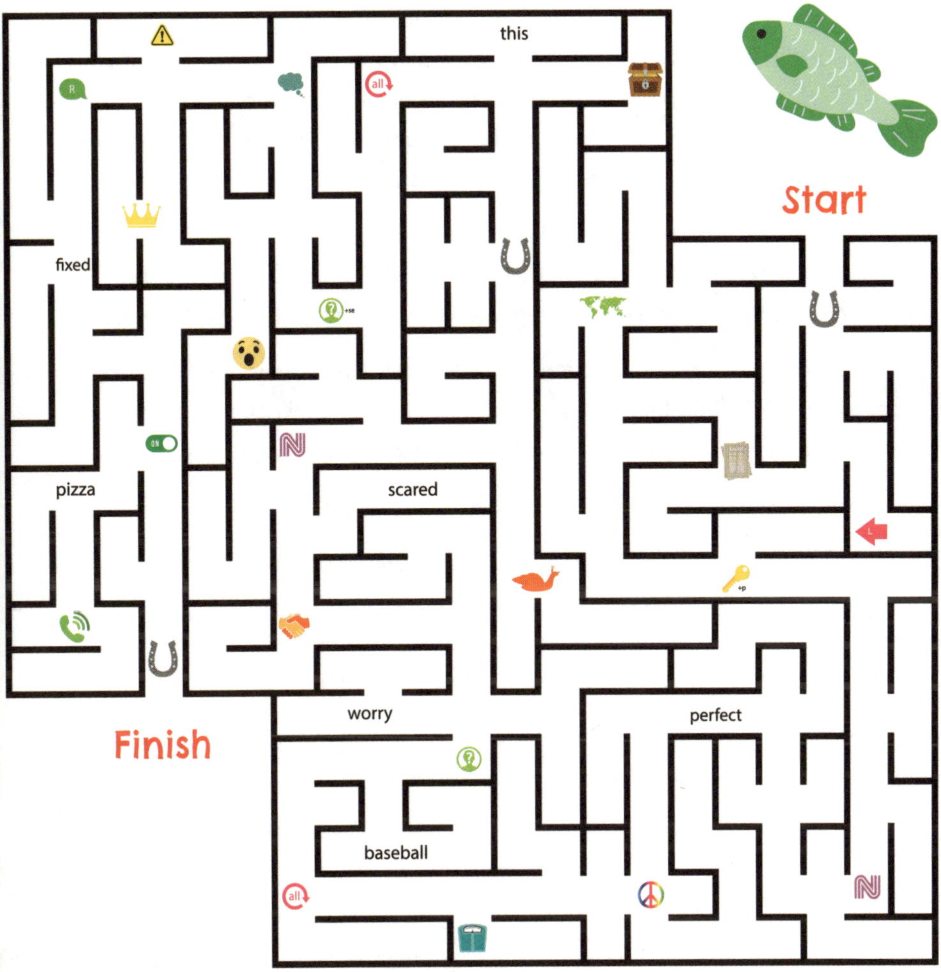

____

____

____________________________ Isaiah 26:3

Answer Key on page 379.

DAY 4: Practice Makes Perfect

The summer sun glinted off the water as Eden and her grandfather pulled their fishing poles out of the water and placed them at the back of the boat. Eden had just told her grandpa she was worried about being in a new class. She felt shy around kids she didn't know already, and all of her friends were in a different class.

Once they settled back in their seats, Grampy started the engine. They slowly headed back to their cabin's dock. Grampy looked at Eden. "Eden, I want you to think about something. Even if you are a little bit nervous about making new friends at school, do you think you are the only one? Do you think maybe there are other boys and girls who feel just as nervous as you do?" Grampy asked.

Eden was surprised. She'd never thought about that, but it made sense. "I guess so." Doubts crept in again, and she shook her head. "But I get scared! I never know what to say to kids I haven't talked to before," Eden explained.

"Hmm, that is a good point," Grampy said. "Well . . . then why don't you and I practice that? We'll pretend we have never met before. I'll ask you a few questions, and then you can ask me a few questions." Grampy suggested.

"OK," Eden answered doubtfully.

For the rest of the ride to shore, that's just what Grampy and Eden did. Grampy asked Eden a question and she answered it. Then Eden asked a question and Grampy answered her. Before they knew it, Grampy and Eden were talking and laughing together.

After they pulled up to the dock, but before they got off the boat, Grampy said, "I want you to remember one thing, Eden. Keep your eyes and your mind on Jesus and trust him. He will take care of you and your heart won't be worried. I'll bet Jesus will use you to make a lot of other boys and girls feel safe and peaceful, too!"

"I'll try, Grampy!" Eden said happily.

A Prayer of David

DAY 5

Read about It

Psalm 3

Think about It

1. Today's Bible passage is a prayer King David prayed when he was fleeing from his own son, Absalom. In it, David talks about how much he trusts and relies on God, even when he is in danger. What do you think about David's faith in God? How does it make you feel?

2. What did you think when Eden's Grandpa said other kids probably felt nervous or scared, too? Sometimes we have to remind ourselves that if we feel worried or nervous, others probably do, too. What are some good questions you could ask someone to get to know them better?

3. Sometimes when we feel nervous the very best thing we can do is to go find others to talk to and make friends with. We can help them feel better by going up to them and starting a conversation. Have you ever tried to be a friend to someone who was all alone?

Do Something about It

When you feel nervous or worried about making friends, pray and ask God to give you courage to talk with others whom you don't know. Be friendly and ask them good questions so that you can get to know them better.

Pray about It

Dear God, I want to help others feel comfortable and happy. Help me think of some good questions I can ask and get to know others better. I will learn how to be a good listener so that I can be a good friend. Help me remember that when I feel nervous, others do, too. Thank you for helping me have peace because I trust you to take care of me. In Jesus' name, amen.

DAY 6: Go Fish!

Read the visual verse, and then write each word beneath its symbol. Then, on separate index cards, draw each symbol or word from the verse. Break the verse into two- or three-word phrases. Make four sets of cards.

Gather with your family or friends to play a game of Go Fish. (You can find instructions for playing Go Fish online.) At the end of each round (when every player has had a turn and play returns to the first player), say the verse aloud as a group.

Alternate Activity: Use your cards to play a game by yourself. Try Concentration or Solitaire. For Solitaire, write each set of cards in a different color. Instead of putting cards in number order, put them in verse order.

U   Will   key +p   N   perfect   peace

all   who?   handshake   N   U   all

who? +se   thoughts +s   R   fixed   ON   U

_____
_____
_____
_____

Isaiah 26:3

Week 23
THE LORD IS MY SHEPHERD

Look at the visual Bible verse below. Try to figure out what it says. Write the verse words on the blank lines. Use the Visual Bible Verse Dictionary on page 371, if needed.

_____

_____

_____

_____

_____

The LORD is my shepherd, I have all that I need. Psalm 23:1

DAY 1: Twinning

Troy and Tim were brothers who looked like twins. They were both tall and lean, and even made similar facial expressions and sounded like each other when they laughed. Troy was fourteen months older than Tim, but Tim was just as tall. Whenever anyone met the two brothers, they always asked, "Is he your twin?"

Troy and Tim sometimes joked about trying to fool their teachers and their coaches by switching places for a day. How funny that would be! But Tim knew that joke wouldn't work because he wasn't able to do schoolwork as well as Troy did.

One day, Tim and Troy were doing their homework, working as fast as they could. They wanted to get outside to play before dinner was ready.

Tim was struggling with his math, and kept getting distracted by checking Troy's progress. *I'll bet he gets finished way before me and then he'll be outside playing before I can,* Tim thought with frustration. *I wish I was as smart as Troy.*

Tim threw his pencil down when he couldn't understand a math problem. He looked at Troy, sitting across from him at the dining-room table. Troy had already finished his math homework and was starting on a science worksheet.

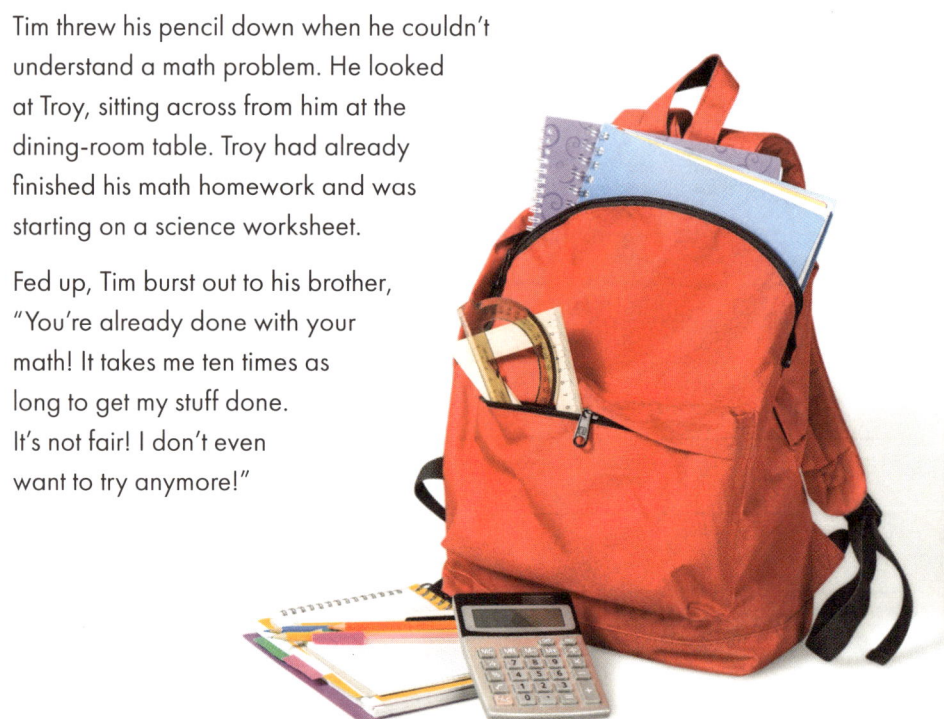

Fed up, Tim burst out to his brother, "You're already done with your math! It takes me ten times as long to get my stuff done. It's not fair! I don't even want to try anymore!"

The Lord Is My Shepherd

DAY 2

Read about It

Psalm 23

Think about It

1. Today's Bible passage is a favorite for many people because of the comfort it gives when you are feeling upset, afraid, or in need. Which part of Psalm 23 is the most comforting to you?

2. This week's verse is from Psalm 23. It tells us that because Jesus is our shepherd we have everything we need. The word *shepherd* is used here to describe how Jesus will lead us, take care of us, and love us. When is a time you have been like a shepherd and taken care of an animal? Or maybe a younger person?

3. Because God knows that we need someone (Jesus) to watch over us every day of our lives, we can feel safe and secure. Jesus is with us in good times and in difficult times. How does it make you feel to know that Jesus is your good shepherd?

Do Something about It

When you start to complain because you are not good at something, stop and thank God for giving you Jesus to be your shepherd. Don't compare yourself to others and get discouraged. Know that he will make sure you have everything that you need.

Pray about It

Dear God, sometimes I feel discouraged and want to give up. There are things others are better at than I am. Help me not compare myself with others. Remind me that you made me exactly the way you want me to be. I have strengths and weaknesses just like everyone else. But sometimes, I do look at my family and friends and wish I was different. Help me to be thankful that Jesus is my shepherd and that I have everything I need. In Jesus' name, amen.

DAY 3: Coloring Verse

Read the visual verse, and then write each word beneath its symbol. Finally, use fine-tipped colored pens or pencils to color in the pictures.

_____

_____

  that

_____

 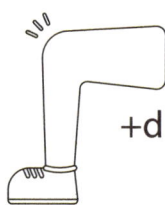

_____

Psalm 23:1

Math and Sports

DAY 4

After Tim complained how Troy was better at schoolwork than he was, Troy looked up, surprised. He said, "I don't know what you are complaining about, you are much better at football and baseball than I ever will be," Troy reminded his brother.

"Yeah, I guess . . . but no one tests you on how well you play football. I have to pass these tests or I won't get to go up a grade." Tim said.

Troy nodded and considered Tim's words. Troy understood that there was a difference between schoolwork—which had to be done—and playing sports—which was fun. Still, Troy didn't like hearing his brother talk about himself in such a negative way.

Troy suddenly smiled. "Tim, I have an idea! How about I help you with your schoolwork and you help me with football and baseball? You're so much better at throwing and catching and batting than I am. I want to get better, but I don't know how," Troy suggested.

Tim glanced over at Troy and thought for a minute. "You mean it? You would help me figure out this math problem so I can get outside and play?" Tim asked.

"Sure," answered Troy. "But you will have to help me too, remember?"

"OK, it's a deal!" Tim agreed.

Troy got up and moved over next to Tim and read through the math problem. It didn't take him long to figure out where Tim was getting confused. Together they worked it out and then turned to their other assignments.

After both boys had completed their homework, Troy and Tim headed out to their backyard to practice throwing and catching and even got in some batting practice before Mom called that it was time for dinner.

When Mom asked them about their day, Tim explained how they had helped each other with homework and sports. "Boys, do you know that you are living out a Bible verse by helping each other? Jesus is using both of you to meet the other's needs." Tim and Troy looked at Mom, and then at each other and smiled.

DAY 5: The Paralyzed Man

Read about It

Mark 2:1–12; Luke 5:17–26

Think about It

1. Our Bible story is about a man who had four friends who worked hard to get him what he needed. What did the man need? Why were his friends so determined to get him to Jesus?

2. This week's verse promises that because Jesus is our shepherd, there is nothing in the world we won't have if we need it. God isn't saying we will get everything we want, but we will have all that we need.

3. Sometimes God uses other people to give us what we need. How did Tim and Troy use their strengths to help each other? They gave each other what they needed by teaching and encouraging. When is a time you were able to give someone something they needed? When is a time someone gave you what you needed?

Do Something about It

When you start to feel scared or discouraged, pray and ask God to help you be thankful for what you do have and for the things you are good at. Then find someone to encourage by helping them with your gifts. It will encourage you, too!

Pray about It

Dear God, please help me to be thankful for the way you created me. Help me to not look at what others can do, and then complain and feel bad if they are better at something. I need to use the strengths you have given me to help and encourage others. Please help me to remember that you made me exactly the way you planned and you have great things for me to do. Give me the courage to do them. In Jesus' name, amen.

Sheep Craft

DAY 6

Before starting the craft, read the visual verse on page 164.

Make this fun sheep and set it in your bedroom as a reminder of Psalm 23 and Jesus our shepherd who gives us all that we need.

What You Need

- Sheep Pattern on this page
- tracing paper
- pencil
- scissors
- cardboard
- 2 spring-type clothespins
- black paint
- yarn

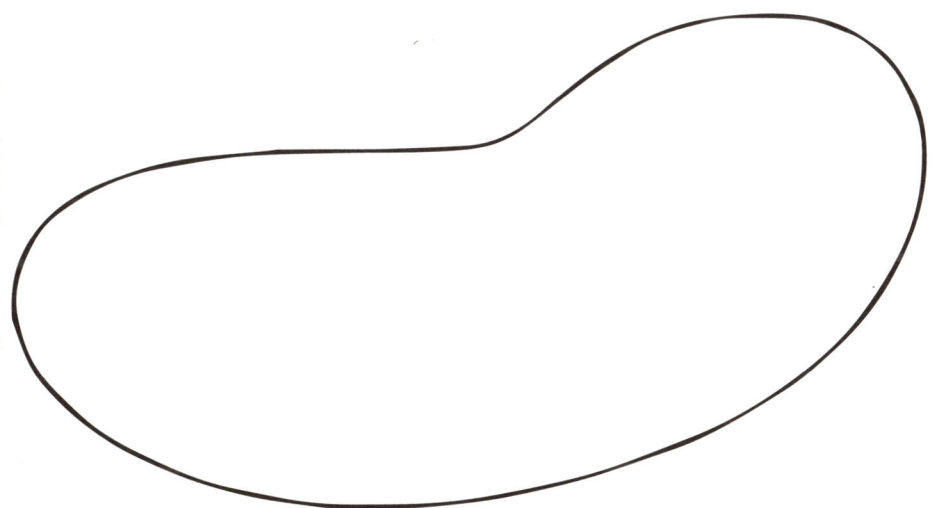

What You Do

1. Trace pattern on this page. Cut out and then trace onto a sheet of cardboard.
2. Paint cardboard shape and two spring-type clothespins black. Set aside to dry.
3. When dry, clip clothespins to cardboard shape to make the legs.
4. Wrap the sheep in yarn until it is fluffy. Tie the end in a knot, trim it, and hide it in the yarn.

Week 24

God Loves and Delights in Me

Look at the visual Bible verse below. Try to figure out what it says. Write the verse words on the blank lines. Use the Visual Bible Verse Dictionary on page 371, if needed.

_____

_____

_____

_____

_____

[God] will take delight in you with gladness. With his love, he will calm all your fears. He will rejoice over you with joyful songs. Zephaniah 3:17

New Clothes

DAY 1

Luna had just plunked out the last few notes of her piano lesson when Becca arrived. Becca had a piano lesson with Mrs. Musgrave right after Luna. Becca always seemed so perfect. Luna always felt invisible when Becca was around.

Luna gathered up her books and backpack as Becca swept into the room. "Hi, Luna!" Becca said happily.

"Hi, Becca," Luna said. She noticed that Becca was wearing a new shirt, pants, and shoes. Luna had seen the outfit in the window of her favorite store the last time she was there. Even Becca's hair had new barrettes holding her perfectly cut hair out of her pretty blue eyes.

Ugh! Luna thought to herself. Every week, Becca arrived in her mom's fancy car and then walked inside with her fancy clothes. *Why can't I have clothes like Becca? Why doesn't my mom let me buy whatever I want when we go shopping? It's not fair!*

Luna shoved her piano books into her backpack and hurried out the door. When she got to her mom's car, she threw her backpack onto the floor and slammed her door shut. "Wait one minute, young lady. What do you think you are doing throwing your backpack like that and slamming the door?" Luna's mom was frowning.

"Mom, I'm just so angry at Becca and at . . . everything! Every week I have to watch Becca walk in with brand new clothes . . . expensive clothes. Today she had on another new shirt and pants and even her shoes were new. I can't stand it! I want to go shopping and buy new clothes like hers," Luna complained loudly.

"Luna, do you remember the conversation we had with you before school started? The decision you had to make about taking piano lessons which would stretch our budget or having more new clothes?" Mom reminded Luna.

"Sort of . . ." Luna answered sheepishly.

"Try and remember then while we drive home." Mom said.

God Loves and Delights in Me • 169

DAY 2: Joseph and the Coat of Many Colors

Read about It

Genesis 37:3–35

Think about It

1. In the Bible story, Joseph had a beautiful coat that made his brothers jealous. God doesn't care how new or beautiful your clothes are! He loves you just the way you are.

2. God is with you. Think about having your family with you. Your friends with you. Then close your eyes and try to imagine God being with you right now.

3. This week's verse says God takes great delight in you. That means God loves everything about you! What are some things that delight you or make you happy?

Do Something about It

When you start to compare yourself and what you have to others, stop and think about how much God loves you. Remember that God promises to be with you. Remember that he is a mighty warrior who wants to save you. Then, remind yourself that God loves you and delights in you no matter what.

Pray about It

Dear God, the Bible tells me that you are always with me. I love thinking about how strong and powerful you are and that you love me so much! Thank you for saving me when I need it. Sometimes I forget that your love for me is better than stuff I can buy with money—please help me remember. Your love will never wear out or get broken. I will never get bored of your love for me. In Jesus' name, amen.

Act It Out

Read the visual verse, and then write each word on the lines below.

      gladness

   calm +r +s

 rejoice   +ful +s

_____

_____

_____

_____

Zephaniah 3:17

Say the verse, acting out the verse phrases as described below.
Repeat the verse and do the actions several times.

"God will take delight in you with gladness"
Smile and hug yourself.

"With his love, he will calm all your fears."
Flex your muscles.

"He will rejoice over you with joyful songs"
Pretend to sing.

DAY 4: New Every Day

Driving home from piano lesson, neither Luna nor her mom spoke a word. Luna's mom wanted to give her daughter some time to think. She'd just reminded Luna about the decision Luna had made to take piano lessons rather have extra money for more new clothes.

Finally, Luna spoke up. "I do remember our deal, Mom. I am glad that I can take piano lessons. But it is still hard when Becca comes in with new clothes every week. I guess I want both," admitted Luna.

"I understand how you feel and sometimes we do feel jealous of what others have, but I think you are forgetting something," Mom said.

"What?" Luna asked puzzled.

"You are forgetting that God's love for you . . . his delight in you . . . is so much better than having new clothes, new toys, new games, and lots of money to spend. God's love is with us always and it never breaks, wears out, or gets ruined like Becca's new clothes will. We never, ever get bored with God's love because the Bible tells us it is new every day," Mom said excitedly.

Luna thought for a minute about what her mom had told her. "So, you mean that even if I had all the clothes that Becca has it wouldn't be enough? That I would still want more?" Luna asked.

"Yes, because it is our heart that needs changing . . . that needs to be content and thankful for what God gives us. When we thank God for what we have—and mean it—he changes us on the inside. We realize that we have all we need because of God's love for us," Mom explained.

"OK, I understand." Luna paused a moment and then spoke softly. "I think I need to go up to my room and ask God for forgiveness for not being thankful."

Mom smiled at Luna in the rear-view mirror. "I think that would make God very happy."

The Prodigal Son

DAY 5

Read about It

Luke 15:11–24

Think about It

1. This Bible story is about a young man who was given everything he wanted. And his life fell apart. God doesn't want us to rely on things for happiness. And we don't have to. Because God's amazing love is something we can truly rely on. When we put God first in our hearts, he fills us up with his love. Can you describe how God's love for you makes you feel?

2. There are so many delight-full things in the world. Yummy food. Beaches and swimming pools. Bikes and scooters. Playgrounds and soccer fields. Dogs and cats. Friends and family. But God tells us that he delights in us more than in anything else in the world.

3. This week's verse is important to memorize and understand because we often feel just like Luna felt about Becca. It's easy to feel jealous of others and then forget all the good things God has given us. Make a list of some good things God has given you. Hint: it doesn't have to be material things—though God gave us all of those, too!

Do Something about It

When you start to forget how much God loves and delights in you, remember that God sent Jesus to die on the cross to pay for all your sins. God loves you so much that he sent Jesus to die for you. Sit in a quiet place, pray, and thank God for loving you so much.

Pray about It

Dear God, sometimes I forget that the most important love in the world is your love for me. I get jealous and upset when I see others with new clothes and toys and games and lots of other things I don't have the money to buy. Please help me remember that your love is the very best thing in the whole world. Your love for me never gets broken, ruined, or old. Help me to say thank you every day for all that you have given me. In Jesus' name, amen.

God Loves and Delights in Me

DAY 6: Verse Tracing

Read the visual verse, and then write each word on the lines below. Next, take a marker and trace around each symbol and word. Then, take another color of marker and trace around the first color. Keep switching colors and tracing around the symbols and words until they all connect together.

Zephaniah 3:17

Week 25
I Don't Have to Worry

Look at the visual Bible verse below. Try to figure out what it says. Write the verse words on the blank lines. Use the Visual Bible Verse Dictionary on page 371, if needed.

❌ 😟 about anything

instead 🙏 about everything

_____

_____

_____

_____

_____

Don't worry about anything; instead, pray about everything. Philippians 4:6

DAY 1

New School

There was a new school that just opened up down the road from Jorge and Lexie's house. Their mom had always homeschooled both of them. But now that there was a new school so close to home, their parents decided Mom would go back to work part-time.

One day, Jorge, Lexie, and their mom woke up early and walked down the block to the school to enroll in classes. The kids were both so excited! But Lexie was feeling something else as well.

Afterwards, as they walked back home, Mom asked, "Are you happy with the classes? I think both of your teachers are going to be great. I've heard lots of wonderful things about both of them. You may even want to join one of the after school sports teams, too."

Jorge was excited about school, but mostly because he could play football and baseball. Lexie wasn't so sure. "I hope I do well, Mom. I've never been in a real school class before. Do you think we learned everything we needed to in homeschool?" Lexie questioned.

"Yes, Lexie. Remember you and Jorge took tests that showed you were both right where your grade level should be in reading and mathematics and writing. No worries!" Mom encouraged.

But Lexie felt doubtful. Lexie kept thinking about all the changes that would happen in the fall. In their homeschool, Lexie and Jorge did their chores, and then they ate breakfast and got dressed. First they did their reading, spelling, and writing assignments. Then they did mathematics. They took a break for lunch and got free play for thirty minutes to do whatever they wanted. Then they did their history and science studies. Last of all they did either an art or music lesson.

Whenever Lexie had questions it was easy to ask Mom to explain. *What will I do when I have a question in school? Will I feel embarrassed asking a question? What if the other kids make fun of me?* thought Lexie to herself.

Mom looked over and noticed that Lexie looked scared. "Lexie, please tell me what you're thinking? Maybe I can help."

Words of Encouragement

DAY 2

Read about It

Philippians 4:4–9

Think about It

1 What happens when we spend time worrying about what may happen tomorrow? We waste today! We don't have the time to be happy, joyful, and thankful for all the good things. What are some things you can do when you start to worry?

2 This week's Bible verse has two important parts. First, God tells us to not worry about anything. God wants us to trust him to take care of us. God doesn't want us thinking about everything that could happen or go wrong. When was a time you worried about something so much that you couldn't stop thinking about it?

3 The second part of this verse tells us to pray about everything. God promises to give us strength, grace, help, and whatever else we need for today. When tomorrow comes, God will give us what we need on that day.

Do Something about It

When you start to feel worried or scared about something that might happen, sit down and pray. Tell God what you are afraid of. Share all your worries and fears with God, and then ask him to help you stop thinking about tomorrow. Ask God to make you brave and know that he is always with you.

Pray about It

Dear God, sometimes I feel worried and scared about what may happen. Sometimes I think and think about changes that are going to happen. Sometimes I feel happy and excited about what could happen tomorrow, but other times I am scared. Please help me to stop worrying about what might happen tomorrow. Help me to be happy and joyful and thankful for all the good things I have today. Please help me to remember that you are always with me. In Jesus' name, amen.

DAY 3: No Worrisome Thoughts

In the thought balloons below, there are worried thoughts a kid your age might have. In the empty balloon, write a prayer that you could pray instead of having worried thoughts.

- Grandma's been really sick lately. I don't know if she'll ever get well!
- I'm scared no one will like me at my new school.
- I can't believe the coach wants me to pitch in our game on Saturday. What if I blow it?

178 • I Don't Have to Worry

Action Against Thoughts

DAY 4

Lexie, Jorge, and Mom were walking home after enrolling in school. Lexie's mom asked her what was wrong.

Lexie wondered how she could possibly explain all her concerns. She blurted out, "I'm scared of going to school next year. I'm worried that I won't know what to do. What if I ask questions and the other kids will laugh at me? I don't want to go!"

Mom looked at Jorge. "Do you feel the same way, Jorge?" she asked.

Jorge shrugged. "No. I want to play sports," Jorge said calmly.

Lexie threw her hands up. "See? Even Jorge isn't worried! "I'm the only one who feels like this. I don't even know what it will be like to be in school all day long."

Mom put her arm around Lexie's shoulders. "Lexie, we can take action with some of the things you're worried about. We can visit the school so that you will know where to go. You can even sit in a class and observe, so you will see what it is like."

Mom continued, concerned, "But you have other worries, worries about things that may never happen. These are things that you need to pray and trust God to take care of. Have you asked God to help you not worry?" Mom inquired.

"No, I haven't. I just . . . I just . . . " Lexie started to say.

"You just keep worrying and thinking and thinking and worrying?" Mom asked.

Lexie sighed. "Yeah. That's about it."

"When you worry about what might happen, it's probably because you've forgotten that God is always with you. God wants you to enjoy today and not worry about tomorrow." Mom said.

"Well, I don't like feeling like this . . . " Lexie answered just as the family walked through the front door.

"OK, then, why don't we take time right now to sit together and pray? All three of us! We will talk to God about all the changes and all the worries you have. And we will thank God for loving us and for taking care of us," Mom said.

"Sounds good to me," Jorge said.

"Me, too," Lexie grinned.

DAY 5: Jehoshaphat Praises God

Read about It

2 Chronicles 20:1–30

Think about It

1. In our Bible story, King Jehoshaphat received the news that armies were coming to attack him and his people. At first, Jehoshaphat was afraid! But then he prayed to God. He encouraged his people to fast and pray. And when the time came to face the armies, Jehoshaphat and his people were so confident in God's love and help, they SANG instead of fighting. What do you think would happen if you sang praises to God the next time you were afraid or worried?

2. When we worry it's as if we don't think God can or will take good care of us. Does that make sense to you? What are reasons you can believe that God can take care of you? What are reasons you can believe that God wants to take care of you?

3. Everyone feels worried when life changes but we must turn our worries into prayers to God. We need to ask him to give us courage and to help us trust him to take care of us. When is a time a kid your age might turn worries into a prayer for help? When was a time you felt worried and afraid, but then God took wonderful care of you?

Do Something about It

When you start to worry about things that might happen, stop and turn your worries into a prayer to God. Ask God to give you courage and to help you remember how faithful he is to you. Thank God for taking good care of you in the past, and for caring for you today!

Pray about It

Dear God, I don't want to worry and feel scared. Please help me to stop worrying and instead turn my worries into prayers. Remind me of all the times you have taken good care of me in the past. Please give me the courage I need today and every day. I want to trust you and not worry. I want to be happy and joyful and thankful today for all the good things you have given me. In Jesus' name, amen.

Scrambled Verse

Read the visual verse, and then write each word beneath its symbol. The verse is all mixed up! On the blank lines, write the verse again, but in the correct order this time.

😥

about   everything   _____

❌

_____   about   instead

🙏

anything   _____

_____

_____

_____

_____

Philippians 4:6

Week 26

GOD KEEPS EVERY PROMISE

Look at the visual Bible verse below. Try to figure out what it says. Write the verse words on the blank lines. Use the Visual Bible Verse Dictionary on page 371, if needed.

 made &

 & everything

 +ps every

_____

_____

_____

_____

_____

[God] made heaven and earth, the sea, and everything in them. He keeps every promise forever. Psalm 146:6

182 · God Keeps Every Promise

Zoo Birthday

DAY 1

Bright and early on Saturday morning, Asher got up and got ready to go. It was his eighth birthday and the only thing Asher had asked for was a trip to the zoo. Uncle Ed had promised they'd go. He was so excited!

He changed out of his pajamas and into his clothes, washed his face, and brushed his teeth. Asher even remembered to comb his hair without his aunt reminding him. "Aunt Lorene, Uncle Ed, I'm ready! Let's go!" cried Asher as he ran to the kitchen.

Aunt Lorene was making Asher's favorite breakfast, cheesy scrambled eggs with bacon and a bowl of fruit. "Here you go, birthday boy! Sit down and eat," Aunt Lorene said as she handed Asher his plate of food.

"Thanks, Aunt Lorene!" Asher said. "I can't wait until we get to the zoo. I want to see every animal in the zoo today," exclaimed Asher.

"We will. We will," said Uncle Ed, coming into the kitchen. "First things first. While you are eating Aunt Lorene and I have a few gifts for you to open," he said.

"Yes!" replied Asher. Aunt Lorene carried three carefully wrapped presents into the kitchen and sat them on the table in front of Asher.

"Open this one first, Asher," Aunt Lorene said, handing him the smallest box. Asher ripped off the gift wrap and inside was a book on caring for hamsters.

"Cool! Thanks, Aunt Lorene. Thanks, Uncle Ed," Asher said.

"Now this one," Aunt Lorene instructed.

Asher tore the wrapper paper off fast and found hamster food, hamster toys, and a hanging water bottle. Asher looked up at his guardians with a question on his face. He could see where this was going . . . *Was it true?* He wondered. *Could they have gotten me a . . .*

"Now this one," said Uncle Ed.

If he hadn't needed his fingers for unwrapping the gift, Asher would have had them crossed. Asher was hoping and hoping he was right about what this gift would be. And he was! "Thank you, thank you, thank you! A hamster of my very own!" cheered Asher.

God Keeps Every Promise

DAY 2: Created by God

Read about It

Genesis 1—2:2

Think about It

1. God is the maker of everything on Earth and in Heaven. Have you ever stopped to think about how amazing it is that God created every living thing? Think about your very favorite kind of animal. Now think about how different this animal is from every other kind. God is amazingly creative!

2. Because everyone is different, we take care of each thing (and every person) in a special and unique way. What do you think Asher will have to learn about taking care of his new hamster? When have you had to learn to care for one of God's creations? (Human, plant, animal, etc.)

3. This week's verse tells us not only did God create everything in the world, but he keeps all of his promises forever. That means there will never be a day when God forgets or just decides not to keep a promise. What is a promise from God that you are happy he will keep forever?

Do Something about It

Take time each day to really look at something God created. It could be a person, plant, or animal. Thank God for being the creator of that thing and of everything on Earth and in Heaven. Thank him for always keeping his promises.

Pray about It

Dear God, please help me to never forget that you made each thing, each animal, and each person exactly the way you wanted. Including me! Help me to treat this world and all the people in it with love and kindness. In Jesus' name, amen.

God's Great Creation

Read the visual verse, and then write each word beneath its symbol.

Set a timer for one minute. In the space below, draw or write down as many animals as you can. Repeat with other created things: trees, plants, food, people, etc. Use another sheet of paper if you run out of room!

Bonus Idea: Make this activity a game! Invite friends and family to make their own lists. When the minute is up, count up how many things are on each person's list. The person with the most items on their list names a new category for the next round.

 made

 everything

  +ps every

Psalm 146:6

God Keeps Every Promise

DAY 4
Animal Care

Asher examined every animal on display: monkeys, zebras, elephants, birds, reptiles, otters, and even a polar bear! Asher didn't want the day to end. "Why does the zoo close so early? " Asher asked.

"These animals need quiet hours away from people like us watching them." Uncle Ed explained. "They also need to be fed and cleaned."

"Plus a veterinarian comes in to make sure each animal is healthy." Aunt Lorene added.

Asher nodded his head in understanding, "Just like I have to go home and study how to take good care of my hamster, right? I have to learn what he needs to stay healthy," Asher commented.

"Exactly. God created the Earth and everything in it, including animals. God put Adam in charge of caring for the animals. We are to continue Adam's work. We need to make sure we do everything we can to help them stay healthy," Aunt Lorene said.

Uncle Ed continued, "It wouldn't be pleasing to God if we didn't care for the animals or the earth or the people he created. Every day we need to think about good ways we can work hard to make sure we are taking care of God's creation," Uncle Ed added.

"I will make sure I take care of my hamster. I promise," Asher agreed.

"We know you will," Aunt Lorene said. "That's why we got one for you. We knew we could trust you to take good care of him." Aunt Lorene and Uncle Ed exchanged a smile.

"Thanks! I love him!" Asher said.

"Now . . . Why don't you start caring for that cute little guy by figuring out a good name for him?" Uncle Ed said as Asher laughed.

"By the way, in case I haven't said so for a while, thanks for promising to take good care of me. You're doing a great job!" Asher told his guardians.

"Oh, Asher!" Aunt Lorene said as her hand went to her heart. "We love you!"

186 · God Keeps Every Promise

God Creates People

DAY 5

Read about It

Genesis 2:4—3

Think about It

1 This Bible passage tells us that God created people. Did you ever stop to think about how amazing our bodies are? Think about the different senses God gave us: sight, smell, touch, hearing, taste. There are so many ways to experience God's wonderful creation.

2 Think about one of your favorite things God created. It could be a person, plant, animal, etc. What do you know about that thing by using each of your senses? What does it look like? Does it make a sound? What does it feel like? How does it smell? What does it taste like? (This is not an excuse to bite your younger brother or sister!)

3 Our Bible passage also tells us that not only were Adam and Eve the first people, they were the first to sin. But all people have sinned, except for one. Who is the only person who never sinned? Read 2 Corinthians 5:21 to find out. What is this verse talking about when it says that Jesus did something for us?

Do Something about It

When you are given the responsibility of taking care of God's plants or animals, read and learn all you can about them. Then do your best to help them grow and stay healthy. Also, look for ways that you can care for the people God put in your life.

Pray about It

Dear God, I am thankful that you created so many interesting and beautiful things for us to take care of and love on the earth. Please help me to do my best to care for animals, plants, and people so that they will grow strong and stay healthy. Help me to be responsible for what you created. I am glad that you created us with five senses to help us understand your creation. In Jesus' name, amen.

DAY 6: Seen in the Scene

Color the scene. The symbols and words of the verse are hidden inside the scene. Circle each one. Then, write the verse words in order on the lines below. **Note:** Some words appear more than once in the verse, but they'll only be in the puzzle once.

_____

_____

_____

_____

Psalm 146:6

188 · God Keeps Every Promise

Week 27
God Protects Us

Look at the visual Bible verse below. Try to figure out what it says. Write the verse words on the blank lines. Use the Visual Bible Verse Dictionary on page 371, if needed.

  am

put

When I am afraid, I will put my trust in you. Psalm 56:3

DAY 1

Brad's Dilemma

Brad was reaching up high to put his books in his locker when he noticed Cody coming toward him. Brad hurried and slammed his locker shut. Brad was afraid of Cody.

Even though Cody had never teased or bullied Brad, Brad had seen Cody make fun of other kids. *I'm getting out of here. Every time Cody is around, something bad happens.* Brad thought as he hurried down the hall away from Cody.

Later that day, Brad was at his locker again. It was time to go home and he was stuffing homework assignments into his backpack. Suddenly, he heard Cody's voice. "Hey, kid . . . give that to me!" Cody snarled. Brad didn't wait to find out to whom Cody was talking or what he was demanding. Brad hurried and went outside to wait for his mom to arrive.

Outside, there were two teachers making sure everyone was safe around the cars. Brad never felt scared outside waiting for his mom. *There she is*, Brad said to himself when he spotted her. He took off running toward his mom's car.

Once inside, Brad sighed with relief.

"That was a big sigh," his mom said. "Is something up?"

"Maybe," Brad admitted. "Mom, does Jesus tell us to love people who are mean to others?" Brad asked.

"Is someone being mean to you?" Mom asked, concerned.

"No, but there's a mean kid named Cody at school and he teases other kids. I'm scared he might tease me, too," Brad answered.

"Well, I'm glad no one's being mean to you, but I'm sad Cody's being mean to others. To answer your question, yes, Jesus does want us to love others. Even others who are mean. In Romans 12:21, the Bible tells us to overcome evil by doing good. Does that make sense to you?"

"I don't know . . . Maybe." Brad said thoughtfully. "Does it mean if someone is being mean, we need to try and be nice to that person?"

"Yeah! That's the idea," Mom said. "Let's talk more about this when we get home. I'd like to read a story to you about a man named Daniel."

Daniel and the Lions' Den

DAY 2

Read about It

Daniel 6

Think about It

1. Today's Bible story is full of courage and faith. Daniel wouldn't stop praying to God, even when the ruler put him in a den with lions as a punishment. The next morning the ruler went to see if Daniel was still alive. He was! God had closed the lions' mouths so they wouldn't hurt Daniel because he had trusted in God to take care of him.

2. When we think about doing something that makes us scared, we should talk to God about our fears and ask him to give us courage. Sometimes God will ask us to do or say something that feels scary. But God understands all our feelings. He wants us to trust him. When is a time you felt afraid? What did you do? Did you pray for courage?

3. Not many people will be thrown into a den with lions like Daniel was, but everyone will have to face some scary things at times. What can you do when God asks you to be brave and say or do something that frightens you?

Do Something about It

When you believe that God wants you to do or say something that scares you, ask God for courage. Pray and tell God all your feelings and ask him to make you brave so that you can obey him.

Pray about It

Dear God, please help me to do the right thing and be kind to others even when they are mean. Help me to be brave and say words that are kind and nice. Thank you for always being with me and protecting me. In Jesus' name, amen.

God Protects Us

DAY 3: Lion Craft

Reread the visual verse on page 189. Then, make this lion as a reminder of how, like Daniel, you can pray and trust God when you are afraid.

What You Need

- Lion Head pattern on this page
- tracing paper
- pencil
- yellow, orange, and red construction paper or cardstock
- scissors
- black fine-tipped marker
- toilet-paper tube
- glue

What You Do

1. Trace pattern on this page. Cut out and then trace onto a yellow sheet of construction paper or cardstock. Cut a 3-inch circle from the same construction paper or cardstock.
2. From a sheet of orange construction paper or cardstock, cut a rectangle 3¾ inches wide and long enough to wrap around your toilet-paper tube. Wrap tube and glue to secure (image a), making the lion's body.
3. Cut strips of orange and red construction paper or cardstock and glue to 3-inch circle to make the lion's mane (image b). Glue lion's head to mane.
4. Draw the lion's face and whiskers on the head.
5. Cut a tail from orange construction paper or cardstock and the tuft at the end of the tail from red construction paper or cardstock. Draw hair on the tuft and glue to tail.
6. Glue finished tail and head to lion's body.

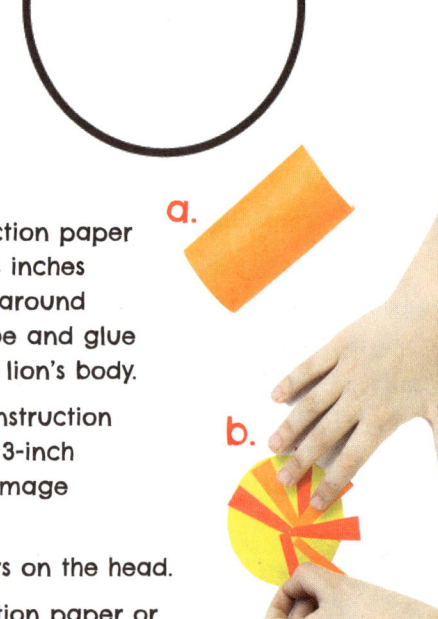

Bravery for Brad

DAY 4

The car grumbled and sighed when Brad's mom turned off the engine. Brad and his mom grabbed their things and went into the house. Mom put out apple slices with peanut butter for an after-school snack.

Mom had her Bible next to her. "Here we go," Mom said as she opened her Bible to the book of Daniel. Mom read the whole story of Daniel praying and then getting into trouble and being thrown into the lion's den.

When they got to the part where the king called into the lion's den and Daniel answered, Brad cheered. "Wow! What a great story, Mom," Brad said.

"Let's talk about how God wants us to love others even when they don't love us. God wants us to trust him even when we are afraid that others will be unkind to us. What do you think God wants you to do about Cody?" Mom asked.

"I think God wants me to talk to Cody and be nice to him. Everyone else is afraid of him and they don't talk to Cody at all," Brad explained.

"Has Cody ever hurt kids? Physically, by hitting or pushing them?" Mom asked. "I don't want you to be in danger."

"No, he's not like that. But he gets in trouble all the time for saying mean things and sometimes he breaks stuff. The teachers all know about him." Brad said.

"Good. Because I don't want you to do anything that might get you or someone else hurt. You be sure to talk to a teacher or other adult at school if Cody threatens you or anyone else."

Brad nodded. "I don't think that will happen. He doesn't hurt kids . . . I mean other than saying mean things, which is bad enough. But if God wants me to be nice to him anyway, I'll try!"

"I'm so proud of you, Brad. Let's pray and ask God to give you the courage to be kind to Cody tomorrow," Mom encouraged. "Dear God, thank you for giving Brad the good idea of talking with Cody. Please help him to have the courage to speak with Cody and not be afraid. If Cody says unkind things to Brad, help him to just walk away and not feel upset. Thank you, God, for being with Brad tomorrow. In Jesus' name, amen."

"Thanks, Mom! But please pray for me after I get to school tomorrow too, OK?" Brad asked.

God Protects Us

DAY 5: Daniel's Dinner

Read about It

Daniel 1

Think about It

1. Today's Bible passage is about a time when Daniel and his friends, Shadrach, Meshach, and Abednego, first started to serve the King Nebuchadnezzar. Even though it could have gotten them in trouble, Daniel and his friends were brave enough to do what God wanted them to do. When was a time you had to be brave to do what God wanted you to do?

2. Sometimes, it's difficult to do the right thing. We might be afraid that others would make fun of us or call us names. Maybe we're afraid of getting punished for doing the right thing. Or maybe we're just not sure what the right thing to do is! What is something you can do in all these situations to help you follow God, even though it is difficult or scary?

3. When we know that God wants us to do or say something that feels scary, we can remember what Daniel did. He kept doing what God wanted him to do. He ate the foods that God wanted him to eat to be healthy. And when it came to praying, not even the lions' den could stop him! What can we learn from Daniel's obedience to God?

Do Something about It

When you know the right thing to do, obey God—even if it feels scary! Read the story of Daniel or other Bible stories to remind you that God will always help you obey him and do the right thing.

Pray about It

Dear God, I know that you are strong and powerful. I love reading about how you protected Daniel in the lions' den, and how Daniel chose to obey you even when it was scary. Help me to trust you to take care of me, too. Thank you for your love and help. In Jesus' name, amen.

Verse Word Search

Read the visual verse, and then write each word beneath its symbol. Then, find each verse word in the word search. **Note:** Some words appear more than once in the verse, but they'll only be in the puzzle once. And don't forget *Psalms*!

Bonus: Find the following words from this week's Bible stories about Daniel and the lions' den: lions, den, Daniel, Shadrach, Meshach, Abednego.

  am

---

put

Psalm 56:3

```
A I G N A R L W I L L X Q E
C G H L I O N S H A D R A C H
Q K G V Q O G X C Z S T M J O
Q X A F N N P S W M Y I A A H
H D F T G P D E L K W H H C M
K D F S I N H A L I C J A K K
A O A U O A S B M V N H F T C
B F K N R P M I J D S Y I K R
E S R J I N M Y J E L Q E Y B
D E N A C E A L M Q Q W R N X
N W J J I Y L C K Z P R Y N U
E H F I F D O P E S G M T N X
G E Y G C O Q U U V H U A I X
O N Q T R U S T D T X U V V X
E T F F F T T T J B J J T B V
```

Answer Key on page 379.

God Protects Us • 195

Week 28
God's Hand Holds Me Up

Look at the visual Bible verse below. Try to figure out what it says. Write the verse words on the blank lines. Use the Visual Bible Verse Dictionary on page 371, if needed.

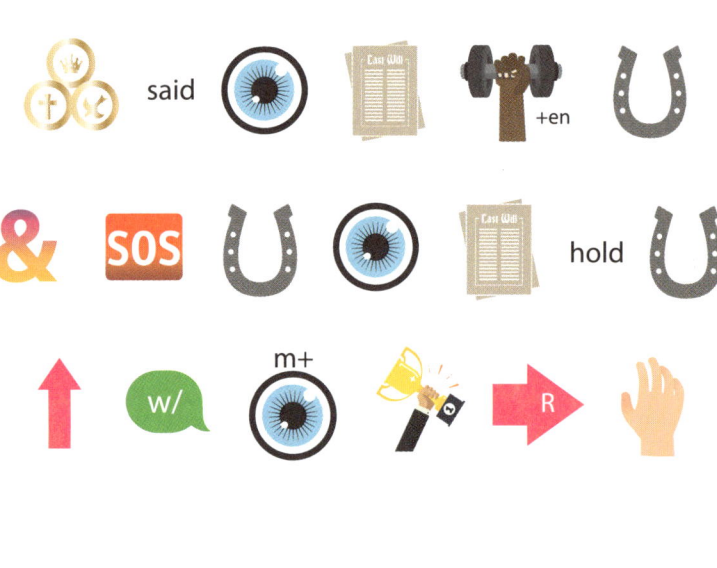

_____
_____
_____
_____
_____

[God said,] "I will strengthen you and help you. I will hold you up with my victorious right hand. Isaiah 41:10

Art and Baseball

DAY 1

When the school bell rang at the end of the day, Derek ran as fast as he could down the marble steps and out the swinging doors to his mom's SUV. Derek jumped inside and sat down gasping for air.

"Good heavens, Derek! What's going on?" Mom asked.

Derek buckled up and he caught his breath. "Mom!" he exclaimed. "You won't believe this. Four of my pictures are going to be included in the art fair! Four!"

"Oh, that's wonderful. You've been working so hard for weeks on those pictures. I'm so proud of you," Mom exclaimed happily as she pulled out of the school driveway.

"One of them isn't even finished yet. But if I finish this weekend, there will still be plenty of time for it to be hung for the art fair," Derek explained.

"I'm going to invite Grandma and Grandpa to come to the art fair, too. I know they will want to see your work," Mom said.

"That would be fun!" Derek agreed. "Call Dad, too. I know he and Angela were excited to see my pictures." When they arrived home, Derek went right into his bedroom and changed into his baseball uniform.

"Ready, Derek? Your game is going to start in twenty minutes," Mom called.

"I'm coming. I just need my bat and mitt," Derek grabbed his equipment and ran to the car.

In the car again, Derek munched on a peanut-butter and jelly sandwich and sipped some water while his mom drove to the ballpark. Five minutes later, Derek was out on the field practicing with his teammates.

Then it was time for the game. Innings one and two flew by as Derek didn't get a chance to bat. Finally, in the fourth inning, Derek was up to bat. Strike one! Ball one! Strike two! *Crack!*

Derek hit that ball so hard it flew into the outfield and off he ran. Sliding into second base, Derek collided with the boy on the base and Derek heard another crack. His arm was bent the wrong way and he doubled over in pain.

God's Hand Holds Me Up

DAY 2

Crossing the Red Sea

Read about It

Exodus 14:5–31

Think about It

1 In our Bible story, God told Moses to hold out his hand over the Red Sea. Moses obeyed. It wasn't Moses' hand that parted the Red Sea, it was the victorious right hand of God, helping Moses and the Israelites. This week's verse tells us some wonderful things about how God will take care of us by strengthening us and helping us. What are some ways you can get strength and help from God?

2 God's promise also tells us that he will hold us up with his victorious right hand. Can you close your eyes and imagine God holding your hand? How does that make you feel? Comforted? Safe? Secure? Loved?

3 When we need God's strength and help, God will always give it. And God always hears us when we ask. Sometimes we may not need physical strength or health. What are some other kinds of strength we might need God's help to have?

Do Something about It

When you feel like you don't have enough strength to do what you need to do, pray and ask God to give you the strength you need. Then, close your eyes and imagine that God is holding your hand and taking good care of you.

Pray about It

Dear God, I am not feeling like I have enough strength today for all that I need to do. Will you please help me finish my work? I know that you love me and have promised to take care of me. Thank you for loving me so much and for knowing when I need help even when I forget to ask. I like to imagine you holding my hand when I feel sad or lonely, too. It makes me feel safe and loved. In Jesus' name, amen.

Say, Write, Sing, Repeat

DAY 3

Say the verse; write the verse; sing the verse. Repeat these steps until you know the verse!

1. Say the verse aloud. If needed, review the Visual Bible Verse Dictionary at the back of the book to remember what each symbol stands for.
2. Write the verse on the lines below—as many times as you can!
3. Sing it to "Frère Jacques" ("Are You Sleeping?") or another tune.

I will strengthen   My victorious right hand
You and help you   My victorious right hand
I will hold   Isaiah 41:10
You up with

4. Repeat steps 1, 2, and 3 until you can say the verse without help.

 said   +en

  hold   w/ m+   R

_____

_____

_____

_____

_____

_____

_____

_____

Isaiah 41:10

DAY 4: Broken Arm, Broken Dream

Derek was on the ground at second base, trying to hold back the tears, but it hurt so much! "Derek, are you OK?" his coach called out as she ran to Derek.

"It hurts. Bad," Derek cried. Derek's coach motioned for her assistant coach, Hank, who gently picked Derek up and carried him back to the dugout.

Derek's mom was there waiting for him. "It doesn't look good," Coach said. "You'll want to get X-rays right away."

"We'll go to the hospital right now," Mom said. Looking at Derek, she added, "I'll call your dad when we get there."

"Good idea. Hank will carry Derek to your car," Coach offered.

Derek's dad joined them at the hospital, where a doctor carefully felt all over Derek's arm and ordered an X-ray. Derek had broken his arm.

When they got out of the hospital, Derek's dad said, "I'm sorry about your arm, Derek. But I'll sign your cast when you come over on Saturday." He hugged Derek and then waved as Derek and his mom drove off.

Suddenly, on the way home, Derek started to cry again. "Derek, what's wrong? Is it your arm?" Mom asked.

"Mom, I won't be able to finish my picture! I broke my left arm! I can't paint with my right hand, and now I can't lift my left one," Derek said unhappily.

"Honey, you're right. I'm sorry. It's a bummer, but at least you have three other pictures that are finished," Mom reminded him.

"I know, but I wanted to show all four. I worked so hard on them," Derek said.

"Let's remember something important. When we feel sad or discouraged, God has promised to strengthen and help us. God even promises to hold us up with his strong hand!" Mom said with a smile. "Your arm might be broken, but God's hand is strong!"

"I know, Mom. I know you're right," Derek agreed. Then he grinned. "Since it's so late, I guess we'll have to pick up pizza for dinner," he suggested.

"Pizza? You think you can handle eating pizza with your right hand?" Mom laughed.

"Oh, I know I can eat pizza with my right hand!" Derek joined her laughing.

Aaron & Hur Lend a Hand

DAY 5

Read about It

Exodus 17:8–13

Think about It

1 In today's Bible story, we read about a time Moses had trouble holding up his hands. So Aaron and Hur helped him. Joshua was winning the battle every time Moses' hands were up. Do you think Moses' hands were helping Joshua fight the battle? If so, how? It was God who was giving Joshua strength to win the battle! Moses' holding up his hands was an encouragement, but it wasn't Moses' hands that were making the difference.

2 God wants us to remember that he will strengthen and help us. Sometimes we need help with work. Other times we need help with our thoughts. And still other times we need help getting over disappointment. God wants us to remember that when we are hurting, he is making something good come from our hurt. Have you ever felt sad when something didn't work out as you hoped? Were you able to find something to be thankful for?

3 It's easy to forget that our strength and help come from God, especially when we've been hurting. Consider what's been happening in your life recently. For what would you like to thank God? What are some ways you can show your thanks to God?

Do Something about It

When you feel disappointed, ask God to help you find something to be thankful for. Don't get stuck feeling discouraged or sad. Pray, and say out loud all of the good things God has done for you.

Pray about It

Dear God, when I am feeling sad and disappointed because something happened that I didn't expect, help me find something to be thankful for. Every day, you give me good things, and I don't want to forget about that. Thank you for always giving me the strength I need. I like to think that you are holding my hand in your victorious right hand. In Jesus' name, amen.

DAY 6: Emoji Emotions

Reread the visual Bible verse on page 196. In the first circle, draw a face that represents how you are feeling right now. Beside the face, write how you would pray about that feeling. For example: If you are feeling happy, you can pray and thank God for all the good things he has done for you. Draw two more faces with emotions kids your age might have: anger, excitement, fear, silliness, sadness, etc. Beside each face, write a prayer you might say if you felt that way.

Week 29

GOD FREES ME FROM MY FEARS

Look at the visual Bible verse below. Try to figure out what it says. Write the verse words on the blank lines. Use the Visual Bible Verse Dictionary on page 371, if needed.

 +ed

  $0.00 +d

from:  +s

_____
_____
_____
_____
_____
_____

I prayed to the LORD, and he answered me. He freed me from all my fears. Psalm 34:4

DAY 1

A New Brother?

In the car, Rachel fidgeted nervously. She and her father were on their way to meet Cindy, her father's fiancée, and her son Matt. Rachel liked Cindy, but had never spent much time with Matt. Rachel was the same age as Matt. After the wedding, they would all be living in the same house, and going to the same school—maybe even be in the same class! Rachel wasn't sure how she felt about all of that.

Today, the four of them were going to spend the whole day together at the park, and then go out for dinner and ice cream. "Rachel, are you excited about today?" her father asked.

"Yeah. I guess so. I think the park will be fun and I love ice cream," Rachel replied.

"I was talking about spending time with Cindy and her son Matt, Rachel. Do you think you and Matt will get along?" Dad asked.

"Sure, Dad," Rachel answered.

Inside Rachel was not so sure that she and Matt would get along. She was a girl. He was a boy. They liked different things. She enjoyed reading and playing board games. Matt like sports—all kinds of sports—playing sports and watching sports on the television.

Rachel thought about Cindy. She liked Cindy. Rachel's mom had died when she was only two years old so Rachel couldn't remember her mom at all. She always missed having her mom around and was glad Cindy would be there. Of course, she also kind of wished Cindy could live at their house without Matt.

"Dad, are you sure Matt is going to live with us, too? Why can't he live with his dad?" Rachel asked.

"I am sure, Rachel. Cindy and I have talked all about this many times. Matt will be living with us during the week and on two weekends a month. The other weekends he will live with his father," Dad explained. He paused, and then continued, "Why do you ask? Are you nervous about having Matt live with us?"

"Yes. No. . . . Maybe?" answered Rachel uncertainly.

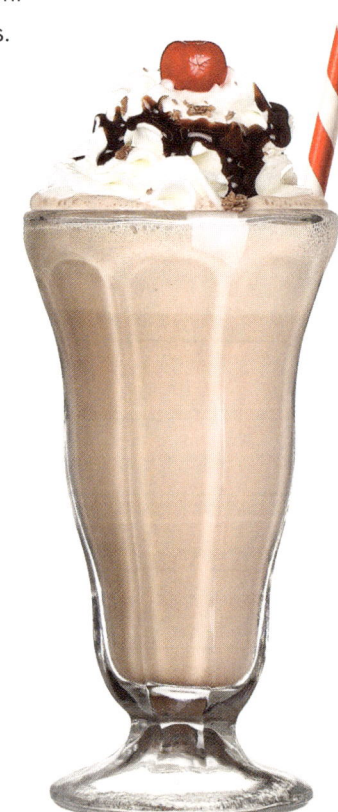

Praise Prayer Psalm

DAY 2

Read about It

Psalm 34

Think about It

1. This week's verse comes from the psalm we just read. Our verse has three parts: our part, God's part, and God's part again. First, it says, "I prayed to the LORD." Going to God for help or answers or just to talk with him is our part.

2. The second part of this verse tells us that God answers us. God hears us when we pray and he listens to us. He loves us and he wants us to know he will take care of us. This is God's part.

3. The third part says that God freed us from all our fears. This is God's part again. Have you ever thought about prayer as having different parts? God's part, our part . . . Both are important.

Do Something about It

When you feel afraid about anything, pray to the Lord. Talk to God about your fears. He will hear you. Do your part by praying, and God will do his part by hearing you and answering you. God will free you from all your fears.

Pray about It

Dear God, sometimes I feel scared and afraid of changes that are going to happen. Please help me remember to talk to you about my fears. Thank you for hearing my prayers and for promising to love and protect me. Thank you for freeing me from my fears. In Jesus' name, amen.

DAY 3: Acrostic Verse

Reread the visual Bible verse on page 203. Write the verse on the blank lines below. Then, look at the acrostic grid on this page. What phrase do the filled-in letters spell? Fill in the empty boxes of the acrostic grid with words from the verse. **Note:** Some words appear more than once in the verse, but they'll only be in the puzzle once. The only word not included is *I*.

_____

_____

_____

Psalm 34:4

206 · God Frees Me from My Fears

Answer Key on page 379.

Full House

DAY 4

Rachel's face flushed red and she put her hands to her cheeks as if to cool them. She felt so embarrassed! Here she was with her dad, driving to see his fiancée Cindy and Cindy's son Matt. And Rachel had just admitted she was concerned about Matt living with them after the wedding.

Rachel looked at her dad. She paused for a moment, and then everything came out in a rush. "I'm sorry, Dad! I'm not sure how I feel about having a brother. Matt is OK. But it's always been just you and me living together. I don't know what it will feel like with other people in our house," Rachel explained.

The car hit a bump as Dad turned a corner and the park was in sight down the block. Rachel continued, "I mean, having a mom could be really cool, but having to share stuff with a brother? And he's going to my school, too—maybe even my class! That could really be a bummer. My whole life could be different. And I'm pretty happy with how things are. So yeah . . . I'm scared."

"Look. I get it, Rachel. And let me tell you a secret. I'm a little scared, too. This is going to be a big change for all of us. If we are feeling scared, do you think that Cindy and Matt might be feeling the same way?" Dad asked.

Rachel listened carefully to her father talk. She'd been wondering about how it would feel to have new people in her house. But Rachel had never stopped to think about how Cindy and Matt might feel about leaving their home and moving into hers.

"Oh, Dad, I bet you're right. Cindy and Matt must be feeling just like we are." She paused as Dad found a parking place.

"What can we do to help them not be scared?" Rachel asked.

"Well, the first thing that comes to my mind is that we pray for our family. And starting now *our family* includes me, you, Cindy, and Matt. Let's ask God to help us learn how to grow into a family together. How does that sound?" Dad asked.

"Great!" Rachel replied. "I always feel so much better after I've told God about my fears," Rachel said firmly. Dad turned off the engine and they prayed.

God Frees Me from My Fears · 207

DAY 5: The Lord Is My Light

Read about It

Psalm 27:1–3

Think about It

1 Today's Bible passage is from another psalm by David. David knew a lot about fear! And he knew that God was the answer to his fears. One of the best parts of this week's verse is the word, *all*. God promises to deliver us from ALL of our fears. Not half of them. Not three-quarters of them. But ALL of them.

2 How do you feel when you take the time to talk to God about your fears? Do you say memory verses out loud? Sometimes it helps a lot to say God's promises out loud . . . as loud as you can!

3 When we feel scared or afraid, we sometimes forget that others feel the same way. Rachel was scared about how her family would change, but she never thought about how Cindy and Matt—or even her dad—might be feeling. Dad was wise to encourage Rachel to think about others and their fears. Have you ever wondered if others feel just like you do? What could you do to find out? What could you do if you found out they were afraid?

Do Something about It

When you feel afraid, pray and ask God for courage. Also pray for your family and friends to have courage, too. Remind yourself that if you feel scared, someone else is probably feeling the same way, too. Help them by praying for them.

Pray about It

Dear God, help me to remember that if I am feeling afraid others might be feeling the same way. Remind me to pray and ask you to help my family and friends to be brave. I want to encourage them to trust you, God. But sometimes I forget to pray and ask for your help. Please help me remember to say your promises out loud . . . very loud . . . to help me feel brave. In Jesus' name, amen.

Missing Word

DAY 6

Read the visual verse, and then write each word beneath its symbol. Color the visual verse. One very important word is missing. Figure out what word is missing and write it in the space. Why do you think this word is so important in the verse? Write your response on the lines provided.

 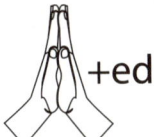+ed

_____

  +ed  +d

_____

 *from*  m+ 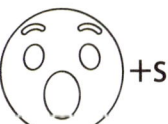+s

_____

Psalm 34:4

_____
_____
_____
_____
_____

God Frees Me from My Fears · 209

Week 30
God Always Knows What I Need

Look at the visual Bible verse below. Try to figure out what it says. Write the verse words on the blank lines. Use the Visual Bible Verse Dictionary on page 371, if needed.

Your Father knows exactly what you need even before you ask him! Matthew 6:8

Science Camp

DAY 1

Jonah ran into the house, almost stepping on his cat, Simon, who was sleeping on the doormat in a patch of sunshine. Jonah jumped over Simon and made his way to the living room. He was so excited to tell his dad about the dates for the science camp. Science camp was Jonah's favorite week of the summer—of the whole year!

In Jonah's bedroom, he had a wall calendar and each day he would mark an X to count down to the days when science camp started. He couldn't wait to write this year's dates on his calendar!

One of the best parts of the week was having his dad go along as a parent leader. Jonah had been outside swinging in his tire swing, imagining it was a rocket ship, when he saw his dad pull into the driveway. That's why he'd come running into the house so fast, and why he was now standing in front of his father, panting to catch his breath.

"Dad . . . it finally came . . ." Jonah said as he tried to catch his breath. "I have the science camp letter here!" Jonah exclaimed.

"Great, let me see it." Dad smiled and started reading the letter. After a moment, his smile turned into a frown.
"Oh . . . no," he said quietly.

"What? What's wrong?" Jonah asked.

"I'm already scheduled for an out-of-town business conference that week. I'm afraid I can't go this year, Jonah." Dad explained. "I'm sorry."

"No!" Jonah was crushed. "Dad, you have to come. We do this together every year. It won't be the same without you," Jonah said sadly.

"I'm really disappointed, too. But, Jonah, I can't miss this conference. I have to attend. You will have a great time at camp even without me," Dad assured Jonah.

"I don't know if I want to go anymore," Jonah said sadly.

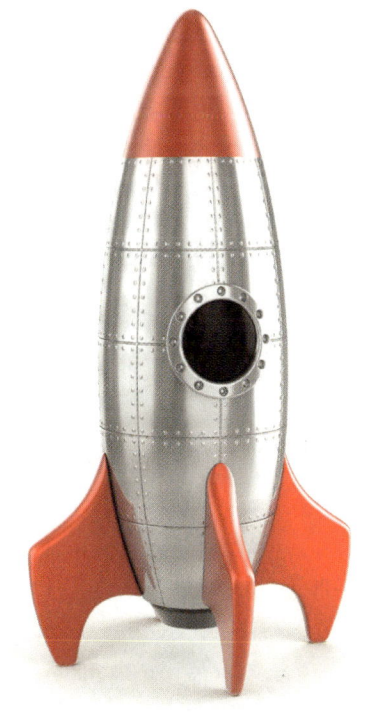

God Always Knows What I Need

DAY 2: The Lord's Prayer

Read about It

Matthew 6:5–13

Think about It

1. Today's passage of Scripture tells about Jesus teaching his friends—and us—how to pray. This week's verse is from this passage. Think about what the verse really means: God is answering your prayers before you even think to pray about it! What would you do if you prayed and asked God for help and God brought help so fast it surprised you?

2. Jonah is disappointed because his father cannot go with him to the science camp. Jonah starts to feel nervous about going alone. God knows what Jonah needs—to trust God to take care of him. What would you say to Jonah to make him feel better?

3. We have to remember that God isn't like us. God is all-powerful, all-knowing, and always sees what is happening in our lives. He knows what we need today and what we will need tomorrow. What is something you might need tomorrow or soon after? Have you prayed and asked God for help with that thing? Why or why not?

Do Something about It

When you need help, pray and ask God for whatever you need. Remember that even before tomorrow comes, God already knows exactly what you will need. Say this memory verse out loud to remind yourself that God is the one who takes care of you.

Pray about It

Dear God, please help me to go to you right away when I have a need. Help me to remember that you are the one who knows exactly what I need today and tomorrow. Even before tomorrow is here and I am worrying about what may happen, you are ready to help me. Thank you for loving me so much. In Jesus' name, amen.

Science Stuff

DAY 3

Color this page of science objects. Circle the hidden symbols and words of the verse. Then, write the verse words in order on the blank lines below.

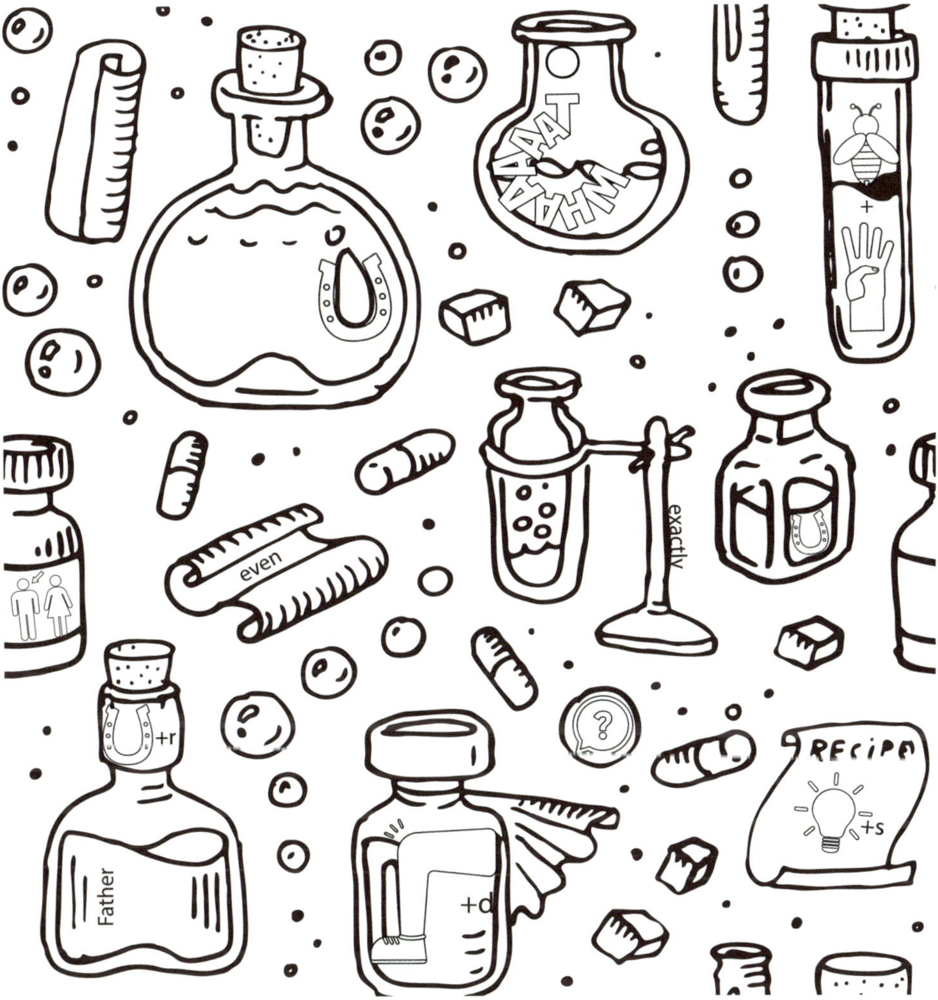

Matthew 6:8

Answer Key on page 380.

DAY 4: Up and Down and Back and Forth

Jonah dragged himself outside to ride his skateboard up and down in front of his house. All the time, Jonah kept thinking to himself how hard it was going to be to go to science camp without Dad. *I want to go. But I don't want to go. Maybe I won't go!* Jonah thought to himself.

Up and down. Back and forth.

Jonah didn't know if he wanted to go to science camp by himself. It had always been the two of them—Jonah and his dad—together at the science camp. He remembered some of the other kids had gotten homesick during camp. They missed their families. Jonah never felt that way because his dad was always close by. *I don't want to feel homesick! Since Dad can't go, I don't think I want to go,* Jonah thought to himself.

Then again, he'd always had such a good time. *Maybe I can handle it, even if Dad isn't there!* Jonah thought.

Up and down. Back and forth.

Jonahs' thoughts kept going up and down and back and forth, too! Jonah kept thinking and riding his skateboard until his mom called him in to dinner. Sitting down to a yummy meal of chicken and rice, Jonah practically forgot about his science camp troubles as he gobbled up the food. Then just as Jonah was standing to take his plate to the sink, his father stopped him.

"Please sit down again, son. Jonah, your mother and I have been talking about science camp. We understand that going without me is disappointing, but we want you to go alone. It might feel a little scary without me there, but God is always with you. We know that you will have a terrific week doing science experiments and learning new skills," Dad said. "What do you say?"

"I want to go. But I don't want to go. But . . . I think I should go?" Jonah said tentatively. Dad and Mom looked at each other and smiled.

"We think you should go, too. And remember this—God already knows what you will need when you are at camp. God promises to be with you and to take care of you," Dad encouraged. "Besides, we're just a phone call away."

"Thanks, Dad. I know you're right," Jonah agreed.

Bread or a Stone?

DAY 5

Read about It

Matthew 7:7–12

Think about It

1. Today's Bible passage is a message Jesus gave to his followers. And it applies to us today. Have you ever needed something and even before you asked for it, someone gave it to you? This is what God does. Even before we ask him for something he is already answering and supplying our need.

2. Jonah feels uncertain about going to camp without his dad because he felt safe when his father was there. When is a time you felt uncertain about going somewhere or doing something because you would be alone? Whenever you feel that way, remember that you're never really alone. God promises to be with you.

3. Do you talk to God every day? You don't need to be alone in a quiet room to pray. You can be playing outside and praying. You can be riding in a car or on a bus and praying. You can be watching television and praying. You can pray in school (especially if you have a test). Praying can happen anywhere and anytime because God is always listening. Where would you like to pray today?

Do Something about It

When you think of something you really need, stop and pray no matter where you are. Remember that you can pray anywhere and at any time. God is always close by and listening to you.

Pray about It

Dear God, please help me to remember that praying and talking to you can happen anywhere and anytime. I don't have to be alone in a quiet room to pray. You are always close by and always listening for my prayers. Thank you for caring for me so much that even before tomorrow comes, you know what I will need. I feel safe knowing that you are with me. In Jesus' name, amen.

DAY 6 Roll On

Read the visual verse, and then write each word beneath its symbol.

Roll a pair of number cubes. Look up the word associated with each number and write it on the appropriate blank line. Keep playing until you have rolled every number that corresponds to the words in the verse.

Challenge: Using separate sheets of paper, play this as a game with family members or friends. See who can complete the verse first!

1 +r   **2** Father   **3** +s   **4** exactly

_____ _____ _____ _____

5    **6**    **7** +d   **8** even

_____ _____ _____ _____

9    **10**    **11**    **12**

_____ _____ _____ _____

_____

_____

_____

Matthew 6:8

Week 31

I Can Speak with Love

Look at the visual Bible verse below. Try to figure out what it says. Write the verse words on the blank lines. Use the Visual Bible Verse Dictionary on page 371, if needed.

  +th

_____

_____

_____

_____

_____

We will speak the truth in love. Ephesians 4:15

DAY 1

Birthday Cake Blues

Selah and her sister, Janna, had come up with a plan to bake a German chocolate cake for their mom's birthday. Selah loved to cook. She was so excited to share her love of cooking with her mom. When the bus finally stopped, Selah scurried off and hurried up the street to her house.

As she walked in the door, Selah saw Janna laying on the couch, watching television. Janna went to the middle school and had a half-day on Wednesdays. Selah was surprised Janna wasn't already in the kitchen getting things set up. Selah called out, "Hey! We gotta get moving if we want this cake done before Mom gets home." Janna stretched and flapped her hand at her sister to get out of her face before standing up and heading to the kitchen.

Once the girls were there, Janna snapped, "Selah, remember we are using Grandma's recipe for this cake for Mom, not some recipe you found on the Internet!"

"I know that, Janna. We already talked about Mom's cake," Selah said with some hurt in her voice.

"And we still have to wrap her presents," Janna continued.

"I know," Selah agreed. "We already talked about all this last night."

"I knooow . . . ." Janna said drawing the word out sarcastically. "I just wanted to make sure you didn't forget and mess up our plans."

Selah didn't say anything to her sister; but inside, Selah was thinking, *Why does Janna have to be so mean all the time? Why does she talk to me like that?*

The girls soon had all the cake ingredients out on the kitchen counter. "We have the flour, baking soda, baking powder, salt, sugar, eggs, vanilla, chocolate, butter . . ." Selah counted off to Janna.

"Stop it! Will you! I'm trying to read the instructions for making the cake. I can't think when you're talking. Be quiet!" Janna said angrily. Selah didn't say anything to Janna as her eyes filled with tears and her lip started to quiver. Turning around, Selah ran up to her bedroom and shut the door. "What's wrong with you? Where are you going? Selah! Selah! Answer me!" shouted Janna.

Mary and Martha

DAY 2

Read about It

Luke 10:38–42

Think about It

1. The Bible passage is about two sisters just like Janna and Selah. In the Bible story, Jesus spoke kindly to Martha to help her see that what Mary was doing was good. Jesus was demonstrating what this week's visual verse is all about: Speak the truth in love. God expects us to use our words to speak the truth and not lie to others. And we are to speak the truth with love, which means to speak kindly. When is a time someone had to talk with you about something difficult? How did they speak to you—kindly with love or harshly with anger?

2. Have you ever said words to someone that were truthful, but you spoke them with unkindness, impatience, or anger? How could you have said the same thing while saying the words kindly?

3. Think about a time when someone spoke to you in a way that hurt your feelings. Why were your feelings hurt? Were they saying words that were truthful? Did they say the words in a way that showed they were upset or irritated or angry with you? If the words were true, how would you have rather heard those same words spoken to you?

Do Something about It

When you are speaking to others, speak the truth and don't lie. Be careful to say your words kindly and gently so that you won't hurt the person's heart.

Pray about It

Dear God, please help me to speak the truth in love. Help me to always speak words that are truthful and not lie. Sometimes, even when my words are truthful, I say them in a way that is not kind. I need you to help me be both truthful and kind when I speak to others. It hurts me when others talk to me unkindly or in anger and I do not want to speak that way to anyone. In Jesus' name, amen.

I Can Speak with Love

Criss-Cross Verse

Reread the visual verse, and then write each word on the lines below. Next, solve the puzzle by filling in the words of the verse. Don't forget to use *Ephesians*!

Ephesians 4:15

Answer Key on page 380.

Truth Talk

DAY 4

After Selah ran off to her room, upset at the way Janna was speaking to her, Janna felt defeated. She really needed Selah to help her with the cake. Selah was good at following recipes, and Janna just couldn't seem to. *That's just like her!* Janna thought angrily. *She talks me into doing something I'm lousy at but she's good at, and then she bails on me!*

Janna tried to talk to Selah through her bedroom door, but it was no good. No matter how much she yelled at her, Selah wouldn't budge. Before Janna knew it, their mom came home from work and found Janna alone in the kitchen, cake ingredients all over the counters, bent over Grandma's recipe card, trying to figure it out. "Janna, where is your sister? I thought you were both going to make my birthday cake together." Mom asked.

"Selah acted like a baby and ran to her room crying. She always gets upset and runs away. So I have to do everything by myself," complained Janna.

"Oh, Janna . . . I think there might be more to the story than you're telling me." Mom suggested. "Am I right?"

"Well . . . I did sort of snap at Selah. She was talking when I was trying to read the instructions for making the cake and I told her to be quiet," defended Janna.

"And you spoke to her kindly and patiently?" Mom asked.

"Uh . . . I guess I could have been nicer. But Selah is too sensitive. She always makes a big fuss about nothing," said Janna in anger.

"Janna, I think you need to consider who was really making a big fuss. And I think you need to think about how people feel when you speak to them unkindly." Mom continued in a softer tone, "Janna, remember the verse your Sunday school class memorized last month? It was the verse about telling the truth, but speaking kindly?" Mom asked.

"I think so . . . 'Speak the truth in love.' That's it," Janna replied.

"I want you to go to your room and really think about what that verse means. Then, I want you to think about how you spoke to your sister. After that, you, Selah, and I are going to have a talk," Mom instructed.

"And then after that, maybe we can finish the cake," Janna suggested.

"Well, I certainly hope so!" Mom laughed.

DAY 5: Paul Speaks the Truth

Read about It

Acts 17:16–34

Think about It

1. In our Bible passage, Paul spoke important truths to the people of Athens. He didn't insult them because of their beliefs. He simply told them the truth in a kind and loving way. Everyone needs to practice speaking the truth in love. Let's practice! Imagine a family member or friend is playing a loud video game while you're trying to read. What would you say? Were your words kind and loving? If not, try again!

2. Practice telling your friend that she hurt your feelings when she shared a secret with another friend. What would you say? Were your words kind and loving? If not, try again!

3. Practice asking your mom or dad for forgiveness because you lied about breaking a plate. What would you say? Were your words kind and loving? If not, try again!

Do Something about It

When you have to speak words that might be hard to say because you did something wrong and need to ask for forgiveness, pray and ask God to help you before you speak. If you need to tell someone some difficult truths, pray and ask God to help you before you speak. Practice saying truthful words in a way that is kind and gentle.

Pray about It

Dear God, sometimes I struggle to say truthful words in a kind and loving way. I may feel upset or angry, but I want to speak the truth in love. Please help me to speak the truth. Please teach me to say words kindly and nicely. Help me know when I need to wait until I calm down to speak. It is hard for me to be nice when I'm feeling hurt on the inside. I'm glad that you will help me. In Jesus' name, amen.

Visual Verse Cut-Outs

Read the visual verse, and then write each word beneath its symbol. Next, look through old magazines or newspapers for the key words to this verse, cut them out, and glue them in order in the space below.

_____

_____

Ephesians 4:15

Week 32

The Fruit of the Spirit

Look at the visual Bible verse below. Try to figure out what it says. Write the verse words on the blank lines. Use the Visual Bible Verse Dictionary on page 371, if needed.

The  produces this  of

 +s

+ness +ness +fulness +ness  self+

_____

_____

_____

_____

_____

The Holy Spirit produces this kind of fruit in our lives: love, joy, peace, patience, kindness, goodness, faithfulness, gentleness, and self-control. Galatians 5:22-23

Sand-Pit Capers

DAY 1

Brielle and Quinn would be coming home in a few minutes. Their grandma was in the kitchen just starting to make an after-school snack of fudge brownies. Grandma went to the sink to wash off a spoon, and looking out the window, noticed two boys sneaking in through the gate to the alley. As she watched, the boys quickly ran to the sandpit, grabbed some toys, and took off running through the gate again.

"Hmm, I wonder who those boys were?" Grandma said out loud.

About an hour later, Brielle and Quinn raced each other in the front door. "Grandma, what did you make for us today? Cookies? Popcorn? Cupcakes?" asked Brielle.

"Well, let's just see what I do have for my two best girls," Grandma held up the plate of brownies, as the girls exclaimed happily. "I made a pan of homemade brownies because your daddy loves them, too. But before you get any brownies, go wash your hands, please."

The girls ran to the bathroom, washed their hands, and were back in the kitchen before Grandma had even set the plates and drinks on the table—though their hands might not have been completely dry. "OK, girls, let's thank God for our snack," Grandma said.

After a quick prayer, Brielle and Quinn told Grandma all about their day at school. When they were finished, Grandma remembered the boys who took some toys from the sandpit. "Girls, two little boys came in the back gate and ran off with some toys from your sandpit. Do you know who they are?" Grandma asked.

"Oh, no!" moaned Brielle. "Not again!"

"It's our new neighbors. They keep sneaking over and taking our stuff when we aren't home. Dad and Mom are going to have to talk to their parents again," explained. Quinn. "Let's go outside and see what they took this time, Brielle."

"Be right back, Grandma," Brielle called out over her shoulder.

The Fruit of the Spirit • 225

DAY 2: The Good Samaritan

Read about It

Luke 10:25–37

Think about It

1. Today's Bible passage teaches us that everyone is our neighbor, so we should show the fruit of the Spirit to everyone. *Fruit* means all the good things that grow from having the Holy Spirit live inside of our hearts. Who do you think of when you think of the word *neighbor*?

2. The fruit of the Spirit is love, joy, peace, patience, kindness, goodness, faithfulness, gentleness, and self-control. Think about how you can show all of these different "fruits" by the way you speak to and treat others. Do you think it is easier to show the fruit of the Spirit to people who act that way toward you or to people who don't?

3. When we love Jesus, believe he is the Son of God, and ask him to forgive our sins, we can join God's family. Then God gives us the Holy Spirit to be with us and help us grow God's good fruit. The Holy Spirit is always working inside of our hearts to teach us and comfort us and encourage us to make good choices. When is a time someone showed a fruit of the Spirit to you?

Do Something about It

Think about how you talk to and treat some of the people in your life—family, friends, teachers and coaches, etc. Now think about the fruits of the Spirit. How many of the fruits do you show in your interactions with these people? Pray and ask God to help you show these fruits every day so that others can understand God's love for them.

Pray about It

Dear God, I am thankful that you sent your Son, Jesus, to die so that we can be members of your family and have the Holy Spirit with us. I know that the Holy Spirit teaches us and comforts us and encourages us to make good choices. Help me to remember that I can show God's love by speaking and acting in ways that are loving, joyful, peaceful, patient, kind, good, faithful, gentle, and show self-control. In Jesus' name, amen.

Fruit of the Spirit Tree

DAY 3

Circle each symbol and word from this week's verse.
Then, write the verse words on the blank lines.

_____

_____

_____

_____

_____

Galatians 5:22-23

Showing the Fruit of the Spirit

After Grandma had told them the neighbor boys had stolen some of their toys, Brielle and Quinn ran out to the sandpit in their backyard. They looked for their favorite shovels and rakes and sand toys for making sandcastles. They were all gone!

The girls moaned and ran back inside. "Grandma, those boys took all of our sand toys. ALL of them!" squealed Brielle.

"Why do they think they can steal our things?" Quinn asked.

"I hate them! I wish they had never moved onto our street," complained Brielle.

"Girls, girls, . . . sit down. Let's talk about this together," Grandma said calmly. "First, we don't say we hate anyone, right?"

Brielle hang her head. "Sorry, Grandma."

Grandma continued, "And what does God say we should do when someone hurts us? I know you remember because I heard you both saying the verse at your Bible quiz competition," Grandma said. "It's found in Romans 12:21 . . ."

"Oh! I remember!" Brielle said. She started saying the verse as Quinn joined her, "Don't let evil conquer you, but conquer evil by doing good!"

"Good! Now, let's talk about how God would want you to respond. Remember the fruits of the Spirit? Can you name them all?" Grandma asked. "The fruit of the Spirit is . . ."

"Love, joy, peace," Quinn started.

"Patience, kindness, goodness," Brielle continued.

"Faithfulness, gentleness, and self-control," Brielle and Quinn finished together.

"Wonderful!" Grandma gave them both a big hug. "Now . . . about those boys . . . we will explain what happened to your parents when they get home. I'm sure your father and mother will have a talk with the new neighbors. But I want you two girls to think about the fruit of the Spirit and how you can treat those boys in a way that shows God's love to them," Grandma encouraged.

The Woman at the Well

DAY 5

Read about It

John 4:1–42

Think about It

1 Today's passage is about how Jesus showed the fruit of the Spirit to a Samaritan woman. In Bible times, men didn't talk to women and Jewish people didn't talk to Samaritans. Jesus had more than enough reason to ignore her. But he didn't. And her life changed! Which fruit of the Spirit do you think Jesus showed the woman? There's more than one right answer!

2 God wants us to show his love to others by making good choices in what we say and do. By showing the fruit of the Spirit others can understand God's love for them. Sometimes when others hurt us, it can be hard to love them by speaking kindly and treating them lovingly. What can you do to help show the fruits of the Spirit to others even when you feel upset or hurt?

3 Think about a time when you said something that hurt another person. Do you remember how they responded to you? Did they show you the fruit of the Spirit by forgiving you and loving you? What could you have done differently that would have shown at least one fruit of the Spirit?

Do Something about It

When you are feeling upset or angry with someone, pray and ask God to help you show the fruit of the Spirit. Ask God to help you show love and joy, give you peace and patience, speak kind and good words, be faithful to him, and react with gentleness and self-control.

Pray about It

Dear God, sometimes it is hard to show the fruit of the Spirit to someone who has hurt me. Please help me remember that I have hurt others, too. I need their forgiveness for my bad choices. Please help me to forgive, and then show the fruit of the Spirit in what I say and do. In Jesus' name, amen.

DAY 6

Complete the Comic

Read the visual verse and write the words under the images. Next, imagine a situation in which you might need to show one or more of the fruit of the Spirit. Then, show the situation by completing the comic strip using your own words and drawings. Draw mouths on the characters in the first square. Are they smiling? Frowning? Singing?

  produces this of

   +ness +ness +fulness +ness

Galatians 5:22-23

230 · The Fruit of the Spirit

Week 33
God Will Comfort Me

Look at the visual Bible verse below. Try to figure out what it says. Write the verse words on the blank lines. Use the Visual Bible Verse Dictionary on page 371, if needed.

 comforts

    that

 comfort others

_____

_____

_____

_____

_____

_____

[God] comforts us in all our troubles so that we can comfort others. 2 Corinthians 1:4

DAY 1

Moving Day

Addison and Aaron were moving away to a big city. Today was the boys' last day to see their friends from church. In Sunday school, they had been given a big card that everyone signed and put their contact information in. Addison and Aaron hugged each of their friends and teachers and said good-bye before leaving the classroom for the last time.

As Addison and Aaron were getting into their car, Addison started to cry. "I don't want to move. I don't want to leave our church! I don't want to leave my friends," Addison said through tears.

"I know. I know," Mom said sympathetically as she buckled their baby sister, Ashley, into her car seat. "Leaving is hard, Addison. We are all feeling the same way."

Aaron piped up, "I'm not sad. I'm angry! Why can't we stay here? Nobody asked Aaron and me if we wanted to move," he complained.

Dad looked in the rearview mirror at Aaron and frowned. "Aaron, you know why we are moving. My employer didn't give me any choice. I have to move or I would lose my job," Dad explained.

Driving along, everyone in the car was quiet. No one felt like talking. Dad, Mom, Addison, and Aaron were all busy thinking about what they would miss most when they moved away.

Later that afternoon, with their moving truck all packed up, Addison and Aaron climbed into the backseat of Dad's truck and Mom sat in the front beside Dad. Dad said a prayer before they started, "Dear God, Please help us to travel safely today. Please protect others and us on the highway. And above all, help us to trust you with this move. Help us to be on the lookout for ways to be helpful to others we meet. In Jesus' name, amen."

232 • God Will Comfort Me

Abraham and Lot Move

DAY 2

Read about It

Genesis 12:1–4; 13

Think about It

1. Our Bible passage tells of a time Abraham was told by God to move to a new place. It couldn't have been easy to move from a place where Abraham and his family had always lived, but Abraham had God's promises to comfort him. When is a time that God's promises comforted you?

2. When God promises to comfort us, he is saying that he will help us feel safe, secure, peaceful, taken care of, loved, and cherished. Can you think of any other words that describe comfort?

3. God wants us to trust him when we feel afraid or upset because he will comfort us. But the next part tells us that because God gives us comfort, we can comfort others who need it. When is a time you have comforted someone else? Ask God to show you ways to comfort others.

Do Something about It

When you are feeling afraid or sad or upset, pray and ask God to comfort you. Say this verse out loud so that you remember God is always close by when you need him.

Pray about It

Dear God, sometimes I feel afraid and sad and upset. Please help me to remember that you have promised to comfort me when I need it. I want to be brave and trust you for every new change. And I want to be able to comfort others who need it, too. Please show me ways that I can comfort others and give me the courage to do it. In Jesus' name, amen.

DAY 3: Verse in Motion

Read the visual verse, and then write each word beneath its symbol. For each phrase, write down some motions you can do as you say the verse. Then, practice saying the verse and doing the motions several times. Say it and do the motions in front of a mirror, for your family or friends, or for your stuffed animals. Teach it to someone else and video yourselves saying the verse and doing the motions. Keep it up until you know the verse by heart.

comforts US

_____

_____

N (all) ⌛ ⚠+s

_____

SO that WE

_____

_____

comfort others

_____

_____

2 Corinthians 1:4

A New Church

DAY 4

It was a week after Addison, Aaron, their parents and baby sister had moved to a big, new city. Addison and Aaron walked into their new church with their mom and dad. Mom turned to Dad and said, "I'll take Ashley to the nursery. Please take the boys to find their classes."

Addison was in a different class from his brother Aaron. Their grades had been combined at their church in the small town they'd moved from. It was weird to think they'd be making not just new friends, but different friends.

"I wish we could go in together, Aaron," whispered Addison.

"Me, too," replied Aaron.

"Here we are, boys," said Dad, pointing to the two different directions. "Addison your classroom is down the hall and Aaron's is here. Addison, you're old enough to find your own way, right?"

"I guess so," Addison said.

"Great! See you afterwards at the car," Dad said before going into Aaron's room with him.

Addison continued down the hall, found his Sunday school room, and walked in. Immediately, the teacher introduced himself to Addison and then to the class. He showed Addison where to sit as they started the lesson.

Sitting down, Addison noticed a girl sitting next to him trying to hold back tears. Addison looked over and smiled, "Hi," Addison said.

"Hi," sniffed the girl.

"I'm Addison. This is my first day," Addison explained.

"I'm Karley and today is my first day, too. My family just moved here," Karley said.

"My family just moved here, too. Where are you going to school?" Addison asked.

"I . . . I don't know the name of the school . . . I can't remember . . ." Karley said starting to sniffle again.

"Don't cry, Karley. You and I can be new friends in a new place together!" Addison encouraged.

God Will Comfort Me

DAY 5 Hannah Prays

Read about It

1 Samuel 1

Think about It

1. In the Bible story, Hannah was in distress because she wanted a son so badly. She was teased by Peninnah, but Elkanah tried to comfort Hannah. However, it wasn't until something happened at the Tabernacle that Hannah felt real comfort. What happened that comforted Hannah?

2. There is a saying, "God never wastes our pain." Have you ever heard that before? God never allows us to go through something that is hard and hurts without making us stronger so that we can comfort others. Saying kind things is one way to comfort others. What are some other ways you can comfort someone?

3. Think about this: God always wants us to be looking for others to love and comfort. When is a time someone comforted you? When is a time you comforted someone else?

Do Something about It

When you feel sad or want to be comforted, pray and ask God to show you others who feel the same way. Ask God to help you use words and acts of comfort to show God's love to others.

Pray about It

Dear God, please help me know that you are close by and ready to comfort me. When I understand how much you love me, I want to show that great love to others. Help me to be kind and loving and speak words of comfort to everyone I meet. In Jesus' name, amen.

Fill In the Blank

What word is missing from our verse? For each of the verses below, in the yellow bubble, fill in words that can be substituted for the missing word.

  US   +s

---

 that  comfort others

---

  US

   comfort others

---

 comforts US  +s

---

 that   comfort others

---

2 Corinthians 1:4

God Will Comfort Me

Week 34

Troubles Become Glory

Look at the visual Bible verse below. Try to figure out what it says. Write the verse words on the blank lines. Use the Visual Bible Verse Dictionary on page 371, if needed.

_____

_____

_____

_____

_____

Here on earth you will have many trials and sorrows. But take heart, because I have overcome the world. John 16:33

The Play's the Thing

DAY 1

Max ran as fast as his legs could carry him. He was running to his mom's office. Max's mom was a counselor at his school. Max could go see her when he needed her. Or when Max had some great news!

"Mom! Mom! I am going to be in the school play. I got the part I wanted!" Max yelled.

"Shh, Max. Not so loud," his mom said. "But I am so happy for you, Max!"

"Thanks, Mom," Max beamed.

"You have worked so hard preparing for your audition. Your father will be so proud of you!" Mom said happily.

"I have to go eat now. See you after school!" Max exclaimed.

Several hours later, Max's mom was standing by the front lobby of the school waiting for Max. *Where is he?* She wondered. School had ended fifteen minutes earlier. Sometimes, Max talked with his friends. Mom decided to go look for him.

She went to the playground. No Max. In the library. No Max. She called into the bathroom. No Max. Finally, she found him. "Max, why are you sitting in the cafeteria by yourself? On the floor?" When she got closer, she added, "And why are you crying?" She knelt next to him and put an arm around her son.

"Because, I didn't get the part I wanted. Jude got it. My teacher made a mistake telling me I had the part. It was Jude who got it," Max said through his tears.

"Oh Max, I'm so sorry. I know how disappointed you must be. Will you get to play another part?" Mom asked as she hugged Max tightly.

"Our teacher said I have to learn Jude's part in case he gets sick. So probably not. I'll have to memorize all those lines, and then not get to use them," Max explained.

"Oh . . . I see." Mom murmured. Then she stood up. "Well, let's go home now and we'll talk more later," Max's mom said pulling Max to his feet.

Troubles Become Glory · 239

DAY 2: Sadness Will Be Turned to Joy

Read about It

John 16:16–33

Think about It

1. This Bible passage contains this week's visual verse. It is from the Last Supper, when Jesus was preparing his disciples for what was about to happen—his death and resurrection. Jesus' resurrection was one proof that he has "overcome the world!" How does that make you feel to know that Jesus can overcome any difficulty you might face? Is there anything going on right now that you'd like to talk to Jesus about?

2. This week's verse tells that there will be times when something bad or hard happens to us. When bad things do happen to us, we might feel sad, angry, or disappointed. But God not only will comfort us when we are hurting, he will find a way to make the difficult things into something good. Can you think about a lesson you learned after going through a difficult time?

3. When we go through something that hurts, God wants us to trust him to turn the difficult thing into a good thing. What difficult thing are you going through right now? Pray to God that he will make something good out of it.

Do Something about It

When you feel sad, angry, or disappointed, trust God to turn whatever is upsetting you into a good thing. Think about how God can change something difficult into an important lesson about life.

Pray about It

Dear God, I am feeling sad and angry and disappointed. I don't want to feel all these things. I want this problem to go away. Please help me, God, to trust you even when my feelings are all mixed up. Help me to trust you to change the difficult things into good things. In Jesus' name, amen.

Jar Words

On each jar is a symbol or word from the verse. Write the verse word on the blank line under each jar. Then, circle the jar with the first word of the verse. Draw a line from that word to the jar with the next word. Continue until you have completed the verse with the reference.

DAY 3

John 16:33

DAY 4

Understudy Understanding

Max and his mom walked quietly into their apartment. After a few minutes, Mom went to the kitchen table with some popcorn and juice.

"Come here, Max, let's sit down, have a snack, and talk about what happened," Mom encouraged.

"I don't think I want to talk about it. I want to forget all about it!" Max said. But he moved to the table to have the snack.

"I understand you might not feel like talking, but talking about difficult things can make them easier to understand. You worked hard and you feel disappointed."

"I have even more work to do! I have to learn the whole part and still don't get a part!" Max complained.

"You may not have the part you want, but you do have a part. You have the part of being the understudy. Imagine what might happen if no one was the understudy and the day of the play, Jude couldn't be there. What would happen?"

Max looked surprised. "I never thought about that. I guess we couldn't do the play."

Mom nodded, "That's right. And imagine how all your classmates would feel." Max's eyes got big and he stopped eating. "And what about the audience?" Mom finished.

"Wow! I never thought about any of that." Max said.

"But I don't want to kid you, Max. There are times you might feel discouraged that you didn't get the part. Trust that God will comfort you, Max. He loves you and understands all your feelings. Sometimes we won't have answers to why things happen, but that is when we have to trust God. We need to remember that God is always working toward something even better than we can imagine," Mom said.

"OK. I want to trust God, but I want to be in this play, too! I want to believe that God can turn this difficult thing into something good, but right now I just can't . . ." Max said.

"God understands, Max. Let me pray for you and we will trust that God will help you find something good. And remember that God will always be close by to comfort you," Mom assured him.

Jesus Raises Lazarus

DAY 5

Read about It

John 11:1–44

Think about It

1 Today's Bible story is a great one for remembering that there isn't anything that God can't fix! Even when we might think nothing good can come from a situation—God can make something good. No one in this story could figure out what Jesus was doing or thinking, even when he told them. Even if we don't know how good can come from a bad situation, we can still pray and thank God.

2 When something difficult happens, God asks us to trust him. Max's mom was right to remind him that God turns difficult things into good things, but it doesn't always happen today. Or even tomorrow. Sometimes we have to wait a long time before we understand what God is doing.

3 Think about a time when you were disappointed. Did you pray and try to trust God with your difficult thing? Did God change the difficult thing into something good?

Do Something about It

When you don't understand what God is doing, pray and ask him to help you trust him. Ask him to help you be patient as he works to change the difficult things into good things.

Pray about It

Dear God, I don't always understand what you are doing in my life when difficult things happen. I want to trust you all the time, but I need your help. Please help me to be patient as you work to turn difficult things into good things. I may have to wait a long time, but I believe you are always working to make things good because you love me. In Jesus' name, amen.

Troubles Become Glory

DAY 6: Scrambled Verse

Read the visual verse, and then write each word beneath its symbol. The verse is all mixed up! On the blank lines, write the verse in the correct order.

_____ _____ _____ _____ _____

 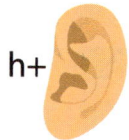  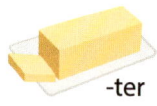 

_____ _____ _____ _____ _____

   sorrows

_____ _____ _____ _____ _____

 trials

_____ _____ _____

_____

_____

_____

_____

John 16:33

244 · Troubles Become Glory

Week 35
I Can Love What Is Good

Look at the visual Bible verse below. Try to figure out what it says. Write the verse words on the blank lines. Use the Visual Bible Verse Dictionary on page 371, if needed.

_____

_____

_____

_____

_____

DAY 1

Spelling Woes

Connor was bent over his book. It was the last assignment of the day—spelling, one of Connor's weaker subjects. He was trying to find all the spelling words before the final bell rang. If he didn't finish in time, then Connor would have to take his spelling home with him.

Connor wanted to go with his friends to a ballgame after school. The last thing he wanted was to be stuck inside. Doing homework. Doing SPELLING! *I'm almost half done. I think I can get it done,* Connor cheered to himself.

"Ha! Look at Connor." He looked up to see a girl from his class pointing at him. "He doesn't want to be the only one with homework tonight! He'll never get it done in time! Connor's too slow," Morgan teased.

Connor's face turned bright red. He felt embarrassed and ashamed. *Why does Morgan always say mean things to me?* Connor wondered.

Trying to ignore Morgan's taunts and nasty comments, Connor bent his head over his book and tried to find another spelling word. Just then the bell rang. Connor slowly looked up at the clock and then closed his book. He would have to take his spelling work home with him . . . again.

Maybe Morgan was right. Maybe I am slow, Connor thought as he gathered his books in his backpack and zipped it up.

Walking to the car, Connor saw Morgan outside yelling at some girls in a younger grade. One of the girls was crying. "You cry baby! What's wrong with you?" sneered Morgan.

Connor then saw a teacher walk up to Morgan and take her inside the building. *Finally! Morgan is in trouble for being so mean. I'm glad!* thought Connor.

By Our Love

DAY 2

Read about It

John 13:31–35

Think about It

1. This Bible passage is from the last supper Jesus had with his disciples before his death. He tells them that others will know they are his followers by the way they show love to each other. This week's verse starts out saying, "Don't just pretend to love others. Really love them." What would it feel like to think someone loves you, but then find out that they don't? God doesn't want us to just act like we love people. He wants us to feel it, too!

2. The second part of this verse tells us to "Hate what is wrong." God wants us to run from wrong things—not join in. It's OK that Connor didn't like what Morgan was doing. Do you think it was OK that Connor was happy Morgan was in trouble? Why or why not?

3. Finally, this verse tells us to "Hold tightly to what is good." Reading the Bible every day helps us to know the difference between good things and wrong things. We need to understand what God calls wrong and what he calls good. That way, we can obey him by making good choices. "What are some things that God wants a kid your age to hold tightly to and do?"

Do Something about It

Take time every day to read the Bible to know what God calls good and what God calls wrong. Then, make good choices by running away from evil and clinging to what is good.

Pray about It

Dear God, I know that you want me to cling to what is good. Loving others is one of the good things you want me to do. That means I should pray for people who do wrong things. Help me to forgive people who do wrong things to me. Help me remember to pray for them. In Jesus' name, amen.

Verse Pictures

DAY 3

Read the visual verse, and then write each word beneath its symbol. In each circle, write or draw what you think of when you think about those words from the verse.

✖ just pretend ✌🏾 ❤️ others

Really ❤️ THEM

_____
_____

h8 ❓ is wrong

_____
_____

Hold tightly ✌🏾 ❓ is 👍

_____
_____

Romans 12:9

248 • I Can Love What Is Good

Happy Time?

DAY 4

When Connor's mom pulled up and he got into the car, his mom greeted him. "Hey, kiddo! You're looking happy today. What's up?"

"Well, remember that mean girl in my class that is always picking on kids? Morgan? She said some nasty stuff to me when I was trying to finish my spelling words," Connor explained. "Then after school, I saw her being mean to girls in a younger grade. Then a teacher came out and took Morgan back inside the building. I bet she is in big trouble!" Connor said gleefully.

"Oh, I see," Mom replied. "So you're glad that Morgan got caught teasing the girls?"

"More than glad! I'm stoked! She deserved to get punished," Connor stated.

"I agree that she needed to be stopped. But do you think God is happy that Morgan is being punished?"

"Huh? . . ." Connor had never considered such a thing. "Um, I guess not exactly *happy*. . . . God loves everyone so he must love Morgan, even if she is so mean. But he must be happy those girls won't be picked on anymore, right?"

"I'm sure you're right about that," Mom said. "But is it appropriate to be happy that she's in trouble? Do you think God might want something else for her?"

Connor thought about it. "I guess God would want her to be forgiven."

"Exactly!" Mom continued gently, "Remember, Morgan's no different than any of us. We all do wrong things. We all need forgiveness. We all need God's love."

Connor looked out the window and thought about what Mom said. He knew she was right, but something else was going on. "It's just . . . I hate being teased! And I'm still glad Morgan is getting in trouble for it," Connor shared.

"I get what you're feeling. I do! But when we are happy about another person getting into trouble, are we sincerely loving that person?" Mom asked. "How would you feel if your best friend was in trouble? Would it make you happy?"

"No . . ." Connor said slowly. "I'd feel pretty lousy."

"The Bible tells us to love everyone—even people who aren't nice. Can you love Morgan by forgiving her?" Mom asked Connor.

"I'll try, Mom. I'll try . . ." Connor agreed.

I Can Love What Is Good · 249

DAY 5 Noah's Ark

Read about It

Genesis 6:11–13, 22; 7:1–24

Think about It

1 This week's visual Bible verse has three key parts that work better together than apart. First, we must have love that is real. We ask ourselves if we truly do love another person, even if that person has hurt us. Be honest! What would be difficult about loving someone who has hurt us?

2 Next, we must hate what is wrong. That means when others do wrong things, we don't join in. And we don't let them influence us to do something else that is also wrong. Today's Bible passage tells the story of Noah. The people at his time were always doing wrong things. But Noah didn't. He chose to obey God. Have you ever been asked to do something wrong with someone? What did you do?

3 Finally, we must hold tightly to what is good. How can we know what is good? We can read the Bible every day. We can make good choices like telling the truth; giving back what isn't ours; loving people and forgiving them. Have you ever loved someone even after they have hurt you?

Do Something about It

When you feel upset or angry at someone and are tempted to hurt them like they hurt you, stop and pray. Ask God to help me to cling to what is good. Do not fight back. Love and forgive.

Pray about It

Dear God, please help me to be a good forgiver. Help me to not yell or hit or scream at someone who has hurt me. Give me the courage to walk away and then talk to a teacher or family member about what happened. Help me to hate what is wrong and to hold tightly to what is good. In Jesus' name, amen.

Backwards Words

DAY 6

The words to this week's verse are spelled backward. Write each word correctly on the blank line next to it. Then, match each word to its symbol on the right.

really _____
is _____
them _____
don't _____
tightly _____
good _____
others _____
love _____
what _____
pretend _____
love _____
hold _____
just _____
is _____
hate _____
to _____
wrong _____
to _____
what _____

Romans 12:9

I Can Love What Is Good · 251

Week 36

Jesus Knows Me

Look at the visual Bible verse below. Try to figure out what it says. Write the verse words on the blank lines. Use the Visual Bible Verse Dictionary on page 371, if needed.

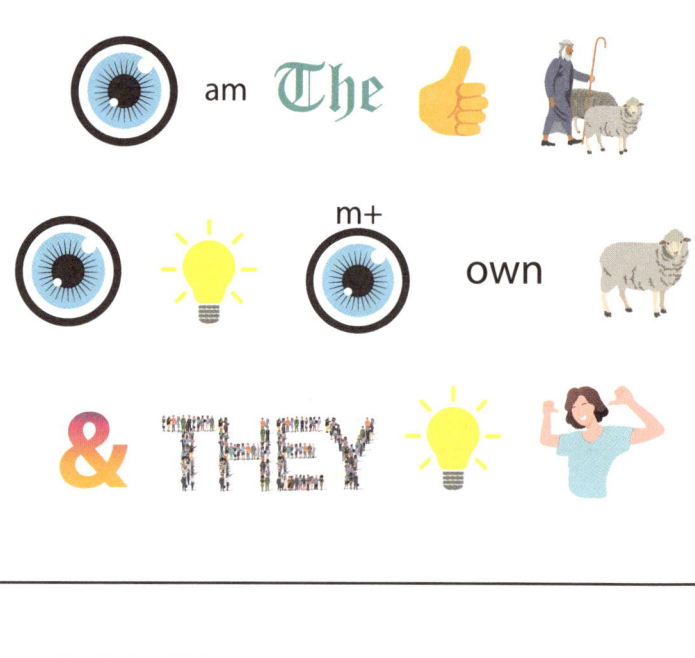

_____

_____

_____

_____

_____

I am the good shepherd. I know my own sheep, and they know me. John 10:14

Time with Trapper

DAY 1

Maggie pulled her barn boots on one at a time, grabbed her leather gloves, and headed out to the barn. It was time to muck out her pony's stall before school. Every morning and evening, Maggie had to clean out her pony's stall, feed and water him, and brush him down. That might sound like a lot of work, but Maggie loved every minute of it.

Looking at the clouds forming in the sky got Maggie thinking. *I hope it doesn't rain this afternoon, I want to take Trapper out for a walk in the woods.* She took another look at the sky. It didn't seem hopeful. Already dark skies were forming as thunder clouds gathered into ominous clumps.

The barn door squeaked and groaned as she opened it. "Here boy," Maggie coaxed as she swung the gate to Trapper's stall. She lead Trapper out to the pen. He couldn't be in his stall while she cleaned it.

"Here you go, breakfast is here," Maggie said. She poured grain into the bucket and pitched some hay into a nearby horse trough. Trapper whinnied in response before lowering his head into the bucket.

Maggie always enjoyed hearing Trapper munch away at his breakfast while she cleaned the stall. Mornings were busy for Maggie so she didn't have extra time to brush and comb out Trapper's hair, mane, and tail. "Come here, Trapper. Good boy. That's it," she encouraged him as she led him back to his stall. "You want a sugar cube before I leave?" She pulled off one of her gloves and pulled a sugar cube from her pocket. "Here you are," Maggie said. She smiled as Trapper's nose nuzzled the treat in her open palm.

Being careful to both close and lock the pen gate, Maggie headed back to the house to get ready for the school bus to arrive.

DAY 2: Jesus Is the Good Shepherd

Read about It

John 10:1–18

Think about It

1. This Bible passage includes this week's verse. It's Jesus teaching, explaining that he is our good shepherd. Do you know what a shepherd does? He takes care of his sheep! Just like Maggie took care of Trapper by feeding, watering, cleaning, and loving him, Jesus promises to be our shepherd and take care of our every need.

2. This week's verse says that Jesus knows his sheep. This means that Jesus knows what we need to live. Jesus also knows what makes us happy and sad. He knows when we feel afraid and scared. Jesus knows everything about us. Since Jesus already knows all about us, why is it important for us to pray?

3. Finally, this verse says that we know Jesus. We can know who Jesus is and we can ask him to lead us all of our lives forgive us for our sins. Jesus promises to forgive us and make us a member of God's family. All the members of God's family will live with him in Heaven forever. How does it make you feel to know that you can live with Jesus forever in Heaven?

Do Something about It

When you feel alone, say this verse out loud to remind yourself that Jesus promises to be your good shepherd. He promises to take good care of you because he knows all about you. Take time to learn more about Jesus.

Pray about It

Dear God, I sometimes feel like no one understands what I need. Please help me to remember that Jesus promises to take good care of me and be my good shepherd. Jesus knows me and I know him. This makes me feel safe and loved. I am glad that Jesus knows everything I need because sometimes I am not sure what I need. But Jesus is close by, watching over me just like a shepherd. In Jesus' name, amen.

Say, Write, Sing, Repeat

Say the verse; write the verse; sing the verse. Repeat these steps until you know the verse!

1. Say the verse aloud. If needed, review the Visual Bible Verse Dictionary at the back of the book to remember what each symbol stands for.
2. Write the verse on the lines below—as many times as you can!
3. Sing it to the tune of "Frère Jacques" or another tune.

I am the good	A-and they-ey know me
Sheh-eh-perd	A-and they-ey know me
I know my own sheep	John 10:14
I know my own sheep	John 10:14

4. Repeat steps 1, 2, and 3 until you can say the verse without help.

 am

 own

_____

_____

_____

_____

_____

_____

_____

John 10:14

DAY 4
Rain, Rain, Go Away

Maggie's school day went by in a blur of activity. She had tests and quizzes and gym time and before she knew it, the last bell of the day rang. She hurried to her locker, grabbed her things, said good-bye to her friends, and then made a bee-line to her bus.

It's not raining yet. I hope I can take Trapper out when I get home! Maggie thought anxiously. A few moments before Maggie's bus pulled up to her house, there was a loud clap of thunder and a few drops of rain began to ping down on the bus. "Oh, no! I wanted to ride Trapper!" Maggie moaned to her friend Talia, sitting next to her. "Maybe if I move fast and the rain doesn't get worse, I'll get a chance."

She made a mad dash through the cold pellets of rain to the safety of her home. As soon as she ran inside, Maggie threw down her coat, took off her shoes, and put her backpack on the chair near the door.

"Hi, Maggie," Mom called from the basement. "I'm down here folding clothes."

"Hi, Mom. I'm going out to see Trapper," Maggie said.

Maggie pulled on her barn boots and put on a raincoat, too. Out the door she ran. "Hi, boy! Hey, Trapper! Trapper!" Maggie called out as she ran toward the barn. The rain was picking up. It starting coming down harder. Trapper was smart. He stayed inside the barn and didn't even come out to the pen to greet Maggie.

Maggie ran into the barn and gave Trapper a big hug. She thought about how much she wanted to ride Trapper. And she thought about how it could be bad for his saddle and the reigns if they got wet. She thought about how they both could get sick being outside in the wet and cold weather. She sighed and went to get his brushes.

Maggie began brushing Trapper. When she got to his head, she looked him deep in the eyes. "I wanted to take you out for a ride today, but it's raining pretty hard, Trapper. I know you don't like the rain." She stroked his nose. "I don't want either one of us to get sick. We will just stay inside the barn where it's dry and warm, OK?" Maggie leaned her head against Trapper. He whinnied, as if he were thankful that Maggie knew how to take good care of him.

The Lost Sheep

DAY 5

Read about It

Luke 15:4–7

Think about It

1. This Bible passage is about a shepherd who left ninety-nine sheep to find the one that was lost. We are like that lost sheep to Jesus. He seeks you out because you are important to him. How does it make you feel to know that you are important to Jesus?

2. Isn't it comforting to know that Jesus knows everything about us? He does! He knows what we need and how we feel. Jesus is always ready to listen to us when we want to talk with him. Jesus is never far away or too busy. What is something you'd like to talk to Jesus about right now? Go ahead and take a moment to pray.

3. Jesus knows all about us, but how well do you know Jesus? What are some ways you can get to know him better? What can you learn about Jesus by reading your Bible? By praying? Where can you go, and who can you talk to to learn more about Jesus?

Do Something about It

Read about what earthly shepherds do and study how they care for their sheep. Then you will better understand how Jesus promises to take of you.

Pray about It

Dear God, I am one of Jesus' sheep. Help me to understand everything this means. Jesus promises to be my good shepherd and I know he is. Jesus knows everything that I need and everything that I feel. This makes me feel safe. Help me to spend time getting to know Jesus better by reading the Bible every day and praying about what I read. In Jesus' name, amen.

DAY 6

Shepherd Maze

Find your way through the maze from start to the finish. Along the correct path, you'll find symbols and words for today's verse. Write each verse word in the order you find them on the blank lines below.

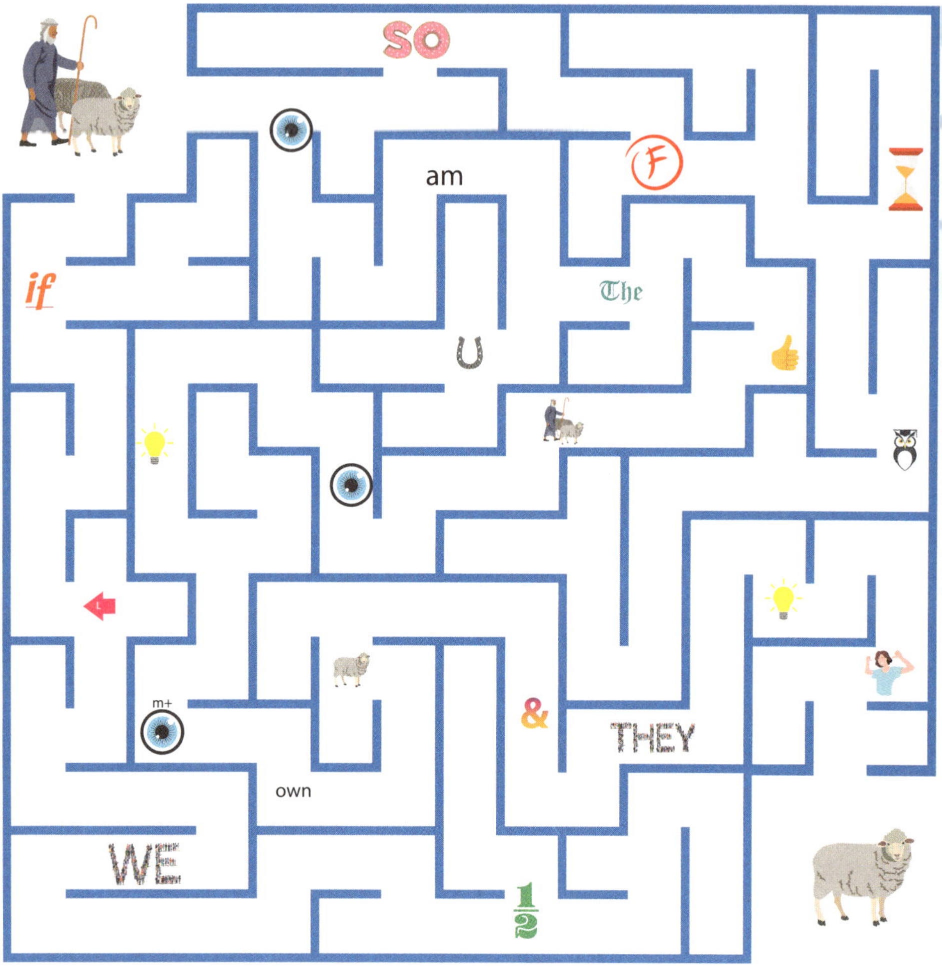

John 10:14

Answer Key on page 380.

Week 37
GOD UNDERSTANDS EVERYTHING

Look at the visual Bible verse below. Try to figure out what it says. Write the verse words on the blank lines. Use the Visual Bible Verse Dictionary on page 371, if needed.

   absolute

understanding  comprehension

_____

_____

_____

_____

_____

How great is our Lord! His power is absolute! His understanding is beyond comprehension! Psalm 147:5

DAY 1

Afternoon Blues

Nico wandered around the school. After the final bell rang, he always took his time gathering his lunch container, backpack, and other things. Nico was the last one to leave his classroom and the last to leave the school building.

As he slowly walked home, he wondered to himself, *What should I do today?* He kicked a red stone off the sidewalk. *I've done all my homework. I went to the library yesterday. Tomas can't do anything. He's got homework from being sick. Alan said he's going somewhere with his mom. Guess I'm on my own.* Nico picked up a stick and tossed it at a tree. "I'm so bored!" Nico said aloud.

Nico continued walking home kicking at stones and tossing sticks up into the air. When he walked to the end of his street, he stopped cold. He could see Nancy's car in the driveway. He balled his hands into fists and frowned. *Not again!* Nico thought angrily.

Stomping in to the house, Nico threw down his things. He went straight upstairs to his room without greeting Nancy. Nancy was Nico's family's housekeeper and sometimes his babysitter. At the moment, she was in the kitchen, making something for him to eat.

"Hello, Nico! I made you a snack," Nancy called up the stairs listening for a response. Hearing none, Nancy walked up the steps. She knocked softly on Nico's bedroom door. "Nico, are you in there? I have a snack for you." Nancy said. "Nico?"

"I'll be right down," Nico replied impatiently.

Nancy could tell that Nico was upset about something. "Lord, help me to find out what is upsetting Nico. Please let us have a good conversation. In Jesus' name, amen."

Praise the Lord!

DAY 2

Read about It

Psalm 147

Think about It

1 Today's Bible passage is a psalm, or song, of praise to God. It tells us three important things about who God is and how he keeps us safe.
- God is great.
- God is absolute (mighty).
- God comprehends everything—The word *comprehend* means understand. God understands everything.

How does it feel to know he understands everything—including everything about you?

2 Because God is great and mighty, he can do anything and everything we might ever need to be protected. Have you ever thought about God being both great and mighty? How does it make you feel?

3 Isn't it wonderful to know that God understands everything we think and feel and do? He is so great and so mighty and God understands everything. When you talk to God in prayer, remember he already knows what you are thinking and feeling. What do you want to talk with God about today?

Do Something about It

When you talk to God, remember that he already understands everything you are thinking and feeling. God is so great and mighty that he is able to do anything and everything you need to take care of you. Remember how great and mighty God is when you feel alone and sad.

Pray about It

Dear God, sometimes I feel alone and sad. I know that you already know what I am thinking and feeling, but telling you makes me feel better. I know that you understand everything I am going through and you want to help me. Please help me to trust you even when I feel so discouraged and alone. You are my great and mighty God! This is a wonderful thing. In Jesus' name, amen.

DAY 3

Hot Potato

Read the visual verse, and then write each word beneath its symbol. Next, gather your family members or friends together. Show everyone this page and review the Bible verse with them. Repeat the verse a couple of times.

Next, sit or stand in a circle and toss a beanbag, small ball, or even a potato back and forth to each other. Each time the Hot Potato is caught, the catcher says the next word in the memory verse. Be sure to have this book open to this page so you can help anyone who has trouble. Continue until as a group, you can play the game and say the verse without help.

   absolute

---

understanding  comprehension

---

Psalm 147:5

An Understanding Ear

Nico decided he'd waited long enough. He got up, went out his bedroom door, and headed downstairs, stomping on each step.

As he went, he mumbled under his breath. "I can't believe Nancy's here to babysit me. Again! I wish I didn't have to be here—alone with a babysitter!" Nico quieted as he neared the kitchen and then stepped through the doorway.

"Hi, Nico! I have one of your favorite snacks all ready for you. Your parents won't be home until later, so you won't be eating dinner until after 7:00," Nancy explained.

"Late? Again?" Nico complained. "Why can't they get home on time? I'm always here by myself. They care more about their jobs than anything else."

"I'm sorry, Nico. I know your dad and mom work a lot of hours and it's hard for you. But I know they love you," Nancy assured him.

Nico didn't say anything. He just took a plate to the kitchen table, sat down, and started munching on his veggies and hummus. Nancy brought over a glass of lemonade, sat it down in front of Nico, and took a seat next to him. "Here you go, Nico. Want to talk about what's on your mind?" Nancy asked gently.

Nico thought for a moment. Nancy really was very nice. "I just hate coming home from school every day and my parents not being here!" he blurted out angrily. "I want to spend time with them, but they are always at work or busy somewhere else. It isn't fair!" Nico groaned.

"I know how you feel, Nico. My father died when I was young so my mother had two jobs and I hardly ever saw her. It was hard on all of us," Nancy shared. Nico looked up. Nancy did understand. Maybe he could tell Nancy everything he was thinking and feeling. Nico smiled at Nancy. Nancy smiled back.

After a moment, Nancy broke the comfortable silence. "OK, so what do you want to do after your snack?" Nancy asked. "Do you have any homework?"

"Nope. Did it all," Nico said.

"Well, then, how about a video game?" Nancy suggested.

"Only if you want to lose again!" Nico laughed.

"We'll see about that!" Nancy said, laughing, too.

DAY 5

The Sun Stood Still

Read about It

Joshua 10:1–14

Think about It

1. In today's Bible passage, Joshua needed help. So he talked with God and God told Joshua that he would be victorious. God then went to work in great and mighty ways to give Joshua and the Israelites victory over their enemies. If God would stop the sun to help Joshua, what limits are there to what he could do for you? What's something you'd like to talk with God about today?

2. God is great. Tell someone why you think God is great. God is mighty. Tell someone why you think God is mighty.

3. God understands everything. Have you ever been feeling alone or sad and then something good or surprising happened and you felt better? Did you just think it was a coincidence or did you see that God was at work? Maybe God brought a friend or a family member over to encourage you? Maybe God had someone call you or send you a funny card? The next time something surprising like that happens, thank God!

Do Something about It

Spend time this week thinking about why God is great and mighty. Consider how God has proven that to you. Remember all the times God sent someone to encourage you because he understands what you are thinking and feeling.

Pray about It

Dear God, I am so thankful that you understand everything about me. It makes me feel safe and secure. I'm glad that you understand everything I am thinking and feeling. You send people to encourage me! You are a great and mighty God. Thank you for proving your great love to me by sending Jesus to die for my sins. Thank you! In Jesus' name, amen.

Hummus and Veggies

DAY 6

Read the visual verse, and then write each word on the lines below. When you're done, make and enjoy a snack like the one Nico had. Be sure to have an adult like Nancy with you to use the blender. While working together, discuss some of the reasons you have to praise God.

What You Need

- 1 14-ounce can cooked chickpeas
- 3 tablespoons extra virgin olive oil
- 1 tablespoon lemon juice
- 1 teaspoon tahini
- 1 garlic clove, crushed
- Dipping Snacks (carrot sticks, pita wedges, etc.)

What You Do

1. Drain the liquid from the can of chickpeas into a bowl and set it aside. You may need it later.
2. In a blender, place all the ingredients except the olive oil and the liquid you set aside. Begin to blend.
3. A little at a time, drizzle in olive oil. If the hummus seems too thick, add a little of the liquid you retained from the can of chickpeas. Continue blending until smooth.
4. Serve with carrot sticks, pita wedges, cucumber slices, crackers, celery sticks, or whatever fresh veggies you have on hand.

absolute  understanding  comprehension

_____

_____

_____

Psalm 147:5

Week 38

God Is My Hiding Place

Look at the visual Bible verse below. Try to figure out what it says. Write the verse words on the blank lines. Use the Visual Bible Verse Dictionary on page 371, if needed.

_____

_____

_____

_____

_____

You are my hiding place; you protect me from trouble. Psalm 32:7

Grace the Worrier

DAY 1

Scrunching up her eyes in concentration, Grace mouthed the verse words silently. Finished, she peeked at her verse card to check if she had it right. "Yes! Done!" she exclaimed happily. Her puppy Buster looked up from where he was curled up next to her on the bed. He wagged his tail as she gave him a congratulatory hug.

Grace was memorizing the Bible verses that her Sunday school class had been given for the month. "I've memorized all ten of the verses. Now I'm two weeks ahead of everyone else in the class," Grace told Buster happily. "I don't have anything to worry about for a while."

Grace worried a lot. She always tried to do her schoolwork ahead of her class. Grace did her Pioneer Girls achievement work ahead of time. And now, Grace even started memorizing all her Bible verses ahead of time.

Bouncing down the hall, she poked her head in her big sister Emily's room. "Guess what. I have all my verses memorized—for the whole month! I feel so much better now," Grace told Emily.

"That's great, Grace! But what are you going to do now that you are so far ahead in school . . . and Pioneer Girls . . . and your memory verses?" Emily teased.

"I . . . I . . . don't know," replied Grace.

"I have an idea. Why don't you start reading through those memory verses and really think about them. I mean, memorizing them is great, but they'll only really help you if you understand what they mean. Think about how God wants his promises to change your life." Emily suggested.

"What? I don't understand." Grace was confused.

"You memorized the words, but do you understand what they mean? Do you know what God promises you?" Emily asked patiently.

DAY 2: Psalm of Protection

Read about It

Psalm 32:7–11

Think about It

1. When God tells us he will be our hiding place, God doesn't mean a real building or place to hide. God is talking about helping us feel safe and secure. God wants us to take all our fear and worry and give it to him. He will comfort us and give us peace.

2. God is our hiding place. God protects us from trouble. Sometimes we may feel afraid and worried. When we do, God wants us to go to him so that he can protect us from trouble. What does it mean to you to say God is your hiding place?

3. When is a time God protected you or someone you love? Sometimes we can remember when God protected us even when we didn't think we needed protection. God knows everything that is happening even before it happens. God knows just when to bring the protection we need.

Do Something about It

When you feel afraid or worried, take time to say memory verses that promise God's protection. Think about all the words in each promise and ask God to help you understand them. Pray and ask God to show you how his promises can change you and your life.

Pray about It

Dear God, sometimes I feel worried and afraid. Please help me to understand all the promises you have in the Bible for me. Help me to know what they mean and how these promises can change my life. Thank you for being my hiding place where I can feel safe and secure. In Jesus' name, amen.

Acrostic Verse

DAY 3

Reread the visual verse on page 266, and then write each word on the lines below.

Look at the large acrostic grid on this page. What phrase do the filled-in letters spell? Fill in the empty boxes of the acrostic grid with words from the verse. Then, take the remaining words and fill out the small acrostic grid. Finally, write the remaining word in the two boxes at the bottom.

Note: Even though the word *you* appears in the verse twice, you will only use it once in the acrostic grids.

Psalm 32:7

Answer Key on page 380.

Safe from Worry

As she walked back to her room, the words her older sister had just said echoed in Grace's mind. "Grace, you spend so much time making sure that everything is done so you won't worry . . . but you do worry! Have you ever memorized a Bible verse about worry?" Emily asked. "Maybe you can slow down and take a few moments to really think about what that verse means."

Grace sat down on her bed and took out all her Bible memory cards. She began reading them—really reading them. Grace reread each promise. As she said the words out loud, she tried to think about how God could change her life.

After a while, she gathered up a few of the cards and went back down the hall. She poked her head in Emily's door and asked, "Can we talk some more?"

"Sure thing," Emily said, patting the bed next to her. Grace sat next to her sister.

"Some of these memory verses . . . Well, I understand some better than others. Why is understanding so much harder than memorizing?" Grace asked her sister.

"Memorizing is great, but if you don't understand what the words mean or if you don't understand what God is promising, these verses won't bring you much help when you need it," Emily explained. "And that's kind of the point of memorizing Bible verses. So you'll know God's promises when you need them the most."

"I'm not sure I understand," Grace said, puzzled.

"Think about this verse, Psalm 32:7. 'You are my hiding place; you protect me from trouble.' What does that make you think of?" Emily asked.

"A hiding place?" Grace thought for a moment and suddenly got an idea. "I guess it's like when there's a tornado warning and we go to the basement to be safe."

"Yeah!" Emily said. "This verse is saying God is like a place you can go and hide when you're in trouble. Just like how we feel safer to be in the basement when there's a tornado outside, God makes us feel safer when we go to him when we feel scared . . . or WORRIED!" Emily and Grace laughed.

"Yup!" Grace said. "That's good for me to know!"

Emily continued, "God wants you to trust him when you feel worried or afraid. This verse is great to remember and say out loud any time you start to feel worried or afraid. God wants you to believe every one of his promises. You can even pray these verses back to God!"

The Lord Is My Rock

DAY 5

Read about It

Psalm 18:1–3

Think about It

1 Today's psalm tells us more words used to describe how God is like a hiding place: Count them all! Write them down and look at them every day. This week's verse describes God this way, "You are my hiding place." God is our hiding place when we pray and tell him we need him. God wants to protect us from all our worries and fears.

2 "You protect me from trouble." God promises to protect us from trouble, but he expects us to make good choices. If we make bad choices and do wrong things, we shouldn't expect God to protect us from the consequences of our actions. God will protect us, but we must do our part and make good choices.

3 When we say our Bible verses out loud, pray, and ask God for help and protection. God always hears us. But sometimes we need to ask family members, friends, teachers, or other trusted people for help and protection, too. Who are some of the people you can go to for help? Thank God for each one.

Do Something about It

When you feel worried or afraid, pray and ask God for help and protection. Remember to make good choices. God promises to protect you. One way he does that is by giving you people who will protect you. Make sure to talk with those people and let them know what you are thinking and feeling—both good and bad!

Pray about It

Dear God, I am so glad you are my hiding place. Sometimes when I feel worried or afraid, I need you to hide me away from these feelings. I need your protection from feeling scared all the time. Please help me to remember that you use other people to help me, too. Thank you for all the ways you care for me. In Jesus' name, amen.

DAY 6

Hiding in a Birdhouse

Find the symbols and words of the verse on the birdhouses. In the circle next to each birdhouse, number them in verse order. Then, write the verse words in order on the blank lines below.

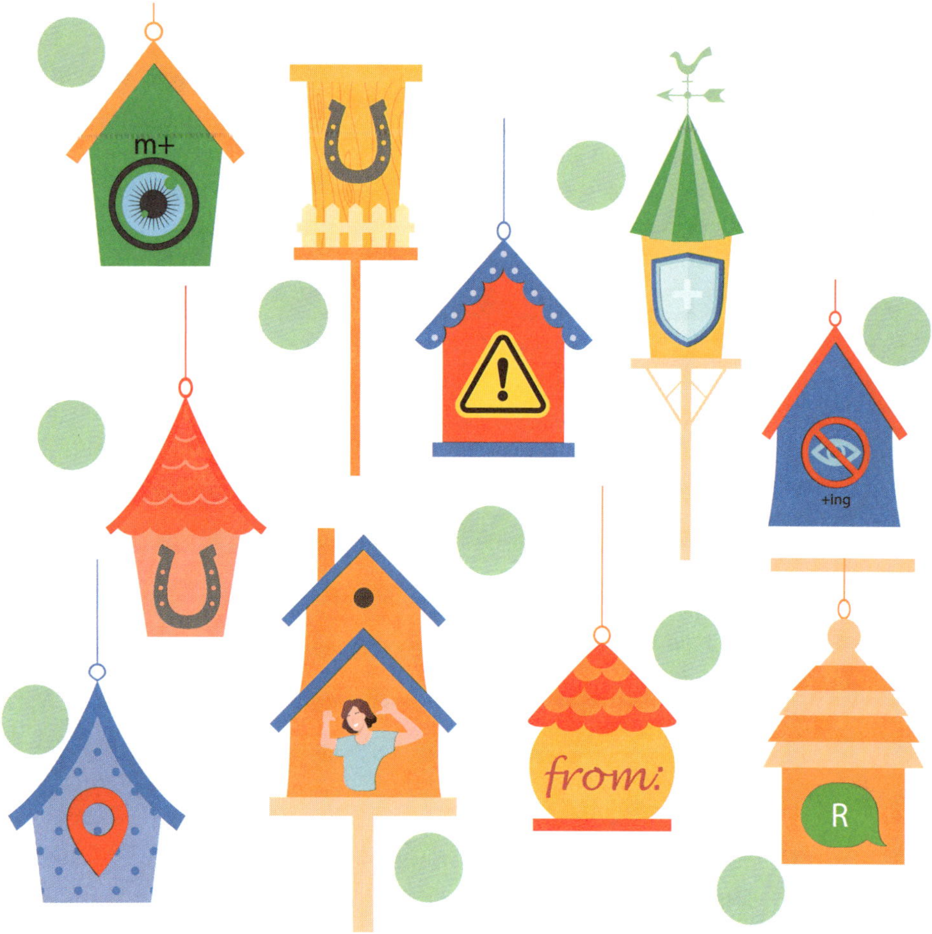

Psalm 32:7

Answer Key on page 381.

Week 39

TELL THE TRUTH TO EACH OTHER

Look at the visual Bible verse below. Try to figure out what it says. Write the verse words on the blank lines. Use the Visual Bible Verse Dictionary on page 371, if needed.

 The  +th

 each other

_____

_____

_____

_____

_____

Tell the truth to each other. Zechariah 8:16

DAY 1 — Getting It Done

Every Saturday morning, Angie had a list of chores to do. These chores were to sweep the kitchen floor, unload the dishwasher, and wipe down the cabinets, counters, and the refrigerator. Angie didn't really mind doing chores, but she just loved it when her Saturdays were free of extra work so she could sleep in and have a lazy day.

In order to make that happen, Angie often did her Saturday morning chores on Friday afternoon, especially since she rarely had homework on Fridays. One Friday afternoon, as soon as she'd put her backpack in its place in the hall closet, Angie decided to get a jumpstart on her chores.

It took a moment to find her Mom, but Angie discovered her working in the backyard garden. She stuck her head out the backdoor. "Hi, Mom! I'm going to do my chores now instead of tomorrow morning," Angie called out to her mother. "Is that OK?"

"Go right ahead! I'll be out here working for quite a while," Mom answered.

Great! Angie thought as she closed the door and turned to survey the kitchen. *I've got the whole kitchen to myself. I'll get my chores done faster with no one else inside getting in my way.* Angie got the broom and dustpan and got busy sweeping.

"That's done! Now to wipe everything down," Angie said aloud. Spray and wipe. Spray and wipe. Before Angie knew it, she had finished that chore, too!

Only one to go! Unloading the dishwasher is the easiest chore of all, Angie thought happily. Angie removed all the utensils, plates, and bowls and placed them in their proper places.

Almost done! All I need to put away are these mugs, Angie thought. Suddenly . . . *Crash!*

"Oh, no, Mom's favorite mug! I broke it!" Angie moaned out loud.

Jacob Tricks Isaac

DAY 2

Read about It

Genesis 27:1–41

Think about It

1 Today's passage tells of the time Jacob lied to and tricked his father into giving him the inheritance due to his brother Esau. Jacob's lies caused so much pain to the entire family! That's why this week's verse is short and simple. Speak the truth to each other. God wants us to know how much he values telling the truth. Speak the truth to each other. Have you ever not spoken the truth to someone? What happened? How did you feel about it?

2 Sometimes we might think a lie is an easy way to get what we want. But when we lie, God is not pleased and our lie will cause others to not trust us. Has someone ever lied to you? How did it make you feel when you found out?

3 When we speak the truth all the time, God is pleased because we have obeyed him. Others can trust us. How would you feel if your family and friends didn't think they could trust you?

Do Something about It

When you are tempted to tell a lie, remember that God wants you to speak the truth all the time. Tell the truth even if it is hard! And even if you might get into trouble. Tell the truth so that others will trust you.

Pray about It

Dear God, please help me to always tell the truth. I want to obey by speaking the truth to others even when I might get into trouble for doing something wrong. If I lie to others, then no one will trust me. I need you to help me be honest and brave with my words. If I have made a bad choice about something I have done, I need to be truthful and ask for forgiveness. Thank you for giving me the strength I need to tell the truth at all times. In Jesus' name, amen.

DAY 3: Rhythm Verse

Reread the visual verse below. Then, say it several times aloud. Finally, come up with motions for each of the three phrases shown below: clapping on each syllable of the word, stomping your feet, hopping on one foot, pumping your fists, etc. Write what you want to do on the lines under each phrase. Then practice saying the phrase and doing the motion several times. After you've practiced, perform your rhythm verse for your family or friends.

    each other

Tell the truth,

_____
_____

To each other.

_____
_____

Zechariah 8:16

_____
_____

Broken Pieces

Angie stood still looking down at the broken pieces of her mom's favorite mug. The bits of pottery were scattered all over the floor she'd just finished sweeping. She couldn't move. She couldn't breathe.

Then Angie took a look to her left. She looked to her right. She listened— hard. Had anyone else heard the crash? Angie didn't think so.

She quickly took in the damages. *I can't fix it. There are too many pieces to glue together. There's no way I could get away with it. Mom will know I broke her mug!*

She started toward the utility room to get the broom. *Maybe I will just sweep up the mess and throw the pieces away,* Angie thought to herself. Then she stopped walking and began to argue with herself.

Angie knew the right thing to do was to go outside and tell her mom what had happened. But Angie didn't want to tell Mom. "If I go outside and tell Mom I broke her mug, she'll be so disappointed, or even angry. She might think I was hurrying to get my chores done and that I was being careless," Angie whispered to herself.

A few more long minutes passed by. Angie was still arguing with herself about what was the right thing to do. *Well, no matter what, I've got to clean up this mess.* Angie went to the utility room for the broom and swept up the mess into the dustpan.

But Angie didn't throw the broken pieces away. She carefully carried them outside. She walked over to where her mom was tending to the tomato plants. Angie held out the dustpan with the broken mug. "Mom, I'm so sorry," she said softly. "I broke your favorite mug. I didn't mean to do it. But it slipped out of my hand," Angie finished sadly.

"Oh, Angie. Did you hurt yourself?" Mom asked with concern. "Did you cut your hand? Are you OK?"

"Yes, yes, I'm fine. Aren't you angry with me?" Angie fretted.

"Honey, I'm just thankful you didn't get hurt. I can always buy another mug. And . . . thank you for telling me the truth," Mom smiled as she hugged Angie tight.

DAY 5: Ananias and Sapphira

Read about It

Acts 5:1–11

Think about It

1 Today's Bible passage isn't a warning that we're going to drop dead if we tell a lie! It's a reminder that we can't lie to God. He knows when we tell lies, and that's what makes us feel bad inside. Doesn't it feel good when we tell the truth? Do you think that Angie felt so glad that she made the right choice by telling her mom what had happened?

2 When Angie was talking to herself about hiding the broken pieces of the mug, she knew it was the wrong thing to do. The Holy Spirit who lives inside of us helped remind Angie of the right choice. When is a time you were tempted to do the wrong thing, but the Holy Spirit encouraged you to do right?

3 When we tell the truth we are often surprised at others' reactions. Angie was afraid that her mom would be angry, but she wasn't. Angie's mom was thankful Angie hadn't gotten hurt and she was so glad that Angie told her the truth. When is a time things turned out differently than you expected?

Do Something about It

When you start talking to yourself about making the right choice to tell the truth or the wrong one to lie, listen to the Holy Spirit reminding you to do what is right. Pray and ask God to help you tell the truth even when you are afraid of what might happen.

Pray about It

Dear God, I know it is always the right choice to tell the truth. When I feel a little scared, please help me be brave and speak the truth. I will ask for forgiveness when I have done wrong. Please remind me that it is always a good choice to be honest and truthful. In Jesus' name, amen.

Alternate Ending

Read the visual verse, and then write each word beneath its symbol.

On the rest of the page, write an alternate ending to Angie's story. Pretend she didn't tell her mom about breaking the mug. What did she do after she swept up the broken pieces of the mug? Did her mom figure out the mug was broken? How? When? How did Angie feel through everything that happened? Is it a sad or happy story? Illustrate your story with pictures.

   each other

Zechariah 8:16

Week 40

My Body Is a Living Sacrifice to God

Look at the visual Bible verse below. Try to figure out what it says. Write the verse words on the blank lines. Use the Visual Bible Verse Dictionary on page 371, if needed.

_____

_____

_____

_____

_____

Give your bodies to God because of all he has done for you. Let them be a living and holy sacrifice.... This is truly the way to worship him. Romans 12:1

Mirror, Mirror

DAY 1

Kyra frowned before she even looked in the mirror. "I don't like this pair either," she complained. "I hate these glasses! I hate having to wear glasses, Mom!" Kyra took the glasses off and handed them to her mother.

"You know what the doctor said, Kyra. If you don't wear your glasses every day, your eyes will get weaker and your vision will get worse," Mom explained. "You can't even see the board in your classroom anymore."

"I know. I know," Kyra muttered.

"At least we know why your grades have been dropping." Mom continued. "You can't see, honey. It's important that you see well."

Kyra sighed. "I know. I know. But I feel ugly wearing them. No other girl in my class has glasses. I'll be the only one!" Kyra said through her tears.

Mom held Kyra's face in her hands and looked deep into her eyes. "You're beautiful no matter what and no glasses could ever change that." Mom hugged her. "It's not such a terrible thing, Kyra. You need these to see." Kyra nodded.

A few days later, Kyra got dressed and ready for school. She was just starting out the door when her mom called after her, "Kyra, you forgot your glasses."

Uh-oh, Kyra thought. She was hoping to get away without having to wear them. She slowly walked back to the kitchen where Mom was.

"I don't want to remind you about your glasses every morning," Mom said, handing the glasses case to Kyra who reluctantly took it. "Is this going to be a problem?"

"Oh, Mom, I think my eyes are getting stronger on their own. I can see better than ever before. I don't think I need these glasses now," Kyra said sheepishly.

"Oh, really? Well, we can make another appointment with your eye doctor to be sure," Mom told Kyra. "But insurance doesn't pay for that so if the doctor says the same thing, the cost for the appointment will come out of your allowance."

"Oh, don't! We don't have to go to the doctor," Kyra said, giving in. "I'll wear them. I will."

DAY 2: Jesus' Sacrifice

Read about It

Mark 15:21–39

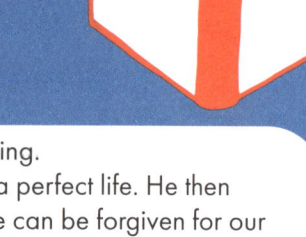

Think about It

1. The word *sacrifice* means giving up something. Jesus came to Earth as a human and lived a perfect life. He then willingly sacrificed his own body so that we can be forgiven for our sins and live with him forever in Heaven. If you would like to know more about Jesus' sacrifice and becoming a member of God's family, talk with an adult family member or whoever gave you this book.

2. One way to thank Jesus for his sacrifice is by using your body as a *living and holy sacrifice*. But what does that mean? Since it's a *living* sacrifice, God doesn't expect us to die like Jesus did. We sacrifice our bodies to God when we use them for his purposes: when we obey his word and when we serve others. What are some ways you can use your body for God by obeying him? By serving others?

3. What does worshiping God look like to you? This week's verse tells us that everything we do is worship, as long as we do it for God. How does it make you feel to know that obeying God and serving others are ways to worship God?

Do Something about It

It's wonderful to worship God by singing and praising him—but we can do even more than that. God created our bodies to worship him. Worship God by the way you work, play, study—everything you do! Every now and then, stop and think about how you can worship God in whatever it is you are doing.

Pray about It

Dear God, *sacrifice* is a fancy word to say that I am sacrificing myself and my body for your purposes. You created me just the way you wanted me to be so that I can love and serve others. Help me to be thankful for how you made me and not look at others and feel upset because I'm different. We are all different! In Jesus' name, amen.

Missing Word

Read the visual verse, and then write each word beneath its symbol. Color the visual verse. One very important word is missing. Figure out what word is missing and write it in the space.

 +r bodies

_____ _____ _____ bodies _____ _____ _____

of   has done

of _____ _____ has done _____ _____

Let    +ing

Let _____ _____ _____ _____

 holy _____ This  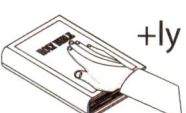+ly

_____ holy _____ This _____ _____

   worship

_____ _____ _____ worship _____

Romans 12:1

My Body Is a Living Sacrifice to God • 283

DAY 4: Seeing Clearly

Kyra left her house wearing her glasses and walked nervously to the corner. She knew as soon as she turned the corner she would probably run into her friend Lauren who lived on that street. As soon as she turned the corner, she took off her glasses and put them in their case.

I hope nobody saw me wearing those ugly glasses, Kyra thought anxiously. She looked around nervously. It looked like the coast was clear! Just then, she saw her friend step out of her house. "Hey, Lauren!" Kyra called out happily. The two friends walked to school together and played on the playground until the bell rang.

Everything was fine at first. But then, Mrs. O'Brein told the class to do the math assignment written on the board. Looking up toward the board at the front of the room, Kyra got scared. *Oh, no! I can't see the problems*, she thought. *Mom was right. I do need my glasses or I can't get my work done.*

For a few minutes, Kyra just sat in her chair and worried about what her classmates would say. Then Mrs. O'Brein noticed she wasn't working. "Kyra, let's get to work on that math assignment," she gently scolded. Finally, slowly, Kyra took her glasses out of their case and put them on.

She looked at the board. *Oh! That's much better. I can read everything now*, Kyra thought, smiling to herself. She looked outside the windows and saw the pretty blue sky with the fluffy white clouds. She heard birds singing and then saw some birds land on the roof of the school. Kyra then noticed the beautiful flowers that were blooming all along the window edge. *Oh, so pretty!* Kyra thought.

Suddenly, Kyra felt sad. She understood what Mom had been trying to teach her. God had made everything special. God had made her special. Before starting her assignment, Kyra took a quick moment to pray.

> "Dear God, please forgive me for complaining about how you made my eyes. I am so happy that I can see the beautiful world you created. Help me to use my eyes and my whole body in ways that will please you. In Jesus' name, amen."

Jesus Washes the Disciples' Feet

DAY 5

Read about It

John 13:1–17

Think about It

1. Our passage today is from the last supper. Jesus washed his disciples' feet as an example of the way they should serve each other. God wants us to love and serve others. He made us the way we are so that we could each serve others in unique ways. Have you ever wished that God had made you different than you are?

2. God thought about us before he created us. God knows the special gifts, talents, and abilities he has for each of us. When we get upset because we can't do something or we don't look like someone, God is sad. He made us perfectly! What are some of the things about you that are unique and different? How can you use those things to serve God?

3. Our bodies belong to God. We can thank God for making our bodies special by serving others. How can you use your body this week to love and serve others?

Do Something about It

When you feel sad or upset because you don't like how God made you, remember that God created you exactly the way he wanted you to be. God has already planned all the good ways he will use your body to love and serve others. Say thank you to God!

Pray about It

Dear God, I know that you have made me exactly the way you want me to be. You created me to look like I do and you have given me gifts and talents to use to love and serve others. Please help me to remember that my body belongs to you! I want to obey you and serve you with my body. In Jesus' name, amen.

Healthy v. Unhealthy

DAY 6

There are a number of different healthy body options shown below. Color all the healthy body options. Cross out the unhealthy options.

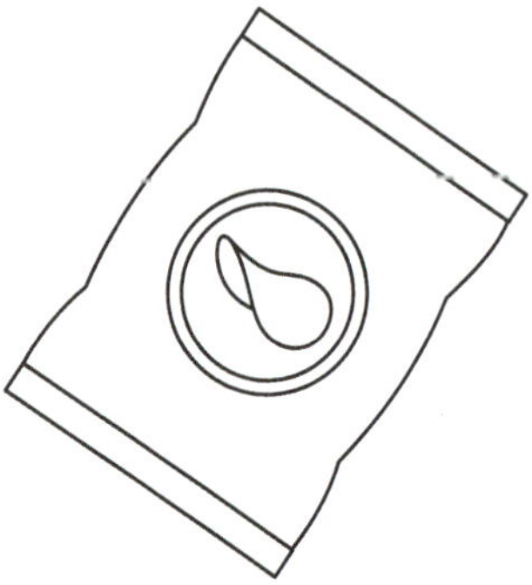

286 · My Body Is a Living Sacrifice to God

Week 41
EVERYTHING BELONGS TO GOD

Look at the visual Bible verse below. Try to figure out what it says. Write the verse words on the blank lines. Use the Visual Bible Verse Dictionary on page 371, if needed.

The   The 's

 everything  it The

  its belong

_____

_____

_____

_____

_____

The earth is the Lord's, and everything in it. The world and all its people belong to him. Psalm 24:1

DAY 1

Jared's Collection

Jared looked at his baseball cards all spread out so that he could see them. Jared loved collecting baseball cards. Every year for his birthday and for Christmas, Jared asked for baseball cards to add to his collection. Jared was crazy about baseball. He loved playing it. He loved watching it.

His brother James collected coins—all sorts of coins from those minted many years ago to brand-new, just-released coins. James loved his coin collection and going to coin stores as much as Jared loved baseball. Jared sighed happily as he looked at his cards. Then, feeling thirsty, he left the bedroom he shared with James to get a water bottle.

As he was filling his water bottle, James came in from taking out the trash. The brothers nodded at each other as they passed. A moment later, James hollered from the bedroom.

"Jared, you need to move your baseball cards off of my bed. Now!" yelled James. Jared had spread all his cards over both twin beds in the room he shared with James.

"Don't touch them. I'll be right back," responded Jared, who was trying to twist on the lid to his water bottle. James looked at Jared's baseball cards all spread out over his whole bed. He wanted to shake them off onto the floor. But he didn't.

Jared hurried back into the room. "Thanks for not touching them, James. I'm putting all my cards in order of their value. The most expensive ones are here," Jared said pointing to the top row of cards on James' bed.

"They all look the same to me," said James, dismissively.

"Are you kidding? Look at each one, they are all unique," Jared said as he passed one to James to study.

"Still don't see why you collect these things. You should collect coins like me. I'll always get my money back, even if it is just the amount of the coin itself. Yours are just pieces of paper," James said unkindly.

Jared didn't reply. He had already heard this before from James, but he didn't care. Jared would collect what he loved most. Baseball cards!

The Earth Is the Lord's

DAY 2

Read about It

Psalm 24

Think about It

1 This psalm makes it clear that God created everything on Earth and it belongs to him. That's why we have to take care of the things he gives us. Have you ever thought about this before? That everything belongs to God, but he gives us things to use? How does that change the way you think of the things that belong to you? Of things that belong to others?

2 God is the creator of everything that lives on Earth, too. This means the plants, animals, and even we, his people, belong to God. God is our creator and we are his creations. How does it make you feel to know that God is your creator and your heavenly Father?

3 Does this make you think differently about the way you treat your things? What about things that are your favorites? What about things you don't really like?

Do Something about It

When you look around at all the things in your room—your clothes, your books, your toys, your games—thank God for giving them to you. When you think about the people in your life—your family, friends, and others—thank God for giving these people to you.

Pray about It

Dear God, thank you for everything that you have given me to use and to enjoy. I know that everything on the earth belongs to you, including me. Thank you for being my creator and my heavenly father. You show me all the time how much you care about me through the creation of this beautiful world. In Jesus' name, amen.

DAY 3 Everything in It

Read the visual verse, and then write each word on the lines below. Finally, use fine-tipped colored pens or pencils to color in the pictures.

The 🌍 is The 👑's & everything in it

The 🗺, & all its 👥 belong ✌ 🧍‍♂️🧍‍♀️

_____

_____

Psalm 24:1

What a Mess!

"Make sure you clean off my bed," James told Jared.

"I will. I will," Jared assured him. He picked up his favorite—a birthday gift from his parents when he first started collecting cards several years earlier. "Let me see how much you're worth now," Jared said aloud. He picked up a book that listed the value of his cards, flipping through the pages until he found what he was looking for. "Wow! You're worth over fifty dollars!" Jared said to the card. "I have to tell Dad!"

Jared raced down to find his father who was in the garage. After Dad had congratulated him, Jared got so excited about how much his card was worth that he decided to tell his neighborhood friends. "Be back in a while, Dad," Jared called.

James had been outside when we saw Jared run down the street. "I'll bet all of his cards are still on my bed," James complained to himself. He peddled for home.

Once in the house, James ran up the stairs to the bedroom, and he was right. All the Jared's cards were still on the bed. "I'll show him," James said out loud. He grabbed the bottom corners of his bedspread, lifted it, and then shook as hard as he could. All of the cards went flying.

"What did you just do?" James' father asked as he looked into the boys' bedroom and saw the mess. He'd come inside to take a shower and had heard James as he was walking down the hall.

James froze under his father's gaze. "I . . . uh . . . I . . ." James stammered. He felt so ashamed of his angry outburst, he couldn't answer his father.

"You know better than that. Those are your brother's cards and you just treated them without any care at all," Dad reminded James. "Do you think God was pleased with what you just did?"

James hung his head. "No." James said. "Dad, I'm sorry. I wasn't thinking."

"What are you going to do about it?" Dad asked.

James sighed. "Well, I'm guess I'm going to pick up the cards," he said.

"That's a good start," Dad responded. "Then what?"

"Then I'll tell Jared I'm sorry I messed with them. I really am sorry, Dad!" James said. "I guess I need to pray and tell God I'm sorry, too. Then I'll help Jared put the cards away."

DAY 5: God of Gods and Lord of Lords

Read about It

Deuteronomy 10:12–22

Think about It

1. Today's Bible passage states again that everything in Heaven and Earth belong to God. Because the earth is the Lord's, how can we show God through our actions that we appreciate the world he created?

2. How can we show God we understand that everything on Earth belongs to him? Think in terms of sharing with others and respecting their things. How might this understanding change your actions?

3. How do you care for all the living things (that includes people!)? Are we loving and kind? Or do we only think about ourselves? What kinds of actions show that we are caring for living things?

Do Something about It

Take good care of everything God created. Be loving and kind to the people God created.

Pray about It

Dear God, please help me find good ways to take care of this world. When I see trash, please remind me to pick it up. When I see something that is broken, help me to try and fix it. When I see someone who has a need, help me share what I have with them. Teach me to understand that because you created this world, you expect us to take good care of it and everything in it. In Jesus' name, amen.

Verse Stack

DAY 6

Carefully look over each symbol in the vertical column. Say the word for each symbol aloud. Fill in the missing words on the blank lines. Next, say the entire verse aloud, write it in the empty space, and then make up motions to do with the verse. Repeat saying and doing motions with the verse until you know it by heart. Finally, in whatever space remains, draw pictures of or write about things this verse reminds you of.

Psalm 24:1

Everything Belongs to God

Week 42

We Should Speak as God Would Speak

Look at the visual Bible verse below. Try to figure out what it says. Write the verse words on the blank lines. Use the Visual Bible Verse Dictionary on page 371, if needed.

 as though   + self

were  +ing

_____
_____
_____
_____
_____

Speak as though God himself were speaking through you. 1 Peter 4:11

Chase Chases

DAY 1

"Chase! Leah!" Hearing their names coming from their aunt in that particular tone was enough to make the brother and sister stop arguing immediately. They'd started out planning to play a video game together and then ended up yelling at each other about which game they would play.

"That is enough," Aunt Susan said firmly. "I have been listening to the two of you argue and interrupt each other all morning. Go outside and find something to do," Aunt Susan ordered.

Chase and Leah gave each other a nasty look, but they didn't argue with their aunt. They knew better.

As soon as the door swung shut behind them, their aunt shook her head. She prayed that both Chase and Leah would learn to talk kindly and listen to each other. Neither of them talked in a way that would please God. And neither Chase nor Leah listened to the other at all.

Outside, things weren't going any better than they had inside. Chase grabbed his scooter and off he went. Leah jumped on her scooter and followed Chase.

"Get away from me!" Chase yelled at Leah.

"Make me!" challenged Leah.

"OK, I will," Chase said. He turned around and began to chase Leah. She turned and took off as fast as she could.

"Stop it. Stop it! You're going to make me fall," Leah cried as Chase got closer and closer.

"You started it!" Chase said.

Aunt Susan stood at the window, looking out. She had heard the entire conversation. She went to the front door, opened it, and called out to her niece and nephew. "Chase! Leah! Come back here right now!" Aunt Susan called.

We Should Speak as God Would Speak · 295

DAY 2: Good and Helpful

Read about It

Ephesians 4:25–29

Think about It

1 Today's passage is teaching from the apostle Paul. It's all about handling anger and using words wisely. We have a choice to make about speaking. We can choose to stay quiet. Sometimes the best choice is to stay quiet. This is especially true if you feel upset and angry and are tempted to use your words to hurt someone else. When have you said something in anger that you wish you hadn't?

2 Our visual Bible verse tells us that when we do speak, we should think about our words before we say them. Every word we say will either help someone or hurt them. When have you spoken before you thought about what you were saying? Did it help or hurt the situation?

3 Our words should always show God's love to others. When we speak, we are talking as if we represent God because we do. Our words need to be truthful and loving. How will knowing that you represent God when you speak change the way you talk to others?

Do Something about It

When you feel upset or angry, pray and ask God for the self-control to stay quiet. Wait until you can talk lovingly and truthfully. Remember that your words represent God and his love.

Pray about It

Dear God, sometimes I feel upset and angry. When I do, it is hard to stay silent! I need your help to be quiet until I calm down. Help me remember that all of my words represent you and your love for people. Thank you for helping me to think about my words before I say them. In Jesus' name, amen.

What Can You Say?

Read the visual verse, and then write each word on the lines below. Then, read the descriptions below of two different situations. Write or draw your response in the space provided.

 as though         were   +ing

_____

_____

1 Peter 4:11

When your best friend borrows your video game and loses it . . . What can you say?

When your baby sister has drawn all over your favorite book . . . What can you say?

We Should Speak as God Would Speak

DAY 4

Straight Talk

Chase and Leah sat down on the couch like Aunt Susan had told them. "Let's talk about how you are both using your words," Aunt Susan started.

Chase immediately piped up. "She started it," he said, pointing to Leah.

"No, I didn't," Leah said. "It's his fault!" She pointed at Chase.

"It doesn't matter who started it. You're both responsible. Do you think that the way you both were speaking to each other was loving or kind?" Aunt Susan waited for an answer. Chase and Leah looked at her, at each other, and then shrugged.

"Let me put it this way: Chase, think about some of the things you said to Leah. Would you want someone to talk to you that way?" Chase hung his head. "How about you, Leah? Would you want someone to say the words you said and use the tones you used with your brother today?"

"No," Leah whispered.

Aunt Susan nodded before continuing softly, "Do you think God was pleased with how you treated each other?" Chase hung his head lower. Leah looked up, saddened. Neither of them looked at Aunt Susan because they were ashamed of how they had been acting.

"Well, I should have been nicer to Leah," Chase admitted.

"I shouldn't have followed Chase down the street. I knew it would make him angry," Leah shared.

"OK . . . well, admitting what you did wrong is a good start. But I want you both to understand that every word we speak should show God's love to others," Aunt Susan said. Chase and Leah looked at each other. They hadn't said one nice thing to each other all morning!

"We have to make good choices whenever we speak." Aunt Susan explained. "Sometimes it is better not to talk at all if we are angry. But God wants us to understand that all words are his words. We use the words to represent God to everyone we meet."

"I get it. I'll try harder to speak kindly," Chase said.

"So will I," Leah agreed.

Controlling the Tongue

Read about It

James 3:1–12

Think about It

1. Today's Bible passage has a lot to say about how our words can affect others. This week's verse also encourages us to speak as if we are speaking for God. As God's people, what we say reflects back on God. What are some thing you can say that would reflect God's love for others?

2. If we're not sure what to say, we always have the option of staying quiet and not saying a word. Can you remember a time when you should have stayed quiet because you were too upset to talk kindly? Did you speak or did you stay quiet? What happened?

3. When we speak, God tells us we are to say words that help and encourage others. What are some helpful and encouraging words you can practice saying right now?

Do Something about It

When you say something, remember that all words are really God's words. Take care that your words represent God's love to whomever you are talking.

Pray about It

Dear God, all words are your words. You gave us words to use to help and encourage each other. Sometimes I don't use my words to be helpful. I use them to hurt people when I am angry. Please help me not to use angry words. I want to speak kindly and lovingly. In Jesus' name, amen.

Word Hunt

DAY 6

This week's verse is all about finding the right words to say. Find the right words from the visual Bible verse in the words below. Circle each verse word. Number the words in verse order. Finally, write the words in verse order on the blank lines at the bottom of the page.

_____

_____

_____

1 Peter 4:11

Week 43

WE CAN BE STRONG IN GOD'S MIGHTY POWER

Look at the visual Bible verse below. Try to figure out what it says. Write the verse words on the blank lines. Use the Visual Bible Verse Dictionary on page 371, if needed.

 mighty

_____

_____

_____

_____

_____

Be strong in the Lord and in his mighty power. Ephesians 6:10

DAY 1

The Tryout

The sun was warm on her back as Meg sat on the bench waiting for her turn to go up to bat. Her team had already been out in the field. She was assigned to left field, where she had done her best to catch balls that batters hit her way. Meg hadn't caught a single ball. Not one. So she was really anxious about being up to bat.

I have to hit the ball. I have to hit it so far out that the outfielder will have to run hard to get it, Meg chanted in her head. *Or better yet, a home run! Yeah . . . Like that could happen!*

It was especially important to Meg that she play well today. This was a tryout. All of Meg's friends were on her school's traveling softball team. All of them. Except for Meg. This meant Meg was often left at home alone on weekends while her friends were away playing softball for the traveling team.

Her best friend Dee encouraged Meg to try out. Meg was super nervous about trying out. She knew she wasn't as talented as her friends.

"Come on, Meg! You have to at least try to get on our team," Dee told Meg. "I want you to be with us when we play games out of town. If you make it, then we will all be together on the weekends, too. Please try!"

Meg didn't really want to try out. In her heart she knew she wasn't a fast runner. She wasn't a great catcher. She wasn't a good batter. Those were all pretty important to being a good softball player.

But, Meg so wanted to be with her friends, she had agreed to try. *Dee talked me into trying out, but I knew I wasn't as good as the other team members. I'm going to embarrass myself when I step up to bat. Oh, I wish I hadn't listened to Dee! This is so hard,* Meg thought to herself.

302 · We Can be Strong in God's Mighty Power

The Whole Armor of God

DAY 2

Read about It

Ephesians 6:10–20

Think about It

1 This week's verse is from today's Bible passage, a very popular passage of Scripture. It helps all of us in God's family know how to equip ourselves to face difficulties in our lives. It helps us to understand how we can be brave when we need to be. Our verse tells us it isn't about our own strength, our own power. It is God's power! When is a time you needed strength from God? What did you do?

2 There will be times we all feel weak and afraid. We will be certain that we can't do something on our own. At those times it's important to remember to pray and ask God for his strength. What is something you'd like to ask God for his strength about today?

3 Think about a time when you needed to be brave and to be strong. God wants us to remember that when we feel weak, he will help us. But even when we feel strong, we still need God's help! God is our strength and he is our mighty God every day of our lives. How can remembering God is the true source of strength help us even when we feel strong?

Do Something about It

When you feel weak, pray and ask God to give you the strength you need. When you feel strong, pray and thank God for giving you what you need. Remember to pray at all times, because it is God who gives you what you need every day of your life.

Pray about It

Dear God, sometimes I feel weak and scared before trying something new. Help me remember to talk to you in prayer about how I am feeling. Please give me your strength to do whatever you call me to do. And help me to remember that even when I feel strong, I still need your strength every day of my life. In Jesus' name, amen.

DAY 3

Verse Cross

Write the words of the verse both vertically and horizontally on the lines given. The verses form a cross at the word *Lord*. That reminds us that it's because of Jesus' death on the cross that we can have strength and power from the Lord.

What are some things you would like God's strength and power to do? Write or draw about them in the space available. Then, take a few minutes to pray and talk to God about them.

🐝 💪 IN The 👑 & IN HIS mighty ⏻

_____

_____

_____

_____

LORD

_____

_____

_____

_____

_____

Ephesians 6:10

304 · We Can be Strong in God's Mighty Power

At Bat

How am I ever going to get through this? Meg wondered. Then, she remembered God's power and how it can make you strong.

Meg squeezed her eyes shut and quickly prayed silently. *Dear God, please help me be strong. Help me hit the ball at least one time! Please, God, please!*

Meg took her stance and concentrated on the ball. Strike one! Another ball whooshed right by her bat. Strike two! A third ball was coming straight for her . . . Meg swung . . . Strike three! "You're out," called the umpire.

Meg froze in place. She was so sad and defeated. It was like the world blurred away. *I failed! I'm the worst at softball!* Meg sniffled trying to hold back her tears.

The rest of the tryout was more of the same: one missed ball after another when she was in the outfield. The best she did at bat was hitting the ball directly to the first-base player who easily got her out.

"Meg, I know you're disappointed. But you tried your best," Mom encouraged.

"Mom, I did awful! Why didn't God help me?" Meg asked.

"Prayer doesn't work like that. You prayed and asked God for help. But maybe God is giving you strength to accept your failure. Maybe God is wanting you to trust that he has something better for you."

Meg didn't say anything "I was surprised you even wanted to be on the team. You've never been interested in softball before. Why now?"

"Because all my friends are on the team! Dee encouraged me to tryout." Meg suddenly felt angry. "How could she do that to me? I thought she was my friend!"

"Dee is your friend. She wanted you to try out so you could be together more. Don't let your disappointment turn to anger," Mom said.

Meg sighed. "You're right, Mom. Dee is a good friend. And I tried out because I wanted to be with her and our other friends." Mom had pulled into the driveway and put the car in park. She turned to look at Meg.

"Meg, you are good at so many different things. Why don't we sit down and make a list of activities you really enjoy?" Mom suggested. "Let's focus on helping you do those things."

"OK, Mom." Meg paused for a moment and then added, "I really don't like playing softball that much anyway. It's too stressful!" Meg admitted. She and Mom laughed.

DAY 5: Joshua and Caleb

Read about It

Numbers 13—14:9

Think about It

1 Today's Bible passage is just after Moses led the Israelites out of slavery in Egypt. God had promised them a beautiful land to make their home. Joshua and Caleb were confident that God would give his people the strength they would need to take over the land. The other ten men were scared. How would you have felt if you were Joshua and Caleb?

2 God has made each person with strengths and weaknesses. God wants us to discover what we are good at and then do our very best to develop those special gifts and talents. What are some things you particularly enjoy doing? Are there times you fail doing things you're good at?

3 When we try to do our best, God is pleased. Even when we feel discouraged that we haven't done well, God is still pleased. We must remember that God is happy when we try our best. This can help us have good attitudes even if we lose. When have you tried something that you were afraid to try? How did you feel, even if you didn't do well that first time?

Do Something about It

When you try your best, be content even if you lose. Remind yourself that God only expects you to try hard. God doesn't care if you win or lose. He loves you and wants you to discover the special gifts and talents he has given you. When you pray and ask God for strength, sometimes he gives you the strength to accept that you have failed.

Pray about It

Dear God, sometimes I don't do well at the things I try. Help me remember that talking with you helps me feel better. I know that you only want me to do my best. It doesn't matter if I win or lose. Please help me to keep trying different things so that I can discover the gifts and talents you have given me. In Jesus' name, amen.

Symbol Memory

Remember what the symbols are for the verse and draw each one in the appropriate box.

Be **strong** **in**

the **Lord** **and**

in **his** **power**

mighty

Ephesians 6:10

We Can be Strong in God's Mighty Power

Week 44
Love Never Gives Up

Look at the visual Bible verse below. Try to figure out what it says. Write the verse words on the blank lines. Use the Visual Bible Verse Dictionary on page 371, if needed.

Love never gives up. 1 Corinthians 13:7

Violin Practice

DAY 1

Bree finished her song with a final flourish of eighth notes. She had just started the next of her violin recital songs when she heard the door to the garage open. "Dad's home!" Bree squealed and jumped up to welcome him home with a hug.

All morning, after Sunday morning services, Bree had practiced. She hoped she could play her songs for her dad before he had to leave for the evening church service. He was the pastor of their church. "Hello there, Bree." Dad said as she crashed into him with a hug. "I heard your lovely music playing from outside. I had my windows open and it sounded wonderful."

"Thanks, Dad!" Bree beamed.

"Are you excited about your recital this week?" Dad inquired.

"Oh, yes! I am so excited!" Bree exclaimed breathlessly. "I get to play three songs: two by myself and one with my teacher. You are coming to my recital, right?" Bree asked hopefully.

"Absolutely, Bree. I have it on my calendar." He showed her his phone calendar as he recited the facts. "Thursday evening at 7:00 at the library."

"Oh, good. I don't want you to forget!" Bree said.

"Never! I would never forget such an important event as your violin recital. Every day when you practice I'm being reminded," Dad teased.

"Oh Dad!" Bree laughed.

"Is Mom in the kitchen cooking?" Dad asked. "I smell something wonderful."

"I think so, I haven't been in there for a while. Not since I started practicing," Bree replied.

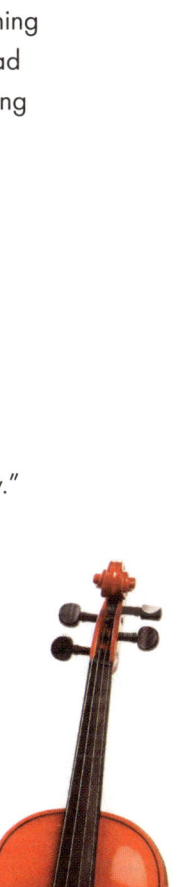

Dad left in search of food, his nose leading him straight to the kitchen. Bree began practicing again. A while later, Bree was still playing when her mom called her in for their Sunday lunch.

"Dinner's ready, Bree!" Mom called.

"Coming!" she replied. *I'm starved. All that practicing has made me hungry*, Bree thought as she hurried to the kitchen.

Love Never Gives Up

DAY 2

The Love Chapter
1 Corinthians 13

Think about It

1 Today's Bible passage includes this week's verse. It's often called "The Love Chapter" because it describes godly love so well. God wants us to show the same kind of forever love to others that he shows us. God always forgives us when we sin or make a bad choice. Always. But when someone hurts us or disappoints us, is it easy to forgive them? What can help you when it's hard to forgive someone?

2 This week's verse is short and sweet.
- Short—Love never gives up.
- Sweet—Love is sweet.

God wants us to understand that his love for us never stops. It doesn't stop when we have sinned. It doesn't stop if we forget to pray. It doesn't stop if we have a bad day. It never stops. God's love is a forever and always kind of love.

3 God tells us that real love never gives up. That means even when someone fails us we shouldn't give up on them, but continue to show them love. God never asks us to do something without giving us the strength to do it. Have you ever felt so upset with someone that you didn't want to show love? What can you do to have the strength to show love even when you don't feel loving?

Do Something about It

When someone hurts you and you are upset and angry, pray and ask God to give you the strength to show that person love. Remember that God always forgives you and he never gives up on you or stops loving you.

Pray about It

Dear God, I want to show the kind of love to others that you show to me. Your love for me never gives up. Your love for me never stops even when I have sinned and done wrong. You are faithful to forgive me and to keep on loving me. Please help me to remember this kind of faithful love when someone hurts me and it is hard to forgive and love. In Jesus' name, amen.

What Love Is

Read the visual verse, and then write each word beneath its symbol. On the rest of the page, write or draw other characteristics of love listed in 1 Corinthians 13.

 never

1 Corinthians 13:7

Sunday Dinner

Bree sat down to enjoy Sunday lunch with her parents. "Yum!" Bree exclaimed. "Barbeque chicken! Thanks Mom!"

Bree's dad prayed, "Thank you, Lord, for this wonderful meal. We thank you for providing so well for us. Thank you for giving us a loving family. Be with us as we enjoy your gifts, and please bless this food. In Jesus' name, amen."

The family passed around the platter of chicken and the bowls of corn and mashed potatoes. The family chatted about church and Bree's recital as they enjoyed their meal.

Suddenly, Dad's phone rang. "Let it ring. I'll check the message after we are finished eating," Dad said.

"This is so good! I was practicing for so long I forgot to get a snack after church," Bree explained as she reached for another piece of chicken.

After lunch, Dad went to check the phone messages as Mom and Bree cleared the table. He began to frown as he listened. Mom noticed his face changing into a sad one.

"What happened? Who was it?" Mom asked when he put down the phone.

"I'm afraid I can't attend Bree's recital on Thursday. There is an emergency meeting the board of elders just set up. Apparently, there is an emergency situation with a member at our church who needs help."

Bree's face fell and she struggled not to cry. Dad went to her and held her hands in his. "I'm so sorry, Bree. I was looking forward to hearing you play," Dad said sadly.

Bree didn't reply. She was so disappointed! But she knew her dad had a very important job. Finally, Bree took a deep breath. "I wish you could be there, Dad. But I know sometimes other people need your help, too. It's OK," she said slowly.

Her dad wrapped her in a deep hug. "I'm so proud of you, Bree! It shows God's love that you care about the needs of others above your own desires."

"I know what!" Mom said brightly. "I'll video the recital! And then the three of us can have our own private recital on Friday evening. We'll make a party of it. I'll make pizza and a special dessert to enjoy while we listen to Bree's lovely music. You can pick the dessert, Bree," Mom suggested. How does that sound?"

"Great!" Bree and her dad answered in unison.

The Lost Coin

DAY 5

Read about It

Luke 15:8–10

Think about It

1. Love never gives up. Our Bible passage today is a story Jesus told to try to explain God's love to others. In the same way, the woman didn't give up and kept searching until she found her lost coin, God's love for us never gives up either. How does it make you feel to know that God loves you so much that he'll never give up on you?

2. Love never gives up. Bree was sad that her father couldn't attend her piano recital, but Bree forgave her dad. She showed God's faithful love to her dad even though she felt sad. She also showed love to the people who needed her father's help. It might have been easy for Bree to get upset and say something unkind, but she didn't. Bree understood that real love sometimes means giving up what we want so that others can love someone in need.

3. Love never gives up. God's love is always strong and faithful even when our love gives up. Sometimes we can give up on showing love, but God's love never does. Have you ever felt so sad that you wanted to give up on loving others? God promises to give us the strength to love and to not stop.

Do Something about It

When you are feeling sad and feel like giving up on showing love to others, remember that God promises to give you the strength and grace to love even when you don't feel like it. Real love never gives up. Pray and ask God for the help you need to love like he does. He promises to give it to you.

Pray about It

Dear God, please help me to show love even when I don't feel like it. Sometimes my feelings are sad or they get hurt, and I don't want to think of good ways to show love. I want someone to love me! But you always love me, God. Your love for me never gives up. Help me to think about this when I don't feel like showing love to others. In Jesus' name, amen.

L Is for Love

Read the visual verse, and then write each word beneath its symbol. Next to each letter of the verse, write a way you can show love that starts with that letter. For example, L is for Lose a bad attitude.

 never

_____ _____ _____ _____

1 Corinthians 13:7

L is for . . . _____

O is for . . . _____

V is for . . . _____

E is for . . . _____

N is for . . . _____

E is for . . . _____

V is for . . . _____

E is for . . . _____

R is for . . . _____

G is for . . . _____

I is for . . . _____

V is for . . . _____

E is for . . . _____

S is for . . . _____

U is for . . . _____

P is for . . . _____

Week 45
I Need Faith to Please God

Look at the visual Bible verse below. Try to figure out what it says. Write the verse words on the blank lines. Use the Visual Bible Verse Dictionary on page 371, if needed.

It    please

_____

_____

_____

_____

_____

It is impossible to please God without faith. Hebrews 11:6

DAY 1

The New Girl

It was a normal morning, but Lizzy could not stop thinking about a new girl her class, Emily.

Lizzy had tried to talk with Emily several times, but Emily never said anything to anyone. During lunch and recess, Lizzy had overheard the other kids talking about Emily. Everyone seemed to think Emily was strange! Lizzy just felt sad for her. She was certain that God wanted her to try and be Emily's friend, but Emily wasn't friendly. Lizzy wasn't sure what she should do next.

"Lizzy! Time to go," Mom called.

"Coming," Lizzy replied and headed out to join her mother in the car.

On the way to school, Lizzy looked out the window. *I just can't figure out why Emily won't talk to me*, she thought as she watched the houses pass by. Lizzy looked at her mom. "Hey, Mom? Can I ask you something?"

"Sure, Lizzy," Mom said.

"Do you remember that new girl I told you about at school? Emily?" Lizzy questioned.

"Sure. I remember you telling me a new girl had moved here," Mom replied.

"Well, I have tried to talk to her, but she won't talk to me or anyone else. It's weird! The other kids in my class are starting to talk about Emily, and they're not being nice," Lizzy shared.

"Well, that's not good. It's too bad the other kids are saying unkind things about Emily. Do you think she just might be shy? Maybe she's too nervous to talk with people she doesn't know," Mom suggested.

"I guess." Lizzy said feeling puzzled. "But how is she ever going to get to know us if she never talks?" Lizzy asked.

"Hmm, well, when I'm not sure about why someone is acting a certain way, I ask myself how I would want to be treated. Then I speak and act toward that person the same way I would hope others would speak and act toward me," Mom said. "Make sense?"

"I know that verse. 'Do to others how you would want others to do to you.' Right?" Lizzy asked.

"Something like that!" Mom said.

The Faith Hall of Fame

DAY 2

Read about It

Hebrews 11

Think about It

1 This week's verse is part of today's Bible passage which gives examples of people who had faith. And their faith led to action! Let's begin with a question. According to this week's verse, what pleases God? Faith! Faith pleases God which means when we believe that God will do what he says he will do . . . that is having faith in God. Why can we believe that God will do what he says he will do?

2 Without faith it is impossible to please God. If we feel we know what God wants us to do—like Lizzy felt God wanted her to make friends with Emily—we have to have faith that God will give us what we need to follow his will. What do you feel God is asking you to do?

3 We need to trust God and believe that he will do what he says by having faith in him. God never lies. God is all-powerful. God is the creator and sustainer of life. If we have trouble-trusting God, we can ask him for more faith to trust him more! What are some other ways you can know more about God? The more you know about God, the more you will trust him and have faith he will do what he says!

Do Something about It

When you are confused about what God is doing in your life, pray and ask God to help you trust him more. Believe that God always does what he promises in the Bible. Even when it is hard to do what you know he wants you to do, choose to trust him. Then take action!

Pray about It

Dear God, please help me to trust you at all times. Help me to be patient and trust you to work everything out for my good, like you promise in the Bible. I want to have a strong faith and to trust and believe in you. Please help me to remember that you never lie, you are all powerful, and you love me. In Jesus' name, amen.

Faith Maze

Find your way through the maze from start to the finish. Along the correct path, you'll find symbols and words for today's verse. Write each verse word in the order you find them on the blank lines below.

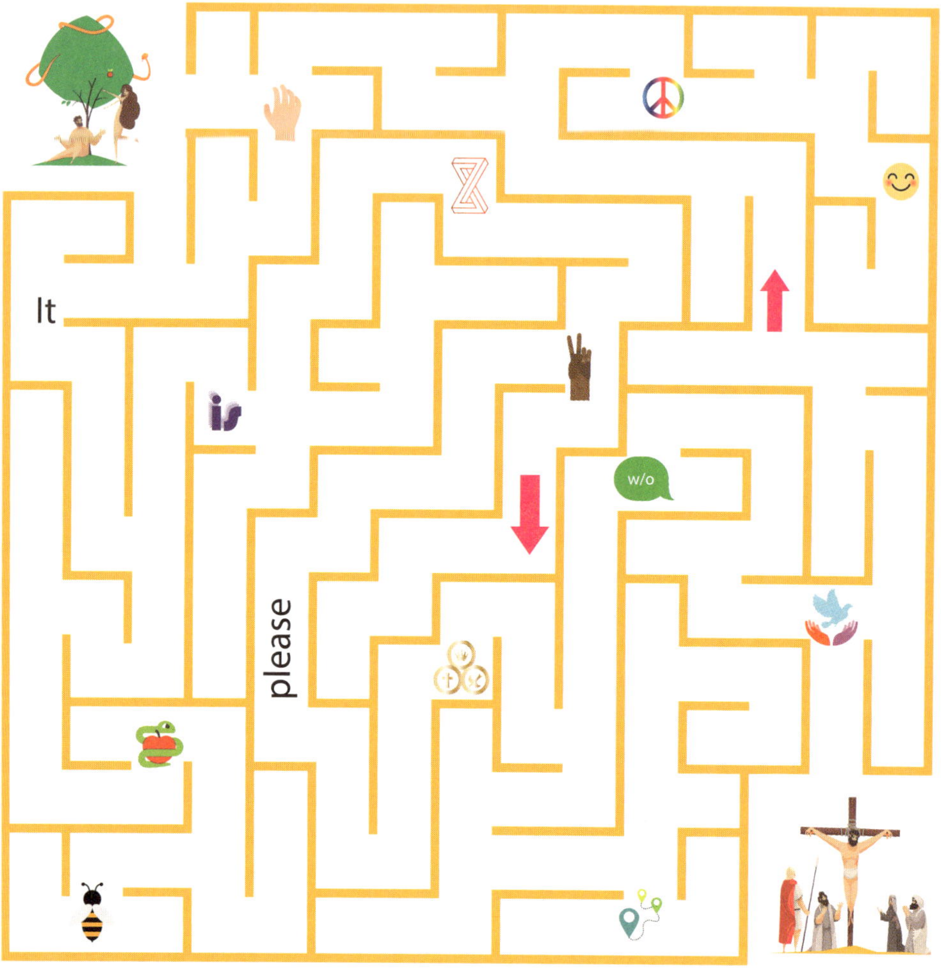

It   is   please

_____

_____

_____

_____

_____

Hebrews 11:6

Taking a Step of Faith

DAY 4

After her mom dropped her off at school, Lizzy thought about what her mother had said in the car. If she were Emily, how would she want to be treated? She'd want someone to be a friend to her! So Lizzy knew what she wanted to do, she was sure it was what God wanted her to do, but she wasn't sure *how* to do it since Emily wouldn't talk to her.

She was also worried what the other kids in class would think. Lizzy knew she needed God's help. While her class was lining up to go in the classroom, Lizzy took a moment to pray. *I know you want me to try again to talk with Emily, God. Please help me to be brave and go up to her today. But I don't want the other kids to start making fun of me,* Lizzy silently prayed. *I trust that you will help me.*

After all the students were seated and attendance was taken, their teacher gave them their instructions for the first hour. "Please go to the shelves and pick out one book to read for the next half hour," Mrs. Hansen said. Lizzy watched as all the boys and girls in her class got up and walked to the back of the room where the reading books were kept.

If I move slowly, Emily will be going back to the books at the same time as me. I'll try again, God, Lizzy prayed again. When Emily walked past her desk, Lizzy got up and started walking next to Emily.

"Hi, Emily," Lizzy said happily. "Do you know what kind of book you're going to choose to read? I like the adventure stories. What do you like best? I love to read. I'm so glad we have such good books in our classroom." Lizzy talked so fast and said so much because she was nervous.

Emily opened her mouth like she wanted to answer Lizzy, but nothing came out.

Lizzy leaned a little closer, "I didn't hear what you said," Lizzy said gently.

"I . . . I . . . I l-l-like-k-k adventur-r-r-re bo-o-oks-s-s, t-too," stuttered Emily.

Lizzy just looked at Emily. Now she understood why Emily wouldn't talk. "Here, let me show you where they are on the shelves!" Lizzy said happily. Lizzy smiled, grabbed Emily's hand, and pulled her to the right stack of books.

I Need Faith to Please God · 319

DAY 5

Rahab Has Faith

Read about It

Joshua 2

Think about It

1. In our Bible story, Rahab showed extreme faith in God when she kept the Israelite spies safe. This week's verse is all about learning to have faith in God and trust him when things are difficult. Do you think it was difficult for Lizzy to keep trying to be friends with Emily when Emily wasn't responding? It was! But Lizzy prayed and asked God to help her have the faith to do the right thing. What is something you'd like to talk to God about today?

2. Lizzy's mom was right to encourage Lizzy to treat Emily just like she would want to be treated. Lizzy did the right thing and was surprised to hear that Emily stutters and that's why she doesn't talk to people. What do you think might have happened if Lizzy hadn't kept trying to be Emily's friend?

3. When we have faith in God and believe what he promises in the Bible, we can have faith that God will help us every day, with everything we do. God wants us to believe that he will always give us what we need to love and serve others. What is a way you can love and serve others today?

Do Something about It

When you know that God wants you to do something, believe that God will give you everything you need to do it. Even when you feel silly or afraid or embarrassed, obey God and do the difficult thing to love and serve others.

Pray about It

Dear God, I know that you want me to be brave and have faith in you even when I feel like I cannot do something. You want me to believe that you will always give me everything I need to get the job done. Help me to have a big faith in you. Help me to remember what a big God you are. Help me to love others and never be afraid to try. In Jesus' name, amen.

Say, Write, Sing, Repeat

Say the verse; write the verse; sing the verse. Repeat these steps until you know the verse!

1. Say the verse aloud. If needed, review the Visual Bible Verse Dictionary at the back of the book to remember what each symbol stands for.
2. Write the verse on the lines below—as many times as you can!
3. Sing it to the tune of "Alouette" or another tune.

   It is impossible
   Impossible, impossible
   It is impossible
   To please God without faith.

   It is impossible!
   It is impossible!
   To please God
   Without faith
   To please God
   Without faith, Oo-oh!

4. Repeat steps 1, 2, and 3 until you can say the verse without help.

It   please

Hebrews 11:6

Week 46

We Must Be Kind and Forgiving to Others

Look at the visual Bible verse below. Try to figure out what it says. Write the verse words on the blank lines. Use the Visual Bible Verse Dictionary on page 371, if needed.

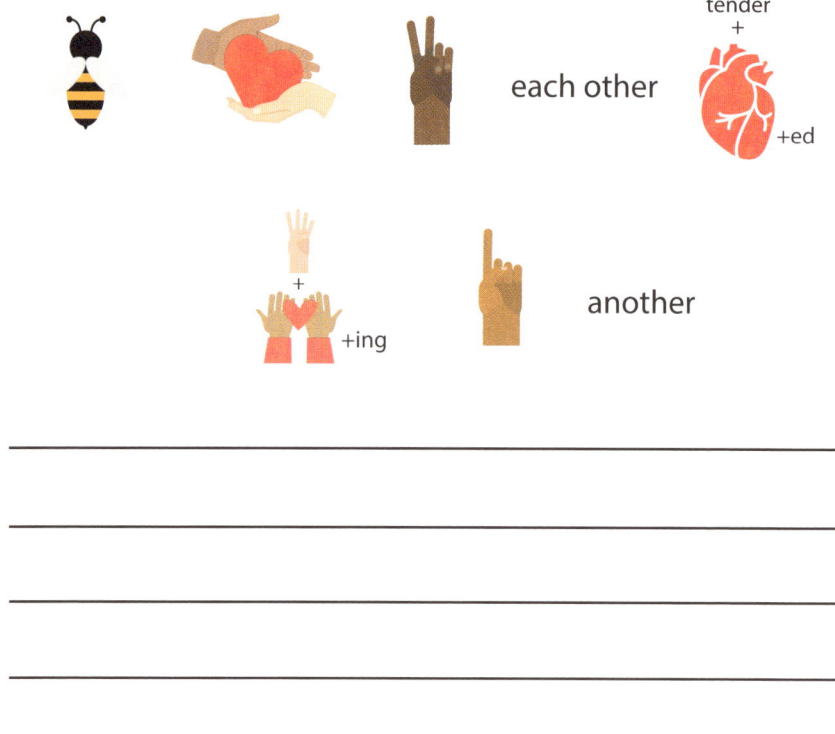

_____

_____

_____

_____

_____

Be kind to each other, tenderhearted, forgiving one another. Ephesians 4:32

Watching Gemma

DAY 1

Whenever Dad had to go downstairs to do laundry, Roman was in charge of watching his little sister Gemma. Today, it seemed to Roman that Dad was always running up and down the basement stairs to put clothes in the washing machine or to transfer wet clothes to the dryer. Finally, it seemed like he had a few minutes to play his video game.

Beep! Beep! Beep! The dryer beeped loudly. "Roman," Dad said, "I'm running downstairs again. Watch Gemma. Don't let her get into anything. Thanks!" Dad said quickly as he headed downstairs.

Roman rolled his eyes and put his game controller down. He glared at his little sister. "I don't want to watch you, Gemma. I want to play my video game." Gemma looked up at Roman from the floor where she was making a mess with her blocks. She also had some musical toys she liked to make a racket with. The almost-two-year-old smiled at her big brother, whom she adored. "Why does Dad always ask me to watch you in the middle of my game?" Roman snapped angrily at Gemma.

Gemma may not have understood every word Roman said, but she did understand his harsh tone. Her big eyes began to fill with tears. Her lower lip trembled. And then it began. "Waah! . . . Waah! . . ." Gemma started to cry.

Oh, no! Roman thought. *Dad's going to be mad!* He got down on the floor with her, picked up some of her toys, and tried to distract her. "Stop crying! Gemma, everything is OK, stop crying!" Roman said anxiously. It wasn't working. Gemma was still crying.

I'll get her some juice, Roman thought. He knew Dad didn't allow Gemma to drink juice in the living room. But surely this time wouldn't matter, right? *Dad won't know,* Roman thought.

Quickly, Roman poured some grape juice into the toddler cup Gemma used. Rushing back to the living room, he held out the sippy cup. "Here, Gemma. Drink this!" Roman said impatiently. Just as Roman was handing the cup to Gemma, it slipped from his hand, the lid popped off, and grape juice spilled all over the carpet. "Oh, no!" Roman cried.

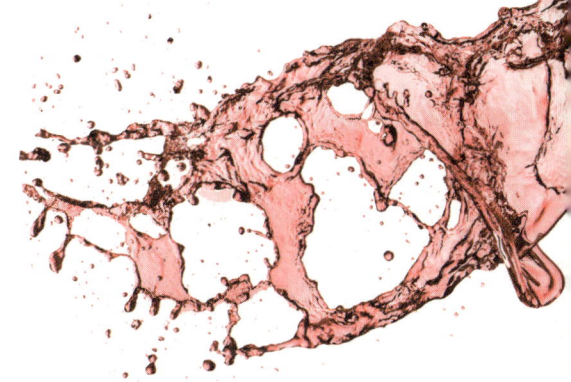

We Must Be Kind and Forgiving to Others

DAY 2: David and Mephibosheth

Read about It

2 Samuel 4:4; 9

Think about It

1 The Bible story tells of a time when King David was kind and compassionate to Mephibosheth, the son of his friend Jonathan. This week's verse tells us we need to be kind to others. What are some ways you can be kind to your family? Which will you do today?

2 In addition to being kind, our verse instructs us to be compassionate, too. Do you know what it means to be tenderhearted? It is a fancy way of saying we should be tender, loving, gentle, and treat others with love and care. Can you think of some ways you can be compassionate to your friends today? Is someone going through a hard time? What can you do to show that you are tenderhearted?

3 God loves it when we learn how to use our words to show we are kind and tenderhearted. Jesus was often kind and tenderhearted to the people that followed him. Even when Jesus was tired and worn out, he spoke kindly and with love. When are times it can be difficult for you to be kind? When you are feeling tired? Grumpy? When else?

Do Something about It

When you are feeling tired or grumpy, ask God for the strength to be kind and tenderhearted. Don't blame others for how you speak and act. Know that God promises to give you the self-control to be loving and kind even when you're not feeling like it.

Pray about It

Dear God, I know that you want me to always be kind and tenderhearted to others. But sometimes I feel so tired and grumpy that mean and unkind words come out of my mouth. Please give me the self-control I need to speak kindly and lovingly even when I don't feel that way. In Jesus' name, amen.

Toddler Toy Time

DAY 3

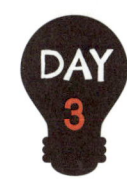

Find the symbols and words of the verse hidden on the toddler toys. Number them in verse order. Then, write the verse words in order on the blank lines below.

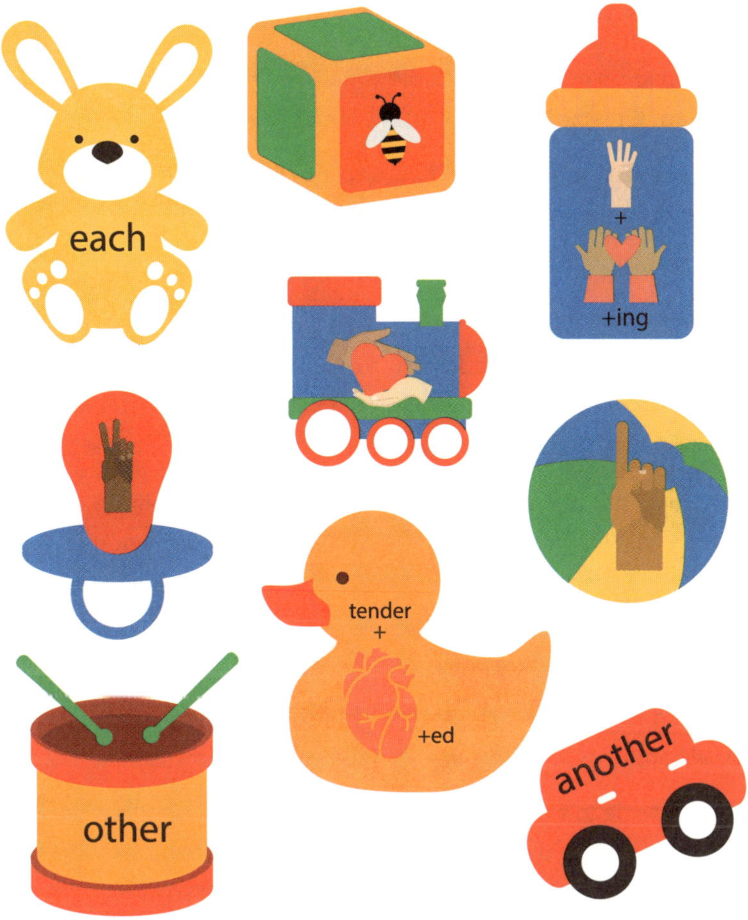
each
+
+ing
tender
+
+ed
other
another

Ephesians 4:32

Answer Key on page 381.

DAY 4

Grape-Colored Carpet

Roman was so upset. His little sister was crying her head off. He got her some juice to quiet her down, and managed to spill it all over the carpet.

Roman hurried to clean up the grape juice that was staining the carpeting. He was desperate to finish the job before his Dad came upstairs.

"Oh, no! I'm going to be in so much trouble with Dad. This has to come out!" Roman despaired out loud. Gemma continued to cry. His distress was adding to hers.

Roman soon realized he needed something stronger than water to clean this mess. "But it's downstairs in the laundry room. That's where Dad is."

Suddenly, Roman was angry again. "Gemma, stop CRYING!"

Just then, Dad walked in the room with an armload of folded clothes. He looked at the scene in front of him with shocked eyes. "Roman, what happened?" Dad put the clothes down on the couch before he dropped them. "Why is Gemma so upset? And how did that grape juice spill all over the carpet?" he asked as he picked Gemma up.

"It's Gemma's fault, Dad! She wouldn't stop crying so I got her some juice. I was just trying to make her stop crying," Roman explained, speaking quickly. "And then the juice spilled and I was trying to clean it up, but Gemma wouldn't stop crying."

"Little children cry, Roman. If you had picked her up and been kind to her, she probably would have stopped crying." Dad soothed Gemma, who had stopped crying and was now sniffling. "What made her start crying in the first place? She was happily playing with her toys when I went downstairs."

Roman didn't want to lie to his father. "I was kind of bugged about having to stop my video game, so I said some things that weren't really nice." He hurriedly excused himself, "But she's too little to understand what I was saying!"

"I think Gemma understood that you didn't want to watch her," Dad said. "And I think she felt your irritability. You haven't been very patient with her lately."

"Yeah. I definitely wasn't very patient. I'm sorry, Dad," Roman apologized.

"Here," Dad said, handing Gemma over to Roman. "Why don't you tell Gemma you're sorry while I put the clothes away. And then I'll get something to help you take this stain out of the carpet."

326 · We Must Be Kind and Forgiving to Others

The Unforgiving Servant

DAY 5

Read about It

Matthew 18:21–35

Think about It

1. Today's story is one that Jesus told to teach his followers to forgive each other. In addition to telling us to be kind and tenderhearted, this week's verse tells us to forgive others. Like the king in Jesus' story, God has forgiven us a huge debt—the price for our sins—because of Jesus' sacrifice on the cross. God wants us to forgive others the way he forgave us. Why does God's forgiveness for our sins make us want to forgive others?

2. God is always ready to help us be kind, tenderhearted, and loving. He is always ready to help us forgive others. But we need to ask for his help. When might it be hard for a kid your age to forgive someone?

3. A big part of being kind and tenderhearted is forgiving others who have hurt us. Is there anyone you need to forgive for something? Pray to God and ask for his help to forgive.

Do Something about It

When you know the right thing is to show kindness and compassion, but you don't want to, ask for God's forgiveness. Then ask God to help you think about what is best for the other person. Ask God to help you love them with kindness, tenderheartedness, and forgiveness.

Pray about It

Dear God, I need your help to really be kind, tenderhearted, and forgiving to others. Sometimes I know the right thing to do but I don't. I pick the easy thing for me. I know that is not right. I want to learn to love and serve others in ways that demonstrate your love for them. I have so much to learn! Please help me to make good and loving choices even when it will is difficult. In Jesus' name, amen.

DAY 6: Verse Word Search

Read the visual verse, and then write each word beneath its symbol. Then, find each verse word in the word search. **Note:** Don't forget to find *Ephesians*!

   each other

tender+ ... +ed

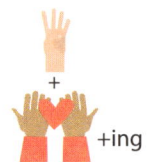  another

+ing

Ephesians 4:32

```
O D A K O K U T T Q J K K L T
Y T K N I I I S F F O X V R E
E B E G Q N P Z O E N B E T E
W A S P I D G M X I A H M E T
S N N L H L K E T N T Q I N R
Z O P T I E J P M O H F F D B
I T O N W Q S H E A A T R E B
B H O F O R G I V I N G S R C
A E N R E L P B A L Z P E H O
U R E D I H K O L N Y T R E N
D F M X V A Y S T C S N V A C
E A C H J D O H R F K X A R T
V H V D E B T E T A T W N T V
I I T I P J M T O S X O T E T
O W K J D X K H K A A L R D Z
```

Week 47

WE MUST LISTEN WELL BEFORE SPEAKING

Look at the visual Bible verse below. Try to figure out what it says. Write the verse words on the blank lines. Use the Visual Bible Verse Dictionary on page 371, if needed.

_____

_____

_____

_____

_____

_____

You must all be quick to listen, slow to speak and slow to get angry. James 1:19

DAY 1

Dirty Clothes

Shannon picked up a sweater and shook the dust off of it. She and her sister Shelby were busy picking up clothes in their bedroom. They had dropped shirts, sweaters, pants, and skirts on the floor—or wherever. Some were shoved under the bed. Others were tucked in between the sheets on their beds. Finally, their mom had had enough and ordered them to their rooms to do their laundry.

"What a mess!" complained Shannon. "Do you ever put your clothes in the right place, Shelby? We have dressers and a closet for our clothes you know," She gingerly picked up a dirty sock. "And a hamper!"

"What about your clothes? I see lots of your school clothes lying all over the floor, too. Even your pajamas are under your bed!" Shelby retorted grumpily.

"I might have a few things lying around, but most of this mess is yours," Shannon replied impatiently.

The girls continued to pick on each other as they picked up and put away clean clothes and put their dirty clothes into piles. Once done, they gave their room a final look to make sure it was all picked up, and then added the clothes that had made it into the hamper into their piles. Then Shannon and Shelby picked them up and headed to the laundry room.

When they got there, Shannon dropped her load on the floor instead of in the basket. "Shannon! You called me messy?" Shelby said in shock. "You just dropped all those clothes on the floor. The laundry basket is right next to you!"

"I always drop them on the floor first. Then I go through each one to see if it needs Mom's stain removal spray on them. Doesn't that make more sense than shoving them all into the washing machine and they won't come out clean?" Shannon replied in anger.

"Just stop criticizing me!" Shannon said before stomping out of the room.

Listening and Doing

DAY 2

Read about It

James 1:19–26

Think about It

1 This week's verse is the first part of today's passage. The verse describes three things that all need to work together.
- First, God tells us that we should be quick to listen.
- Second, we need to be slow to speak.
- Third, we need to be slow to get angry.

Think about these three commands. Which one is hardest for you? Why?

2 When we obey God and use our two ears to listen well when another person speaks, we can often avoid a disagreement or an argument. When was the last time you had an argument? Did anyone say "You're not listening to me" or something like that? How often do your arguments with others contain this phrase?

3 When we use self-control by listening well before we speak, everyone stays calmer. When one person gets angry and says mean words, it is difficult for others to respond kindly. Have you ever stopped an argument by speaking kindly even after another person was unkind to you? If not, what could you do to help you speak kindly in the future?

Do Something about It

When you are speaking with another person, make sure to listen well to what the person is saying before you say anything. Pay attention and try to understand what they are saying and why. If they get upset and angry with you, ask God for self-control to stay calm and not speak unkindly to them.

Pray about It

Dear God, I am trying hard to learn how to be a better listener. I know you have given us two ears to hear so you want us to listen well. When someone is speaking to me unkindly, I need you to help me be self-controlled and not get angry and say words that are unkind. Help me to be slow to speak and to only use my words to love and encourage others. In Jesus' name, amen.

Hot Potato

Referring to the visual Bible verse on page 329, copy the Bible verse words onto a sheet of paper.

Gather your family members or friends together. Show everyone the verse page you created and review the Bible verse with them. Repeat the verse a couple of times. Then, crumple the paper loosely into a ball.

Sit or stand in a circle and toss the paper ball back and forth to each other. Each time the Hot Potato is caught, the catcher says the next word in the memory verse. Be sure to have this book open to this page so you can help anyone who has trouble. Continue until as a group, you can play the game and say the verse without help.

Bonus: When players are saying the first half of the verse, "You must all be quick to listen," toss the paper ball quickly. When players are saying the second half of the verse, "slow to speak and slow to become angry" toss the paper ball in super slow motion! Whenever a player drops the ball or fails to catch it, they uncrumple the paper ball and read the verse aloud.

Doing the Laundry

DAY 4

Shelby looked at her sister's dirty clothes still lying on the laundry room floor and huffed. *Why did she walk out before taking care of her clothes?* Shelby grumbled silently.

Then, thinking about it as she got to work on her clothes, Shelby began to understand Shannon's part in the argument. *I guess both of us weren't being very nice to each other. We didn't listen to each other either. Shannon was angry with me and I was angry with her. I know! I'll wash Shannon's clothes for her!* Shelby decided happily. *Maybe that will show Shannon that I'm not angry at her anymore.*

Later that morning, Shannon was watching TV in the family room and Shelby was quietly reading in their bedroom. Shelby heard when the dryer buzzer went off. Shannon didn't even seem to notice, or maybe she was just ignoring it the way she'd been ignoring Shelby.

Without saying a word, Shelby quickly got up and went to take the clothes out of the dryer. Then she started to fold both her clothes and Shannon's clothes in neat piles. *Almost done,* Shelby thought with satisfaction as she smoothed a few creases from one on Shannon's T-shirts.

A little while later, Shannon came in the bedroom, angry. She had gone in to do her laundry. But it was gone! She was sure Shelby had hidden her dirty clothes to play a trick on her.

Then she saw her clean clothes neatly folded on her dresser. For a moment, she was too stunned to speak. "Ahh, Shelby, did you wash and dry and fold my clothes, too?"

"Yes, I did," Shelby replied.

"Why did you do that?" Shannon asked. "We were fighting."

"I was feeling bad about fighting with you," Shelby said. "So I thought I'd show you I was sorry by taking care of your laundry."

"Aw, that was really sweet. Thank you!" Shannon said. "And I'm sorry for fighting, too." The girls smiled at each other.

"Hey, do you want to play chess?" Shelby asked.

"Are you trying to start a fight again?" Shannon teased. "You know you get mad when I win. You're on!"

We Must Listen Well Before Speaking

DAY 5

Samuel Listens

Read about It

1 Samuel 3

Think about It

1 Today's Bible story is about Samuel and what a faithful listener he was. He listened to Eli, and more importantly, he listened to God. Because Samuel was such a good listener, God trusted him and gave him messages to speak to others. What are some ways you can know the kind of things God wants you to say to others?

2 When we learn to become good listeners before we open our mouths to speak, we can have much more peaceful conversations with others. Did you ever wonder why God gave us two ears to hear but only one mouth to talk? Shannon and Shelby were not listening to each other but they were both talking a lot. How could their conversation have gone better?

3 Think about a conversation you had with someone in your family this week that ended with both of you feeling upset and angry. If you had listened before talking, do you think it might have avoided an argument?

Do Something about It

When you are starting to feel upset and angry with another person, be quiet and pray for self-control. Ask God to help you really hear and understand what the other person is trying to say. If you don't understand, quietly and kindly ask good questions so that you can understand.

Pray about It

Dear God, please help me to listen when I am tempted to talk before the other person is done speaking. Please help me to not interrupt and to not get angry. I want to learn how to become a good listener so that I can understand how to love others. In Jesus' name, amen.

Say What?

Find the correct symbols and words from the visual Bible verse in the conversation balloons below. Circle each verse word. Number the words in verse order. Finally, write the words in verse order on the blank lines at the bottom of the page.

_____

_____

_____

_____

_____

James 1:19

We Must Listen Well Before Speaking

Week 48

BE HUMBLE AND LOOK OUT FOR OTHERS

Look at the visual Bible verse below. Try to figure out what it says. Write the verse words on the blank lines. Use the Visual Bible Verse Dictionary on page 371, if needed.

 humble  +ing of others

as  than  +rselves

_____

_____

_____

_____

_____

Be humble, thinking of others as better than yourselves. Philippians 2:3

Mr. Smarty Pants

DAY 1

"Ooo, fried chicken and green beans! My favorite!" Casey said as he and his sister Kate sat down at the dinner table with their mom and dad. *This is perfect!* Casey thought. *My favorite meal to go with my big announcement!* Casey smiled to himself as he dug into his meal.

The family chatted happily for a few moments before things quieted down. *Now's my chance!* Casey thought. Suddenly, Casey stood up on his chair.

Kate and his parents looked up at him. Kate's mouth dropped open in surprise. No one said a word. "Ladies and gentleman, prepare to be amazed. Here I bring you MY report card!" He pulled his report card from the back pocket of his pants. "Read it. Study it! But do not mess it up! It is a work of art!" Casey said dramatically while taking a bow.

Mom and Dad laughed, and then Dad applauded. "OK, Mr. Smarty Pants, sit down and finish your dinner. We'll look at your amazing report card after the dishes are cleared and cleaned," Dad said with a smile.

During the rest of the meal, Mom and Dad and Casey talked about their day at work, at home, and at school. Kate pushed her food around on her plate, but had lost her appetite. *I wish I was smart like Casey. He always gets the highest marks on his report cards. Not like me. I work as hard as he does. It isn't fair,* Kate thought silently.

"Done already?" Mom asked Kate.

"Yeah, I'm not hungry. May I please be excused?" Kate asked.

"OK, Kate. Just take your plate over to the counter for me please," Mom told her.

"I'm going up to my room and finish my homework," Kate said and rushed away before her family could see her tears.

Be Humble and Look Out for Others

DAY 2: The Pharisee and the Tax Collector

Read about It

Luke 18:9–14

Think about It

1. The word *humble* is a fancy way of saying to not push ahead of others or not brag about what you have done. It means to think about how others feel when you talk and when you do something. The Pharisee in our Bible story didn't care about the feelings of the tax collector as he prayed loudly for everyone to hear. What are some good things to pray about when you pray out loud?

2. In the story, Casey was so excited about his good marks on his report card that he made a big deal about it. Kate felt badly because her brother always did better at school than she did. How could Casey have shared his good news in a way that wouldn't have left Kate feeling so bad?

3. What things come easily to you? When we do our best we can be happy that we have done well. But we need to think about others who struggle and work hard, but don't do well. When we are humble, we remember to use our words in ways that don't make others feel bad.

Do Something about It

When you are excited about doing well at something, be careful how you talk about how well you did. Think about the people who are hearing you and consider if what you're saying might hurt their feelings. Share your good news with others, but be humble when you speak.

Pray about It

Dear God, please show me how to share good news without hurting others' feelings. I want to share good news humbly and not in a bragging way. I need your help to show me how to be sensitive to others who might feel bad if they haven't done well. In Jesus' name, amen.

Crossword Symbols

Complete the crossword puzzle.

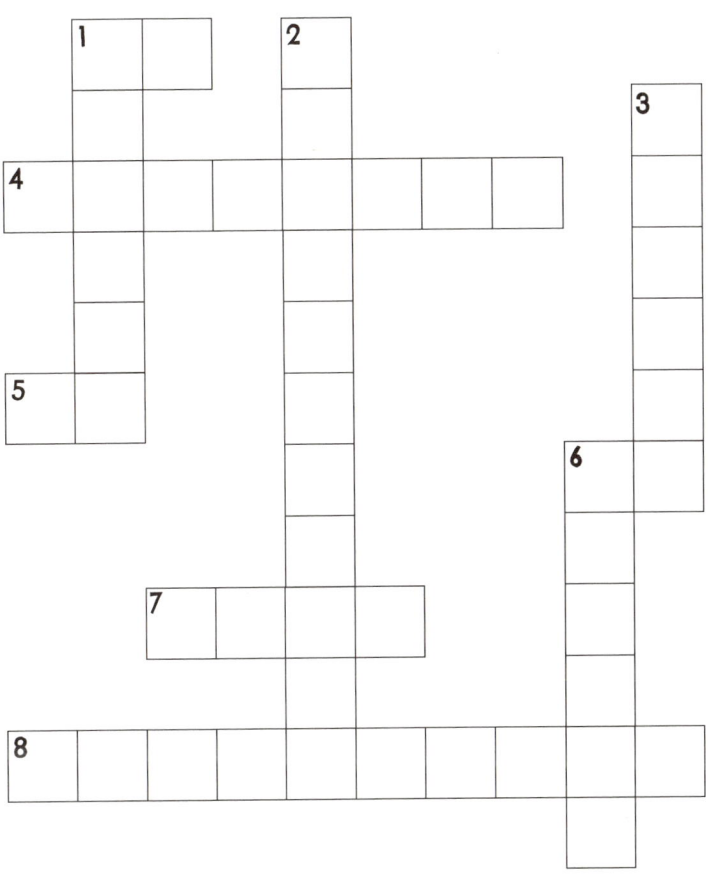

Across

1. of
4. +ing
5. as
6.
7. than
8. +rselves

Down

1. others
2. Philippians
3. humble
6.

 humble +ing of others

as  than +rselves

Answer Key on page 382.

Mrs. Smarty Pants—Not?

Kate went to her room, laid down on her bed, and buried her face in her pillows. She felt so sad and discouraged. She wasn't angry at Casey. She loved her brother and was proud that he did so well in school. But Kate tried so hard to do well, and she just didn't get the same high marks that Casey did.

Kate sighed, sat up, and looked out her window. Kate knew she had some spelling words to write out and a story paper to read out loud. *I'll do the spelling words first. Then I'll ask Mom or Dad to listen to me read my story,* Kate thought. The spelling list didn't take long and Kate was finished.

She went to look for Mom or Dad so that she could read her story out loud to them. She couldn't find them in the house. But she found Casey in the family room, watching a video. "Where did Mom and Dad go?" Kate asked.

"They went for a walk," Casey replied.

"Oh," Kate sighed.

"Why?" Casey asked, pausing his video.

"I have to read my story to them before I'm allowed to play," Kate said a little frustrated.

"Here! Read it to me," Casey offered.

Kate just looked at her brother. Casey was a much better and faster reader than she was. "Well," Kate hesitated. "I don't want to interrupt your video."

"It's alright. I can watch it later. Come on, Kate. Read to me," Casey encouraged.

"OK, but I'm not a fast reader like you are," Kate warned him.

"Kate, when I was in your grade, I could hardly read at all! I'm sure you are much better than I was," Casey encouraged.

"Really?" Kate said, surprised and suddenly feeling much better.

Casey laughed, "Sure!"

Kate sat next to Casey and began to read.

Nebuchadnezzar Praises God

DAY 5

Read about It

Daniel 4

Think about It

1. When this verse tells us to be humble and value others above ourselves, God is saying we need to think about others before we think about ourselves. This is not something that comes easily to a king! Nebuchadnezzar was a very rich and powerful king. But he finally realized he needed to be humble before the one true God. What are some reasons we all should be humble before God?

2. When we speak to others we can choose to use words that encourage and help them or words that could discourage and hurt them. Which kind of words would you rather hear spoken to you? Why?

3. When we are humble and value others above ourselves, we are looking for good ways to love them. We are always trying to find new ways to encourage, help, and bring a smile to another person's face. What can you say today to make someone smile?

Do Something about It

Look for good ways to encourage, help, and bring a smile to someone's face today. Think of something that will help a family member or friend know that you love and care about them.

Pray about It

Dear God, please help me think of good ways to encourage, help, and bring smiles to the faces of my family and friends. Help me to be humble and look for loving ways to show them how much I care. I want my family and friends to know that I think about what is best for them. In Jesus' name, amen.

Coloring Verse

Read the visual verse, and then write each word beneath its symbol. Finally, use fine-tipped colored pens or pencils to color in the pictures.

humble

+ing of

others as

than

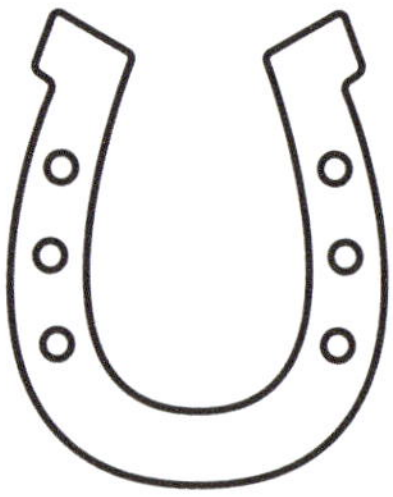

+rselves

Philippians 2:3

Week 49
Don't Be Angry

Look at the visual Bible verse below. Try to figure out what it says. Write the verse words on the blank lines. Use the Visual Bible Verse Dictionary on page 371, if needed.

  by letting

_____

_____

_____

_____

_____

_____

Don't sin by letting anger control you. Psalm 4:4

DAY 1: Christmas Eve

The Christmas tree stood in the front window, colorful and shiny with twinkling lights that flickered on and off. The house was filled with yummy smells of Christmas treats. It was Christmas Eve.

Blaire and Brooke were so excited! When their mom wasn't looking, both of the girls took quick peeks to see what names where on the different presents.

"Oh, this big one is for you, Brooke! I wonder what it is," Blaire whispered.

"This one is so small, I'll bet it is jewelry for Mom," Blaire said.

"The one in the back is so long I can't even guess what might be in it," Brooke told her sister.

"We better leave the gifts alone. Mom doesn't want us touching them," Blaire said getting up off of her knees.

"Girls, time for bed." Mom called. "Go upstairs, change into your pajamas, and brush your teeth. Your father and I will be up in a minute to say goodnight," Mom instructed.

Blaire and Brooke raced up the stairs, quickly put on their pajamas, and then brushed their teeth, just as Mom had asked. They were in bed waiting for their parents—but more anxiously awaiting Christmas morning!

"The sooner we go to sleep, the sooner it will be morning," Blaire whispered.

"I know!" Brooke agreed happily.

Their parents entered their room. "Goodnight, Blaire. Goodnight, Brooke," they both said as they leaned over to kiss each girl goodnight.

"We love you. When you wake up it will be Christmas morning!" Mom said.

"Aren't you excited to finally unwrap those presents you've been looking at for the past two weeks?" Dad teased with a smile.

The girls looked at each other. They were caught! Mom and Dad already knew they had been sneaking peeks at the presents. "Yes, Dad," Blaire and Brooke answered together, laughing. They were so relieved Mom and Dad weren't mad at them for peeking!

Jesus Teaches about Anger

DAY 2

Read about It

Matthew 5:21–26

Think about It

1 Today's Bible passage tells us what Jesus taught about anger. He said that we need to reconcile with anyone we've wronged, and to settle our differences with others. Is there anyone you need to reconcile with? Any differences that need to be settled between you and someone else?

2 This week's verse warns us not to let our anger control us. Have you or someone you know ever said, "I just lost my temper!" When people say they've lost their temper, they really mean their temper got control of them. How often does your anger control you? Every day? More than once a day?

3 How can letting anger control us cause problems? This same verse goes on to tell us to "think about [things] overnight and remain silent (Psalm 4:4). How can thinking about what made you angry help make things better? How could not remaining silent make things worse?

Do Something about It

When you feel angry with someone or something, step away for a while. Avoid the temptation to keep going. Be silent and wait until you have thought about things before you talk to that person or try to do that thing again.

Pray about It

Dear God, help me to not have a hot temper and easily get angry. Help me to be a calm and kind person, God, even when things don't work out like I had hoped. Please give me your self-control to be careful about my temper. In Jesus' name, amen.

DAY 3 Some Kind of Friend

This week's visual Bible verse, Psalm 4:4, says not to be angry. On this page are a number of visual Bible verse words that describe different types of people. Write the words for each symbol on the blank lines. Circle the ones that describe someone you would want to be.

 +ful       +ing

_____   _____   _____   _____

 +ful    +ful

_____   _____   _____   _____

 +ful       +ful    +ing

_____   _____   _____   _____

 +ful    +thful    +ish

_____   _____   _____   _____

346 · Don't Be Angry

Christmas Day

DAY 4

It was finally here! It was Christmas morning, and it had even snowed outside. Blaire and Brooke peeked outside their bedroom window to see all the sparkling white snow that had fallen in the night. Their neighbors had their Christmas lights shining brightly from the night before. It was so pretty.

"Let's go downstairs, maybe Mom and Dad are up," Blaire suggested eagerly. After tying on their robes and putting on their slippers, the girls ran down the stairs. They went straight to the Christmas tree and looked again at the pretty presents. But they didn't touch anything. "Oh when will Mom and Dad get here?" Blaire whispered.

Just then, they heard their parents' bedroom door open. "Girls, wait for us," Dad called. Brooke and Blaire looked at each other excitedly.

Once the family was all together, Dad read the Christmas story about Jesus being born. Then they sang "Silent Night" together. Dad said a prayer and thanked Jesus for coming to Earth to save us all from our sins. Then Mom started handing out the gifts.

"Here is one for you, Blaire. And one for you, Brooke," Mom said. Back and forth the girls opened all their gifts before Mom and Dad opened theirs. When all the presents had been handed out, Brooke kept searching under the tree.

"What are you looking for, Brooke?" Dad asked.

"I'm looking for the one gift I really wanted. I asked everyone for the snowsuit outfit for my doll. I have to have it!" Brooke explained in disappointment.

Mom said, "Brooke, I tried to find that outfit, but it was sold out. I couldn't find one anywhere."

"What?! I told you I wanted it a long time ago. Why didn't you shop right away?" Brooke said in anger.

Dad and Mom looked at Brooke and then at each other. "Brooke, I think you are missing the whole point of Christmas. It isn't about getting what we want and getting angry if we don't. It's about giving," Dad said sternly.

"I think we need to have Dad read through the Christmas story again and have a good long talk about what Christmas is all about," Mom said.

Don't Be Angry · 347

DAY 5

Stop Being Angry!

Read about It

Psalm 37:8–9

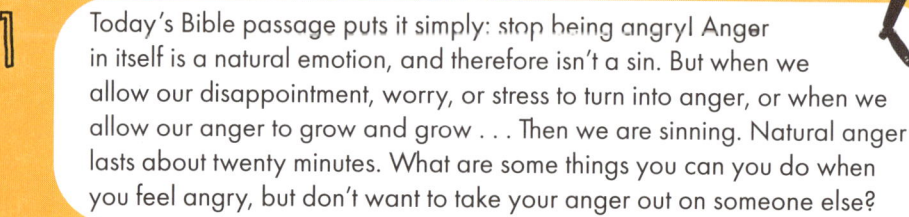

Think about It

1 Today's Bible passage puts it simply: stop being angry! Anger in itself is a natural emotion, and therefore isn't a sin. But when we allow our disappointment, worry, or stress to turn into anger, or when we allow our anger to grow and grow . . . Then we are sinning. Natural anger lasts about twenty minutes. What are some things you can you do when you feel angry, but don't want to take your anger out on someone else?

2 God is not pleased when we act like hot-tempered people who are boiling over in anger. Brooke allowed her anger to boil over because she didn't receive the Christmas present she had asked for. She was not grateful for all she had been given, and that could have ruined Christmas for the whole family. When is a time you were disappointed? Did you allow your disappointment to turn into anger, or did you do something else?

3 When we are not thankful, we can become hot-tempered people because we think we deserve something even when we don't. How else could Brooke have responded to her disappointment? It's OK to feel sad, but when we allow our sadness to turn into anger, God is not pleased.

Do Something about It

When you feel sad or disappointed about something, remember all that Jesus has done for you. Jesus gave his life for you. Learn to be a giver, too. Practice being self-controlled and don't get angry even when you feel disappointed.

Pray about It

Dear God, it is so easy to forget that Jesus gave us eternal life by dying for us. Please help me remember that because Jesus gave his life for me, I need to be willing to give my life for others. That means even when I feel disappointed, I will use self-control and not be a hot-tempered, angry person. Please help me to always be thankful for Jesus and for everything else you have given me. In Jesus' name, amen.

Stop Anger

DAY 6

Reread the visual Bible verse on page 343. Write the verse on the blank lines below. Then, look at the acrostic grid on this page. What phrase do the filled-in letters spell? Fill in the empty boxes of the acrostic grid with words from the verse. The only word not used is *by*.

_____

_____

_____

Psalm 4:4

Week 50

Be Peaceable with Everyone

Look at the visual Bible verse below. Try to figure out what it says. Write the verse words on the blank lines. Use the Visual Bible Verse Dictionary on page 371, if needed.

  harmony

 each other

_____

_____

_____

_____

_____

_____

Live in harmony with each other. Romans 12:16

Rainy Afternoon

DAY 1

The rain hammered at the roof and windows as thunder boomed in the distance. An afternoon thunderstorm had grounded Noah and Parker at home this Saturday. They had been planning to meet up with friends and ride their bikes, but the storm wouldn't allow it. They'd been lying around watching TV all day.

"You boys have watched enough TV already today," Mom said while turning off the television.

"But, Mom . . ." they both protested in unison. But before another word could be spoken, Mom shut them down.

"Nope. I don't want to hear it," Mom said firmly. "Go to the toy closet and pull out some games you haven't played since your last school break," she suggested.

"Come on, Parker. Let's pick some games," Noah said reluctantly. At the closet, the two boys looked over their collection of games. Parker picked out two games. Then Noah picked out two. They carried their choices back into the living room and plopped down on the floor.

Parker started setting up one game while Noah began setting up another. "We're playing my game first, Noah," Parker said.

"No, we're playing my game first, and then we'll play yours," insisted Noah.

"No! I called it first! We are playing this one first or I'm not playing at all," shouted Parker.

"Don't play, then!" Noah responded in anger.

Just then, Mom entered the room. Shaking her head in dismay, she said, "Why are you two arguing? I just asked you to find some games to play. That shouldn't be a reason to start fighting."

"But, Mom, . . . you don't understand," objected Noah.

"Mom, Noah is being bossy!" Parker stated loudly.

Mom shook her head. "Boys, enough." She continued, instructing them, "Pack up those games, and then head to the kitchen. Now!"

Be Peaceable with Everyone

DAY 2: Esau Forgives Jacob

Read about It

Genesis 32:3–21; 33:1–4

Think about It

1. Today's Bible story tells of when Jacob was reunited with his brother Esau. Many years earlier, Jacob had tricked Esau into giving him his birthright. The rift between the brothers had lasted for many years. Finally, they mended their relationship. Is there someone with whom you need to mend a relationship? What could you do to start healing that relationship?

2. This week's verse tells us that we should live in harmony with each other. This means we should live in peace. God wants us to learn how to live with our family and friends without arguing and fighting all the time. Which do you think is happier and healthier—fighting or living in harmony? Why?

3. God wants us to choose to be peacemakers. We cannot control what others do or say, but we are responsible for our own choices. God gives us the self-control to stay quiet and be peaceable even when someone might be angry with us. What is something you could do to keep the peace if someone comes at you in anger?

Do Something about It

When someone is getting angry and upset at you, ask God for self-control to stay quiet and peaceable. Don't start getting angry and yell or say unkind words. Obey God and try to make peace.

Pray about It

Dear God, it is so hard to be quiet and be peaceable when someone is upset with me. I want to defend myself by yelling back at them or telling them to leave me alone. But you want me to be a peacemaker. I need your help and self-control to stay calm and not get angry. Thank you for helping me make right choices. In Jesus' name, amen.

Backwards Words

DAY 3

The words to this week's verse are spelled backward. Write each word correctly on the blank line next to it. Then, match each word to its symbol on the right. Finally, in each conversation balloon, write what you think the person making that face is saying. Is it peaceful? Is it angry? You decide.

ynomrah _____

rehto _____

ni _____

hcae _____

evil _____

htiw _____

Be Peaceable with Everyone · 353

DAY 4
Home Filled with Harmony

Noah and Parker packed up the games they'd been setting up and then went into the kitchen where Mom was waiting for them.

"Boys," She said after they'd sat down at the counter. "I want you to think about how you have been talking and acting toward each other all morning."

The boys looked at each other. "All morning?" Parker asked.

Mom nodded. "Yes, it's been like that all morning."

"But we were planning to go bike riding," Noah said. "It isn't our fault."

"No, but your attitude is your responsibility," she said firmly. "I asked you to find some games to play. And you argued about what game to play!" She shook her head sadly. "It hurts my heart to hear the way you boys talk to each other so disrespectfully. I want you to sit here for a few minutes without talking. Think about what God would want you to do when you speak to each other," Mom said.

Noah started thinking about the Bible verse he had memorized in Sunday school. "Live in harmony with one another." *I remember what my teacher said, too. God wants us to be peacemakers so others will understand God's love,* Noah thought.

Parker sat and looked around the room. *I know I should have let Noah pick the game and played it without complaining. But he wanted to pick the movie this morning, too. He always wants to go first!* Parker thought to himself.

A few moments later, Mom came back to the room and sat next to her sons. "Have you thought about how you should talk to each other? Have you thought about how God wants us to live in peace and harmony with each other? That means sometimes we allow others to pick first, get first turn, and so on. Have you done anything like that for each other today? Even once?" Mom asked seriously.

"No," Noah admitted.

"The rest of the day, I do not want to hear anymore fighting. I want to hear you both being peacemakers," Mom encouraged. "Can you do that?" she challenged.

The brothers looked at each other and smiled. "Yes. Yes, we can!" they said.

Solomon Judges Wisely

DAY 5

Read about It

1 Kings 3:16–28

Think about It

1 Two women came to King Solomon, arguing and fighting over who was the mother of a baby. Solomon was able to determine who the real mother was when she was willing to make peace with the other woman and let her have the baby to save his life. God wants us to make the right choice to be a peacemaker. But being a peacemaker sometimes means we let others have what we want. When is a time you had to give something up in order to keep peace with someone? That was a decision that pleased God.

2 When we obey God and make the right choice to live in peace and harmony with others, everyone around us can see God's love. What are some other ways that kids your age can show God's love to others?

3 Every day is a new day to live in harmony. If you argued or fought with someone yesterday, you can apologize and start over. Pray and ask God to show you if you need to ask for forgiveness from anyone.

Do Something about It

When you wake up in the morning, pray and ask God to show you if you need to ask for forgiveness from anyone for fighting and arguing. Apologize to that person and work harder to be a peacemaker.

Pray about It

Dear God, please help me to become a peacemaker at home and at school. Help me to think about what others need and then help them to get it. I need to let others pick first and be first. Sometimes this is hard to do! But thank you for helping me think about others first. In Jesus' name, amen.

Be Peaceable with Everyone

DAY 6: Verse in Motion

Read the visual verse, and then write each word beneath its symbol. The verse has been arranged in phrases. For each phrase, write down some motions you can do as you say the verse. Then, practice saying the verse and doing the motions several times. Say it and do the motions in front of a mirror, for your family or friends, or for your stuffed animals. Teach it to someone to do with you and video yourselves saying the verse and doing the motions. Keep it up until you know the verse by heart.

● LIVE

_____

[N] harmony

_____

w/ each other

_____

Romans 12:16

356 · Be Peaceable with Everyone

Week 51

Love Is Patient and Kind

Look at the visual Bible verse below. Try to figure out what it says. Write the verse words on the blank lines. Use the Visual Bible Verse Dictionary on page 371, if needed.

_____

_____

_____

_____

_____

Love is patient and kind. 1 Corinthians 13:4

DAY 1

Fixing Cars with Dad

The weekend had finally arrived. Jake was so excited! Jake and his father were going to work on cars in the garage. Jake loved watching his dad use his tools to make the engine work again.

Jake's dad was a mechanic and Jake wanted to be just like his dad. Right now the only thing in his way was finishing breakfast. "Jake, finish up and meet me in the garage," Dad called.

"I'm coming!" Jake replied. Jake shoved the last bit of scrambled eggs into his mouth, wiped his face, dumped his plate into the sink, and ran out to the garage. "What are we going to fix today?" Jake asked as he came through the open bay doors.

"I thought we would get started on checking out your grandfather's old Mustang. Maybe . . . just maybe . . . we might get it running today. I think I know where the problem is and I ordered some new parts to try it out," Dad explained.

"Cool!" Jake said. Jake stood watching his father as he thoughtfully picked out the tools he knew he would need and handed them to Jake.

"Set these down on the bench over there," Dad said pointing to the portable metal workbench near the Mustang.

"OK, Dad," Jake replied.

"Now be careful with these, I had a hard time getting two of these small pieces," Dad said handing each one to Jake. "With all the car parts and hardware lying around this shop, I'd probably never find them again."

"I'll be careful, Dad," Jake promised. But as Jake turned around their family dog, Rip, came barreling into the garage and slammed right into Jake. "Oh, no!" Jake cried as the small parts went flying out of his hands. He watched in despair as the parts rolled across the wood floor of the garage and disappeared into a crack.

Simeon Is Patient

DAY 2

Read about It

Luke 2:25–35

Think about It

1 Today's Bible story is from when Jesus was born. The prophet Simeon had waited patiently for a long time for the Messiah to be born. He was so happy to finally hold Baby Jesus in his arms. Sometimes patience means waiting a long time. Sometimes patience means not getting angry when something goes wrong. God wants us to be patient in both ways. Which way of being patient is more difficult for you?

2 Love is patient. This verse describes what real love looks like in real life. When something happens and it causes a problem, we can get upset or angry. But God tells us that real love is patient . . . even when something goes wrong. Love is kind. A second part of real love is being kind. When someone is unkind to us, it can be very hard to be kind to that person. But God tells us that real love is always kind even when someone hurts us.

3 Love is patient. Love is kind. When was a time you felt impatient, unkind, or both? Did you respond in a way that pleased God? Why or why not? Now that you understand what real love is, you can pray and ask God for patience and kindness!

Do Something about It

When something happens that makes you feel upset or angry, choose to respond with patience and kindness. Ask God to help you to have real love for the other person and not become impatient or unkind.

Pray about It

Dear God, please help me to respond to disappointments and when others are unkind to me by being patient and kind myself. Help me to remember that sometimes I make others upset when I am late or unkind or make mistakes. Real love means I treat others the way I want to be treated. Thank you for loving me with real love all of the time. In Jesus' name, amen.

DAY 3 — Patient Art

Color each verse word by making lots of dots in the letters. Use a different color of crayon or marker for each word. Before you begin coloring a new word, repeat the verse aloud.

LOVE   IS

PATIENT

AND   KIND

1 Corinthians 13:4

Lost Parts

When Jake's dog Rip bumped into him, Jake looked as though he were falling in slow motion. He twisted and turned and tried to hold out his hand to catch those two small parts that Rip had bumped out of his hands. "Nooooooo . . . ." Jake cried.

Suddenly, there was a loud thud. Jake hit the cement floor. Hard. And it hurt. "Ow . . . ." Jake moaned holding his elbow with his hand.

Jake's dad came running. "Are you hurt, Jake?" Dad asked with concern.

"No, I don't think so." Dad was testing Jake's arm, bending it and feeling it to determine if it was broken. "But I dropped the car parts," Jake despaired.

"Let's see if we can find them," Dad said. "Do you know which direction they went?" Jake and his father looked all around the garage, moving car parts around and searching everywhere. After about ten minutes, it was clear the parts were lost.

"We'll never find them, Dad. I'm so sorry!" Jake's eyes welled up with tears.

"Jake, don't worry about the parts. I can always get more. I just want to be sure that you aren't hurt. Stand up and let me check you over," Dad told him kindly.

"But Dad! You told me you had a hard time finding those parts!" Jake protested. "What if you can't get any more? What if we can't fix Grandpa's car? What if . . ."

"Stop. Jake, you are far more valuable than any car or any car part. Stop worrying. Accidents happen. It won't hurt us to wait a few more weeks or even months to order new parts," Dad told Jake. "Now let's see how bruised up you are," Dad said as he looked Jake over closely for bumps and bruises.

As Dad realized Jake wasn't seriously hurt, his poking and prodding turned into tickles. Jake and his father started laughing. Rip ran up and started jumping on and licking them both. "Well, I guess you're going to live," Dad said.

"Oh, I don't know . . ." Jake joked. "I might need some ice cream to survive."

Dad stood up and offered a hand up to Jake, who took it and stood next to his father. "I think we can manage that. Why don't you get in my truck and we'll grab some ice cream after we go to the auto parts store where I found the last ones. Who knows? They might have some extra lying around."

DAY 5: Cornelius Believes

Read about It

Acts 10

Think about It

1 Cornelius didn't know why God wanted him to get Peter; and when Peter received the invitation to see Cornelius, he didn't know why God wanted him to go to Cornelius. Cornelius showed patience by waiting, and inviting his family and friends to wait with them, even though they didn't know why. Both Cornelius and Peter showed patience by obeying God, even though they didn't know what was going on. When is a time you have had to be patient when you didn't understand what was going on?

2 Love is patient. From our story about Jake and his dad, how did Jake's father show patience with Jake after he dropped those car parts? Was Jake's father upset or angry? Did Jake think his dad might be angry? Love is kind. How did Jake's father show kindness to Jake? Jake's dad wasn't concerned about the car parts; he wanted to be sure that Jake was not hurt. Do you think that Jake was surprised by his dad's reaction?

3 Love is patient. Love is kind. When something goes wrong, we feel impatient and disappointed. But we can choose to respond with kindness because God gives us the self-control and the power to do so. What are some ways we can learn to be kind and patient, and show self-control?

Do Something about It

When something goes wrong and you start to get impatient, ask God to help you respond with kindness. Remember what is most important in life . . . people. Don't be selfish and only think about what you want. Look around and try to be patient and kind to others.

Pray about It

Dear God, sometimes I feel sad and disappointed because everything I plan goes wrong. When I am tempted to get angry and impatient with my family or friends, help me to make the good choice of being kind. Thank you for helping me show real love even when it was hard for me. In Jesus' name, amen.

Rhythm Verse

DAY 6

Reread the visual verse below. Then, say it several times aloud. Refer to page 357 if you need help. Finally, come up with motions for each of the three phrases shown below: clapping on each syllable of the word, stomping your feet, hopping on one foot, pumping your fists, etc. Write what you want to do on the lines under each phrase. Then practice saying the phrase and doing the motion several times. After you've practiced, perform your rhythm verse for your family or friends.

Love is patient

_____
_____
_____

and kind.

_____
_____
_____

1 Corinthians 13:4

_____
_____
_____

Week 52

Help Those Who Are Weak

Look at the visual Bible verse below. Try to figure out what it says. Write the verse words on the blank lines. Use the Visual Bible Verse Dictionary on page 371, if needed.

Encourage those   timid

-out
tender of those

_____

_____

_____

_____

_____

Encourage those who are timid. Take tender care of those who are weak. Be patient with everyone. 1 Thessalonians 5:14

Coming Attractions

DAY 1

"Get Your Kicks at the County Fair!" screamed the headline of the newspaper advertisement for the county fair. Marissa and Meg sat on the couch with their heads together so they could both read all about the upcoming county fair.

In particular, Marissa was thrilled to see a list of all the brand-new rides that were part of this year's county fair week. "Ooo . . . look at that one, Meg! Doesn't it look fun?" she exclaimed excitedly. "See, it goes up and down and it twirls around, too. That is the first ride I want to go on."

Meg didn't say a word. She was so busy in her mind thinking about how she could get out of riding any rides this year. Meg loved going to the fair because she loved the animals and other exhibits. Meg was afraid of the rides. They made her stomach feel queasy.

"Meg! Meg! Did you hear what I said?" Marissa demanded. "You look like you are someplace far away. Did you even hear what I said about that new ride?" Marissa asked her sister.

"Yes, I heard you. Yes. It looks like fun," Meg replied. She stood up. "I'm going outside now," she said as she headed to the back door.

That's strange! Marissa thought to herself. "Oh well, at least I'm excited about next week's fair even if Meg isn't," Marissa said aloud, just before Meg went through the door. Meg paused for a moment, looking at Marissa, and then went outside, closing the door behind her. Marissa went back to studying the descriptions of exciting and new things coming to this year's fair.

Meg wandered around the backyard listlessly. *I wish I loved the rides as much as Marissa does. I feel like a baby because I'm nervous about riding them,* Meg thought sadly.

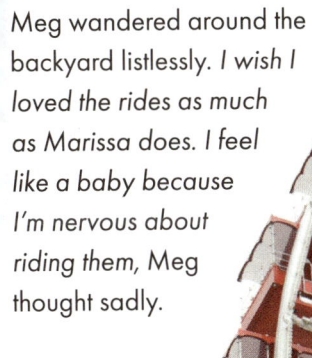

DAY 2: Paul's Final Advice

Read about It

1 Thessalonians 5:12–22

Think about It

1 Today's reading are Paul's final words of advice to the church members in Thessalonica. This week's Bible verse is part of that advice. It breaks things down into three parts. The first part is to encourage those who are timid. Sometimes we may not understand why someone feels sad or scared, but we can try to encourage that person by cheering them up. Who is someone that seems timid that you could encourage this week? What can you do to encourage them?

2 The second part of our verse tells us to take tender care of the weak. Not everyone is strong. Some people are weak. Others get sick easily. But everyone needs help sometimes. Be on the lookout for people you can help this week. And when you do help, do it tenderly. When is a time someone showed tenderness to you when you really needed it?

3 The third part of our verse tells us to be patient with everyone—not just people we like or agree with, but EVERYONE. Being patient can be so difficult! We want to get everything done fast. But sometimes slow is best. What are some things that work better when done slowly, rather than quickly?

Do Something about It

Look around for timid people whom you can help this week. Be patient with them. Help them and encourage them. Remember that every one of us is different and every one of us needs help sometimes.

Pray about It

Dear God, help me to be on the lookout this week for anyone who needs my help. I need to remember that we all need help sometimes and I can patiently be an encourager to someone this week. Thank you God for helping me and for sending others to help me when I am weak. In Jesus' name, amen.

Ferris Words

By each Ferris wheel bucket, you will see a symbol or word from this week's verse. Starting with the word *Encourage*, make your way around the Ferris wheel clockwise. Write each verse word in order on the blank lines at the bottom of the page. But beware: there are some wrong symbols in there!

DAY 3

_____

_____

_____

_____

1 Thessalonians 5:14

Help Those Who are Weak • 367

DAY 4

Swing Time

Marissa had spent half the morning reading about the county fair. She then went to describe what she had found with her mother.

"Mom!" she exclaimed excitedly. "I want to tell you all about the new rides at the fair. And I made a list of the first ride I want to go and . . ." Marissa suddenly paused when she saw her mother had raised her hand, indicating she needed to stop.

"Wait . . . Marissa," Mom said. "I'm glad you found so many wonderful things to do at the fair, but remember we are going as a family. That means we are all going to agree on what we do. We don't have time to see them all," Mom reminded.

"Yeah. Right. I had forgotten about that," Marissa admitted.

"Why don't you try thinking about the fair with everyone in mind," Mom asked.

Marissa walked away, thinking hard about which rides, food, and exhibits were at the top of her list. Then she remembered what Mom said. *Mom wants me to think about what everyone will want to do . . . Meg! I'll ask her what she wants to do right now,* Marissa decided to herself.

She found Meg outside swinging. Marissa took the swing next to her, started swinging, and said, "Mom said we have to decide what we want to do next week at the fair. So what do you want to do?" Marissa asked.

Meg said, "I want to see the animals and I want to get a big cherry snow cone."

"That's it?" Marissa said, shocked. "What about that new ride I told you about?"

"Well . . . I'm not sure," Meg hedged. Then she decided to come clean. "Actually, I AM sure. Marissa, I really don't want to go on that ride. I get sick on those fast, loop-de-loop rides. And they make me afraid . . ." Meg admitted.

"Oh . . ." Marissa said slowly. "I didn't know that." They swung for a few moments in silence. Then Marissa spoke again, "Well, let's see if we can find a ride that both of us will like!"

"Really? You don't think I'm a baby because I don't like the same rides as you?" Meg asked.

"No!" Marissa replied, laughing. Meg joined her and the girls continued swinging and talking about the county fair.

Life on God's Terms

DAY 5

Read about It

Romans 8

Think about It

1. Today's Bible passage describes life as a follower of Jesus. The first part of this week's verse tells us to encourage those who are timid. One of the most encouraging things you can do for a follower of Jesus is remind them of who they are in Christ! What can you do to encourage someone who doesn't know about Jesus?

2. The next part of the verse tells us to take "tender care" of the weak. In our story, Marissa showed real love to her sister, Meg, and suggested they find rides they both liked. In this way, Marissa was helping her weaker sister. Have you ever given up something you wanted because another person wasn't strong enough to do it with you?

3. The third part of our verse tells us to be patient with everyone. Mom was right in encouraging Marissa to remember that going to the fair was a family outing. It wasn't just a trip for Marissa to do everything she wanted to do on her own. Marissa could have gotten impatient with Meg and told her to act like a big girl. But she chose to be patient and show her love instead. When is a time you were patient and showed love to someone else? How did it make you feel?

Do Something about It

When you see someone who needs help and encouragement, find a good way to help them. Ask what they need, and then do it or get help from your family or trusted adults. Remind yourself that we are all different and that is how God made us.

Pray about It

Dear God, remind me that when I am with others, I have to always think about what they want—not just what I would like. Help me to be an encourager and a helper to the weak. I know you made us all different and that is good, but sometimes it is hard to be patient with people who are not like me. I need your help to show real love all the time and to all people. In Jesus' name, amen.

DAY 6: Refrigerator Magnets

Make this fun craft and put it on your refrigerator as a fun reminder to you and all your family to be encouraging, caring, and patient.

What You Need

- Clear, flat-backed marbles
- Paper, white or very light pastel
- Pencil
- Fine-tipped markers
- Scissors
- Glue
- Small magnets or magnet sheets

What You Do

1. Choose a marble and use a pencil to trace its shape onto a sheet of paper.
2. Inside the shape you traced, use fine-tipped markers to write the first word from the visual Bible verse, *encourage*. Make it colorful!.
3. Cut the word, cutting just inside the pencil line.
4. Put some glue over the word and stick it to the back of the marble. That way the word will show through the magnet. If you put glue on the plain side of the paper, the word won't show.
5. Glue a small magnet or a piece cut from the magnet sheet to the plain side of the word.
6. Repeat steps 1–5 with the other words or symbols of the verse.

Bonus: Make additional refrigerator magnets for other verses from this book. Or your favorite verse! If your favorite verse has words that aren't in the Visual Bible Verse Dictionary starting on page 371, them make your own symbol!

Visual Bible Verse Dictionary

A

a:

afraid: 😯

all:

and: &

anger: 😠

angry: 😠

answer: 💬

anyone: ☝️

are: R

ask: ❓

B

be: 🐝

because: bc

become: 🐝

before: 🐝

befriend: 🐝
+friend

believes: 🐝
+🌿

best: 🏅

better:

beyond: 🐝
+ON
+d

but: 🧈
-ter

C

call: 📞

can: 🥫

care:

carry:

Christ: ✝️

cleanse:

come:

control: 🎮

D

delight:

do: ✓

don't: ✗

down:

E

Earth:

east:

eternal: ∞

everyone:

F

fail:

faith:

far:

fear:

fool:

for:

forever: ∞

forgive:

free: $0.00

from: *from:*

fruit:

G

gave:

gentle:

give:

glorious:

glory: *glory*

God:

good:

grace:

great: gr8

guard:

372 · Visual Bible Verse Dictionary

H

hand:
hate:
have: ½
he: He
hear: h+
heart:
Heaven:
heavy: TON
help: SOS
here: h+
hide: 🚫
him:
his: **HIS**
Holy Spirit:
how:
human:

I

I:
if: *if*
impossible:
in: N
is: is

J

joy: 😊

K

keep: 🔑 +p
kind:
know:

Visual Bible Verse Dictionary

L

left: 
life: 
live: 
Lord: 
love:

M

me: 
money: 
my:

N

need: 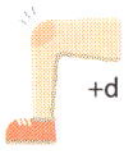
not:

O

on: 
one:

only: 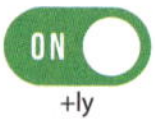
our: 
over: 
overcome:

P

path: 
patient: 
peace: 
people: 
place: 
plan: 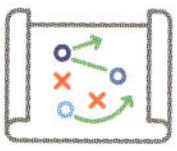
possible: 
power: 
pray: 
present: 
promise: 
protect:

Q

quick:

R

rest:

riches:

right:

S

sea:

seek:

self-control:

sheep:

shepherd:

sin:

slow:

so:

son:

song:

speak:

strength:

strong:

T

take:

tell:

the: The

them: THEM

they: THEY

think:

thought:

through:

to:

together:

trouble:

Visual Bible Verse Dictionary · 375

true:
trust:

U

up:
us:

V

victory:

W

way:
we:
weak:
weary:

west:
what:
when:
who:
will:
wise:
with:
without:
work:
world:
worry:

Y

you:

Activity Answer Keys

Page 45

Page 52

Page 59

Page 62

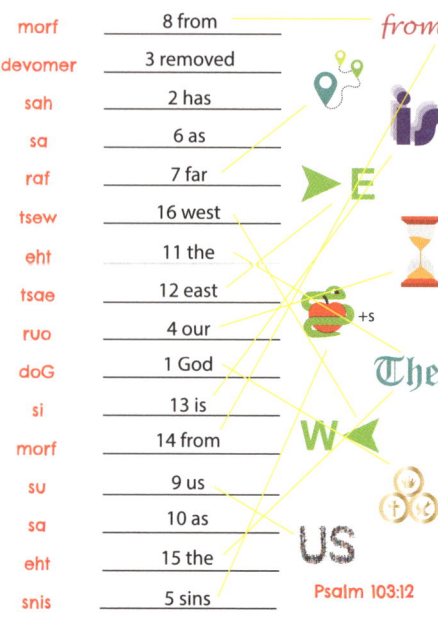

morf	8 from
devomer	3 removed
sah	2 has
sa	6 as
raf	7 far
tsew	16 west
eht	11 the
tsae	12 east
ruo	4 our
doG	1 God
si	13 is
morf	14 from
su	9 us
sa	10 as
eht	15 the
snis	5 sins

Psalm 103:12

Page 69

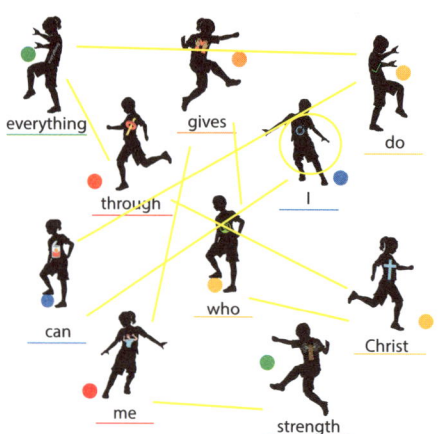

everything, gives, do, through, I, can, who, Christ, me, strength

Page 76

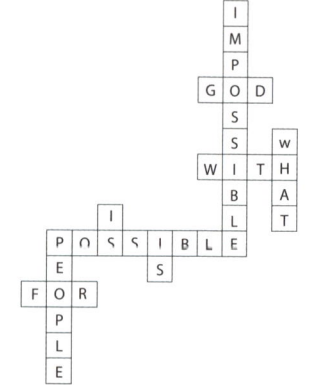

Page 80

Page 101

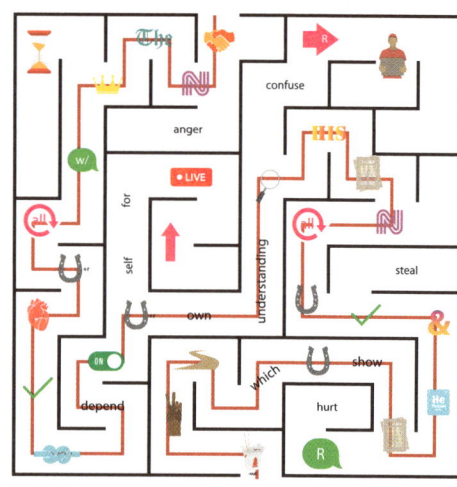

378 · Activity Answer Keys

Page 115

Page 188

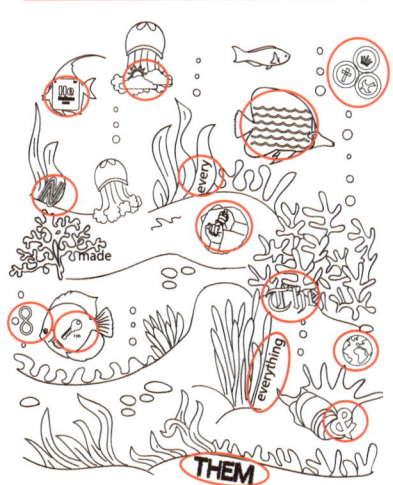

Page 122

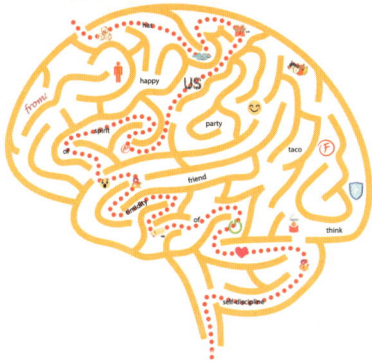

Page 195

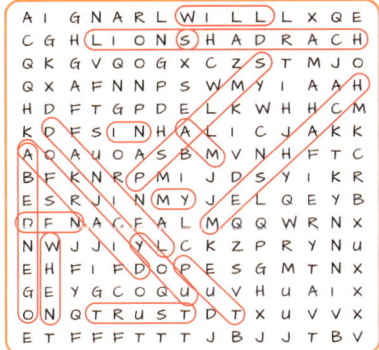

Page 157

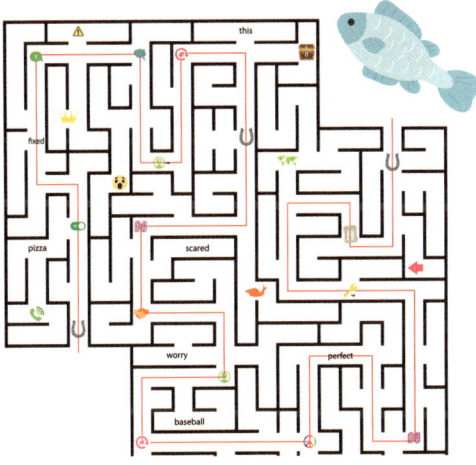

Page 206

Activity Answer Keys • 379

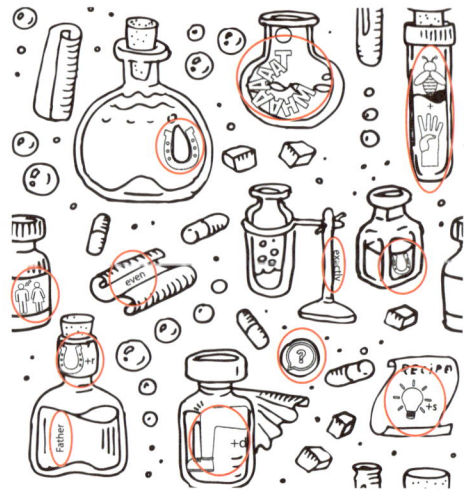

380 · Activity Answer Keys

Page 272

Page 286

Page 300

Page 318

Page 325

Page 328

Activity Answer Keys • 381

Page 335

Page 349

Page 339

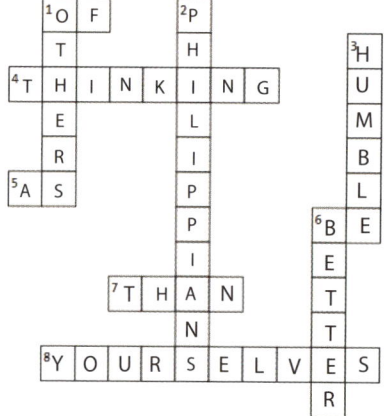

SUPER INCREDIBLE FAITH SERIES FOR GIRLS AND BOYS

Help your children better understand how much God loves them! In these books, boys and girls will be encouraged to develop positive character traits and rely on God to help them in any circumstance.

***Living Bravely*, Ages 6 to 9.**
***Conquering Fear*, Ages 10 to 12**
320 pages, Paperback, Full Color Illustrations

| Living Bravely | L50020 | ISBN: 9781628627800 |
| Conquering Fear | L50021 | ISBN: 9781628627824 |

GUIDED JOURNALS FOR GIRLS AND BOYS

Preteen boys and girls will love these daily devotional journals that really encourage them to dig into the Bible. **Ages 10–12.**

136–160 pages, Paperback, Illustrated

 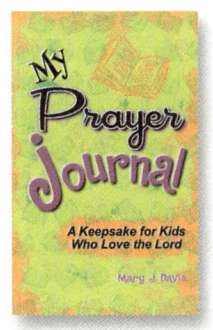

| My Bible Journal | L46911 | ISBN: 9781885358707 |
| My Prayer Journal | D46731 | ISBN: 9781885358370 |

Find more great books by visiting **www.hendricksonrose.com/RoseKidz**.

Moses and Jesus and Me!

Moses and Jesus and Me! brings cool devotionals to children ages 6-9 and 10-12. These devotionals from Gotta Have God devotionals for boys and God and Me! devotionals for girls are packed with insightful stories, meaningful prayers, awesome memory verses, and fun activities that will help boys and girls draw closer to God every day. Each devotional draws on the same Bible content, so boys and girls of different ages can learn the same biblical truths together.

222 pages each, Paperback, Full Color

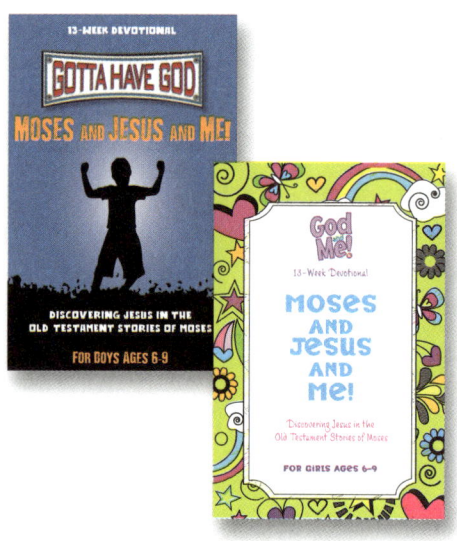
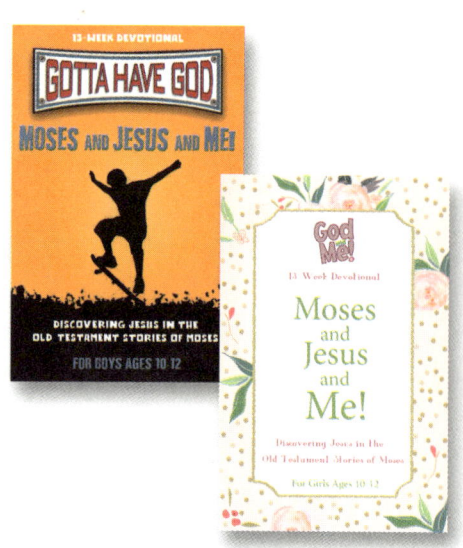

Moses and Jesus and Me! For Boys Ages 6–9	L50035	ISBN: 9781628628135
Moses and Jesus and Me! For Girls Ages 6–9	L50036	ISBN: 9781628628142
Moses and Jesus and Me! For Boys Ages 10–12	L50038	ISBN: 9781628628319
Moses and Jesus and Me! For Girls Ages 10–12	L50039	ISBN: 9781628628326

Find more great books by visiting **www.hendricksonrose.com/RoseKidz**.